Essentials of
Science Classroom
Assessment

Essentials of
Science Classroom
Assessment

Xiufeng Liu
University at Buffalo
The State University of New York

Los Angeles • London • New Delhi • Singapore • Washington DC

KH

For information:

SAGE Publications, Inc.
2455 Teller Road
Thousand Oaks, California 91320
E-mail: order@sagepub.com

SAGE Publications Ltd.
1 Oliver's Yard
55 City Road
London EC1Y 1SP
United Kingdom

SAGE Publications India Pvt. Ltd.
B 1/I 1 Mohan Cooperative Industrial Area
Mathura Road, New Delhi 110 044
India

SAGE Publications Asia-Pacific Pte. Ltd.
33 Pekin Street #02-01
Far East Square
Singapore 048763

Printed in the United States of America

Library of Congress Cataloging-in-Publication Data

Liu, Xiufeng.
Essentials of science classroom assessment / Xiufeng Liu.
   p. cm.
Includes bibliographical references and index.
ISBN 978-1-4129-6101-1 (pbk.)
   1. Science—Study and teaching—Evaluation. I. Title.

Q181.L745 2009
507.1—dc22   2008034297

This book is printed on acid-free paper.

09   10   11   12   13   10   9   8   7   6   5   4   3   2   1

Acquisitions Editor:	Diane McDaniel
Editorial Assistants:	Leah Mori, Ashley Conlon
Production Editor:	Astrid Virding
Copy Editor:	Gillian Dickens
Typesetter:	C&M Digitals (P) Ltd.
Proofreader:	Anne Rogers
Indexer:	Naomi Linzer
Cover Designer:	Edgar Abarca
Marketing Manager:	Christy Guilbault

Brief Contents

Detailed Contents

3 Summative Assessment   45

4 Assessment of Science Inquiry   73

Preface

Assessment is one of most important yet overlooked aspects in science teacher education. Although almost every elementary and secondary science methods course includes at least one session on science assessment, it is most likely that discussions on assessment are sketchy and often rushed. Similarly, popular science methods texts in which assessment is typically one of many chapters only gloss over a wide variety of assessment methods. The outcome is no surprise: Many preservice science teachers develop neither systematic understanding of the role of assessment in science instruction nor competence in applying various science assessment methods. Over the past 15 years, the teaching of science methods courses and graduate science assessment courses in both Canada and United States has convinced me that an urgent need exists for a text that systematically introduces science-specific and practical classroom assessment methods to develop competence in conducting science classroom assessment.

Essentials of Science Classroom Assessment is a supplementary text for use in an elementary or secondary science methods course for preservice science teachers. It can also be a main text for a graduate course in science assessment for inservice science teachers. *Essentials of Science Classroom Assessment* systematically introduces fundamental science assessment methods that are integral of science teaching and learning. It presents not only conventional science assessment methods but also novel and innovative assessment methods that are the results of recent science assessment research. *Essentials of Science Classroom Assessment* intends to bridge science assessment research and science classroom practice and to connect explicitly science assessment and student learning. The ultimate goal of *Essentials of Science Classroom Assessment* is to help preservice and inservice science teachers develop competence in conducting science classroom assessment to support student learning.

Essentials of Science Classroom Assessment follows a constructivist approach to organizing its content. There are three essential components in the constructivist approach to science teaching and learning:

1. Identifying student preconceptions to plan effective science inquiry

2. Promoting and monitoring student conceptual change during inquiry

3. Assessing and reflecting on conceptual change at the end of an inquiry cycle

The above three components correspond to three types of science assessment introduced in this book:

1. Diagnostic assessment

2. Formative assessment

3. Summative assessment

Essentials of Science Classroom Assessment will help science teachers develop an appreciation that science assessment is an integral component of an effective science teaching and learning process and that science assessment is multifaceted in methods (e.g., paper and pencil, performance, concept mapping), time (before, during, and after instruction), and space (individual paper and pencil, collaborative project, computer and Internet based).

ORGANIZATION OF THE TEXT

There are eight chapters in the book. Chapter 1 presents a conceptual framework of science assessment in terms of its relationship with science instruction and its various components. There are seven chapters following Chapter 1. The seven chapters are presented in the order of diagnostic assessment (Chapter 2), summative assessment (Chapters 3, 4, and 5), and formative assessment (Chapter 6). Chapter 7 deals with grading. Chapter 8, the final chapter, deals with a common element of all assessment—data—and discusses ways of using data to improve science teaching and learning. Chapter 8 also presents a rationale of science assessment as an inquiry to integrate all chapters in this book into a coherent conceptual framework. Although Chapters 2 through 6 may be followed in the order above, essentially all the six chapters stand alone; they can be used in any particular order.

FEATURES OF THE TEXT

Essentials of Science Classroom Assessment has the following unique features:

Science Assessment Standards Oriented

Each chapter explicitly addresses specific assessment standards in the National Science Education Standards (NSES). Assessment methods introduced in the chapters are essential for meeting the NSES assessment standards. Each chapter covers not only general assessment methods, such as writing multiple-choice questions, but also science-specific assessment methods, such as Vee diagramming, two-tiered multiple-choice questions, and predication-observation-explanation that have resulted from science education research. Preservice and inservice teachers should benefit from this approach by becoming aware of the expectations in terms of science assessment and being fully equipped to meet the standards.

Competence Based

Each chapter focuses on a few assessment skills that are essential for effective science class-room instruction. Practical examples from both elementary and secondary science class-rooms are used throughout the chapter to illustrate the assessment skills. Checklist and practice questions are available at the end of each chapter for preservice teachers to check their mastery of assessment skills. Throughout each chapter, opportunities for applying the assessment skills are also available. The objective of this competence-based approach is to help preservice and inservice teachers to see the direct relevance of the assessment skills to science classroom instruction and to become competent in them.

Parallel to Method Courses

The structure of this book parallels the structure of a typical elementary and secondary science method course. Assessment concepts and skills in different chapters intend to sup-port various instructional methods and skills introduced in science methods courses. With the exception of Chapters 1 and 8, all other chapters stand alone and can be followed in any order. This feature provides preservice teachers and college methods course instructors maximal flexibility to fully incorporate *Essentials of Science Classroom Assessment*.

Resources to Expand Learning Experiences

Each chapter introduces essential assessment concepts and skills that are only directly rel-evant to elementary and secondary science instruction. It is hoped that preservice teach-ers and inservice science teachers will develop further interest in science assessment and a desire to learn more. Thus, at the end of each chapter, there is a list of annotated bibli-ographies introducing more advanced readings on science assessment. Also, the compan-ion Web site introduces additional resources and tools. At the end of each chapter, preservice teachers should be able to realize that the assessment methods introduced in the chapter are topics of active research in science education and constantly evolving, and it is neces-sary to keep informed continuously.

PEDAGOGICAL FEATURES OF THE TEXT

To facilitate constructive classroom discussion and self-reflection, *Essentials of Science Classroom Assessment* also incorporates the following pedagogical features:

Application and Self-Reflection

After introduction of a major assessment method, a shaded box titled *Application and Self-Reflection* provides an opportunity to apply the method or initiate discussion of critical issues associated with the assessment method. For example, after introducing the technique of constructing a test grid in Chapter 3, an *Application and Self-Reflection* box follows describing an assessment scenario and asking science teachers to develop a test grid to share with the class and critique each other's test grid.

The Cases of Eric and Elisia

Each chapter ends with a case scenario of two imaginary preservice teachers, Eric, a science elementary teacher, and Elisia, a secondary chemistry teacher, on their experiences of learning science assessment. This case scenario box intends to initiate classroom discussion and self-reflection on the assessment skills introduced in the chapter, as well as on the issues that may arise in the classrooms. It is hoped that the case scenarios provide a personal contextualization of assessment skills discussed in the chapter. Through relating to Eric and Elisia's experiences, preservice and inservice teachers will be able to see personal relevance and issues of the assessment methods introduced in the chapters.

Chapter Summary

At the end of each chapter, a brief summary provides a concise review of essential assessment concepts and skills introduced in the chapter. This summary can be used as a guide to review the chapter material before taking a self-evaluation of the mastery of the chapter content.

ANCILLARY MATERIALS

A Web-based student study site further supports and enhances the learning goals of *Essentials of Science Classroom Assessment*. It is located at the following URL: **www.sagepub.com/liustudy.**

This comprehensive study site provides numerous resources to enhance students' understanding of the book's content. Each chapter includes an online quiz designed to test your mastery of essential assessment skills and concepts of the chapter, as well as e-flashcards and Web resources. Other resources include a collection of alternative assessment tasks for teachers to use with students and over 40 abstracts that identify K–12 students' preconceptions of various science topics. Various data analysis tools (e.g., Microsoft Excel data analysis templates) are also available on the site.

ACKNOWLEDGMENTS

I would like to acknowledge the many people who have helped to create this book. First and foremost, my wife Lily Li has been consistently supportive of my work by sparing me from many household chores. My children, Iris Liu (10th grade) and Murton Liu (5th grade), have been a constant source of motivation by talking to me about their schoolwork and sharing with me their assessment experiences as students. Diane McDaniel, my editor at SAGE Publications, has been patient and insightful. Her input throughout the planning and writing of this book has made it a much better product than I expected. My sincere thanks also go to Leah Mori, editorial assistant at SAGE, for keeping things in good order. This book is a result of my teaching science methods courses, particularly LAI 534 Measurement and Evaluation of Science Teaching, at SUNY—Buffalo. Students who took my courses provided valuable comments and suggestions on the materials included in this book and were a constant motivation for me to complete this book.

Many reviewers provided valuable comments about and suggestions to the book proposal and draft chapters. I specifically thank Wali Abdi (University of Memphis), Anjana G. Arora (Richard Stockton College of New Jersey), Katy Bachman (Florida Gulf Coast University), Kimberly Bilica (University of Texas at San Antonio), Alec M. Bodzin (Lehigh University), Wendy M. Frazier (George Mason University), Richard A. Huber (University of North Carolina, Wilmington), Jeanine M. Huss (Western Kentucky University), Sonia Kowalczuk (New Jersey City University), George E. O'Brien (Florida International University), Don Powers (Western Illinois University), Denise Richardson (Jacksonville State University), Barbara R. Sandall (Western Illinois University), Michelle Scribner-MacLean (University of Massachusetts Lowell), John Shimkanin (California University of Pennsylvania), and four anonymous reviewers.

Xiufeng Liu
Buffalo, NY

CHAPTER 1

Assessment for Learning and Teaching

Deciding to become a teacher is a major career decision. With much excitement and anticipation after your acceptance into a teacher education program, your journey toward becoming a science teacher starts in university classrooms. You are taking various courses, including science teaching methods courses. You may not give much attention to science assessment because your teacher education program may not offer a stand-alone science assessment course. From your grade school to university, you have seen your teachers conducting all kinds of assessment: quizzes, exams, standardized tests, and projects, to name just a few. Assessment is a routine task for all teachers; you may think that conducting science assessment requires no more than a commonsense approach, as Elisia and Eric, two preservice teachers think:

ERIC, ELEMENTARY PRESERVICE TEACHER

Eric enters the elementary teacher certification program with a psychology major. Among others, he is taking an elementary science methods course to learn how to teach science. The textbook for the course is a popular one commonly used by many universities and contains a chapter on science assessment. According to the course syllabus, he will have 2 weeks discussing various assessment methods. He knows assessment is an essential part of elementary science teaching because he remembers his experiences as an elementary school student in taking end-of-unit tests and state science exams and, of course, receiving a grade for science on the report card. He basically thinks assessment is a way to assess students and to give students a grade. Beyond grading students, he does not know other roles assessment may play in science teaching and leaning. As far as assessment techniques go, he feels that he has no difficulty in developing a test using multiple-choice questions, short-answer questions, and even a project. Overall, he does not think assessment should play a big role in his teaching of elementary grades, given his belief that students of such young ages need well-rounded education and development, instead of just being good at test taking. At least, he anticipates students will have diverse abilities and backgrounds, and thus no single assessment will fit them all.

(Continued)

(Continued)

ELISIA, SECONDARY CHEMISTRY PRESERVICE TEACHER

Elisia enters the secondary science—more specifically, chemistry—certification program with a major in chemistry. She is taking a secondary science methods course in addition to a number of other courses. Her science methods course also adopts a popular secondary science methods text in which assessment is one of its many chapters. The course syllabus shows that there will be 2 weeks of class time devoted to science assessment. Elisia thinks assessment is an essential component of her responsibility as a secondary science teacher because grades have to be given to students, and their transcripts will be used for many purposes, including applying for university admissions and scholarships. Elisia does not think conducting science assessment is a challenging task because she knows what multiple-choice, essay, project, and even standardized tests are. She is particularly familiar with multiple-choice questions because they are the dominant question type used in her high school and university science classes. Unlike Eric, Elisia believes that assessment should play a very important part of her teaching because high schools should prepare students for life, in which passing tests for various opportunities is a necessity. Thus, it is her responsibility to prepare students for various external tests.

Do Eric and Elisia's cases sound familiar to you? For them, assessment is what a teacher does *to* students. This seems to be the common conception among most preservice teachers and what they have seen routinely in science classrooms from elementary school to university. Can and should science assessment be more than grading students? Should and can science assessment be different in elementary and secondary science classrooms?

RELATIONSHIP BETWEEN ASSESSMENT AND INSTRUCTION

In thinking about how assessment should be conducted in elementary and secondary science classrooms, you first need to consider the relationship between assessment and instruction. The National Science Education Standards (NSES) Teaching Standard C states the following:

> Teachers of science engage in ongoing assessment of their teaching and student learning. In doing this, teachers
>
> a. Use multiple methods and systematically gather data about student understanding and ability.
> b. Analyze assessment data to guide teaching.
> c. Guide students in self-assessment.
> d. Use student data, observations of teaching, and interactions with colleagues to reflect on and improve teaching practice. (National Research Council [NRC], 1996, pp. 37–38)

How does the Teaching Standard C sound to you? Besides assessment of students, Teaching Standard C also suggests assessment to be used to guide and improve teaching. For many beginning science teachers, the role of science assessment in guiding and improving teaching may be unfamiliar. One key characteristic of science assessment implied in the above teaching standard is that science assessment is an integral component of science teaching and learning. Science assessment is not just one activity, such as an end-of-unit test or state exam, but also an ongoing process happening simultaneously with science teaching and learning activities. Science assessment is not only what you do to students but also what you do to inform teaching. A National Research Council committee has called for the design of a science learning environment to be assessment centered (Bransford, Brown, & Cocking, 2000), which best demonstrates the prominent role of assessment in the teaching and learning processes. Science teaching and learning in an assessment-centered learning environment are guided by assessment and, in turn, inform assessment.

Assessment is a systematic, multistep, and multifaceted process involving the collection and interpretation of data (NRC, 1996). There are four components in assessment. The *data use* component refers to the intended use of assessment results such as grading students, planning instruction, improving curricula, and comparing students. The *data collection* component refers to the target on which assessment data will be collected, such as student achievement, science inquiry ability, and attitude toward science. The *methods to collect data* refers to the specific ways to collect data, such as paper-and-pencil tests, interviews, and performance tasks. And the last component, *users of data,* refers to people or organizations that will have an interest in or make use of the data, such as students, teachers, and universities. The combination of the above four components forms assessment. Thus, assessment is a complex process; it entails systematic planning, implementation, analysis, and interpretation. The core of assessment is data, which make assessment empirical or, in other words, a scientific inquiry enterprise.

Assessment includes two processes: measurement and evaluation. **Measurement** is a process of quantifying the degree to which a student possesses a given characteristic, quality, or feature, while **evaluation** is the process of interpreting measurement data based on a set of criteria in order to make certain judgments. A key tool of measurement is a test. A **test** is a set of questions or tasks that elicit student responses plus a set of scoring keys or schemes to score them. A test can include a variety of question formats, such as multiple-choice questions, a concept mapping task, and a performance task.

Although science assessment is integral to science teaching and learning, it is also distinct from science teaching and learning. Guided by the overall purpose for supporting and improving science teaching and learning, science assessment purposefully collects relevant data, as well as analyzes and interprets them to answer specific questions about science teaching and learning. The centrality of data in science assessment requires that data to be collected are of high technical quality (i.e., meeting technical standards). Only when we are sure that assessment data are of high technical quality can we use assessment data to answer important questions about science teaching and learning. Sample questions that may be answered by science assessment are the following: What preconceptions do students bring to the science classroom? How do students' conceptions change during science teaching and learning? And have students mastered the expected learning standards?

Because science assessment and science teaching and learning are both distinct and closely related, we may consider science assessment and science teaching and learning as two sides of the same coin. Without teaching and learning, science assessment is meaningless; without assessment, science teaching and learning is mindless. Therefore, you must consider science assessment and teaching and learning at the same time when planning for effective science instruction.

APPLICATION AND SELF-REFLECTION 1.1

Give two assessment examples you experienced when you were a student, one in elementary school and another in high school, to answer the following questions:

What was the intended use of the assessment?

What was the target of the assessment and how was it measured?

How was the assessment result used?

Are there matters of concern to you from your current perspective as a preservice teacher?

How should the assessment be enhanced?

FOUNDATIONS OF SCIENCE ASSESSMENT

What are fundamental considerations of science assessment? A National Research Council committee on assessment conceptualizes assessment to include three foundations:

FIGURE 1.1   The Assessment Triangle

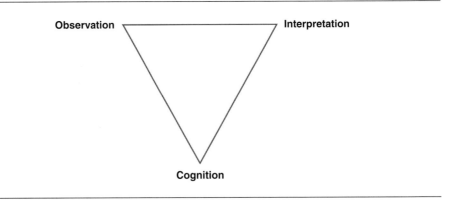

Source: Adapted from the NRC (2001).

In Figure 1.1, **observation** refers to assessment tasks through which students' attainment of learning outcomes is elicited, **interpretation** refers to measurement models through which the assessment data are interpreted, and **cognition** refers to theories on how students learn. Observation and interpretation are related to data collection, analysis, and validation, and cognition is related to science teaching and learning. Observation and interpretation and science teaching and learning must agree with each other.

Assessment Foundation 1: Cognition

Research has suggested that the social-cultural constructivist approach to science teaching is most promising (Tobin, Tippins, & Gallard, 1994). Effective teaching follows the following principles:

- Teachers must draw out and work with the preexisting understandings that their students bring with them.

- Teachers must teach some subject matter in depth, providing many examples in which the same concept is at work and providing a firm foundation of factual knowledge.

- The teaching of metacognitive skills should be intergraded into the curriculum in a variety of subject areas. (Bransford et al., 2000)

In addition, effective teaching takes place in the following learning environments:

- Student centered: Schools and classrooms are organized around students.

- Knowledge centered: Attention is given to what is taught, why it is taught, and what competence or mastery looks like.

- Assessment centered: this consists of formative assessment—ongoing assessments designed to make students' thinking visible to both teachers and students—and summative assessment—assessments at the end of a learning unit to find out how well students have achieved the standards.

- Community centered: Develop norms for the classroom and school as well as connections to the outside world that support core learning values. (Bransford et al., 2000)

Implications of the above principles for science assessment are presented in Table 1.1.

Assessment Foundation 2: Observation

How can we collect data to fulfill the above assessment demands? Different assessment demands require different types of data to be collected. For example, techniques for identifying student preconceptions can be diagnostic inventories, interviews, and free-response writing. Similarly, many techniques are also available for assessing in-depth conceptual understanding such as two-tiered multiple-choice and constructed-response questions. Techniques for assessing application can be performance assessment and Vee diagrams.

TABLE 1.1   Cognitive Principles and Their Implications for Science Assessment

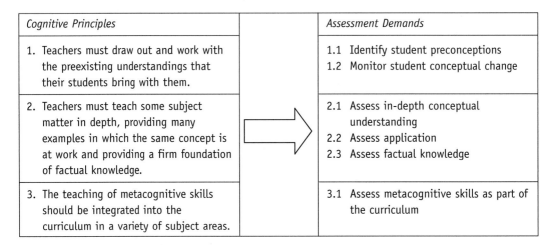

Cognitive Principles		Assessment Demands
1. Teachers must draw out and work with the preexisting understandings that their students bring with them.		1.1 Identify student preconceptions 1.2 Monitor student conceptual change
2. Teachers must teach some subject matter in depth, providing many examples in which the same concept is at work and providing a firm foundation of factual knowledge.		2.1 Assess in-depth conceptual understanding 2.2 Assess application 2.3 Assess factual knowledge
3. The teaching of metacognitive skills should be integrated into the curriculum in a variety of subject areas.		3.1 Assess metacognitive skills as part of the curriculum

Multiple-choice questions are commonly used for assessing factual knowledge. Finally, many techniques such as concept mapping and portfolio assessment are appropriate for assessing and promoting metacognition in students.

Observation may be considered as consisting of multiple dimensions. At least the following dimensions can be conceptualized:

- The medium: Observation can be based on text, audio-video, graphic, and physical action.

- The time: Observation can take place from instant responses to long-term responses ranging from days to months.

- The agent: Observation can take place individually, in pairs, and in groups.

- The construct: Observation may involve the cognitive domain (i.e., knowledge, comprehension, application, analysis, evaluation, and creation), affective domain, and psychomotor domain.

- The content: Observation may involve a single topic or multiple topics.

Assessment Foundation 3: The Measurement Model

The most commonly applied measurement model is the classical test theory (CTT). The CTT has three basic aspects: validity, reliability, and absence of bias. Validity refers to the degree to which inferences made from assessment data are accurate and sound. Assessment validation may be based on content (the alignment between assessment coverage and the intended curriculum), relevant criteria (the correlation between two sets of assessment data), and theoretical construct (the agreement with the hypothesized mental processes or products). Reliability refers to the degree to which assessment data are replicable and consistent across time, contexts, and tasks. Reliability may be established by the internal consistency of assessment items or tasks and the stability of student assessment scores over time, across contexts, or among raters. Absence of bias refers to the positive consequences of inferences and uses of assessment data. Absence of bias may be established by documenting the immediate and long-term effects of assessment result uses.

APPLICATION AND SELF-REFLECTION 1.2

Are you surprised that science assessment can be so complex and there are so many aspects to consider? Read the following two scenarios and examine how each relates to the three assessment foundations described above.

Scenario 1: Ms. A has just completed a unit on living things with her fourth-grade class. Although the textbook unit contains many colorful pictures of various living organisms and descriptions of their characteristics, she decided that a more effective way to teach this unit was to allow students to observe and explore various living organisms they encounter in their daily lives. During the unit, students were asked to select an area (i.e., a mini habitat, in their backyards) and observe and record the behaviors and characteristics of the living things in the "mini" habitats. Class time was given for students to share observations and research questions, as well as to conduct further research in the library and on the Internet. The culminating event of the unit was a poster presentation session open to the public (parents were particularly invited). Assessment was conducted during the presentation. Students were given a grade based on how well their posters were designed and how their presentations were made.

Scenario 2: Ms. P has just completed a unit on Newton's second law to her Grade 11 physics class. Ms. P's approach to teaching physics is based on a strong belief that students learn best by hands-on learning. During the unit, students spent about half the time of the unit doing labs and the other half working on textbook problems involving primarily calculations using the formula. The end-of-unit test was modeled after the state exam consisting primarily of multiple-choice questions. Student unit grades were based on the end-of-unit test scores.

SCIENCE ASSESSMENT AS A SYSTEM

What are the types of assessments you need to consider when you plan for teaching a science unit? The best way to approach planning science assessment is to consider an approach to planning for science instruction. One popular approach for instructional planning is the backward design approach elaborated by Wiggins and McTighe (2005). Briefly, the backward design approach ensures that the planned curriculum will result in real understanding instead of just factual knowledge in students. The backward design approach considers the key to developing real understanding in science as the coherence among curriculum goals, assessment evidence, and learning activities. Although the approach is described as three stages, curriculum planning does not have to follow the stages in sequence—multiple entry points are possible. The three stages are (a) Stage 1—define desired results, (b) Stage 2—identify assessment evidence, and (c) Stage 3—plan learning activities. Based on the backward design approach, a complete assessment plan supporting science teaching and learning should parallel the above three stages. Figure 1.2 shows the assessment types and their correspondence to the backward design approach stages.

FIGURE 1.2   Backward Design Approach and Its Implication for Assessment

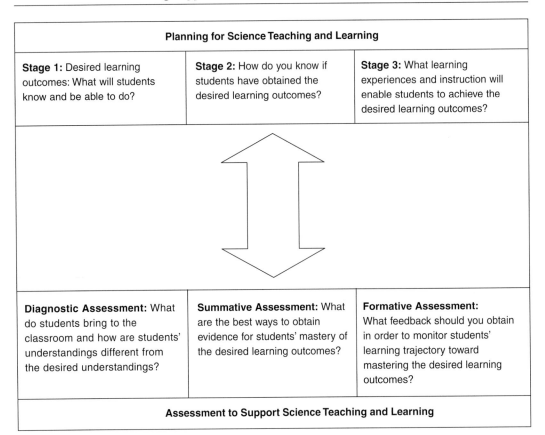

Based on Figure1.2, assessment may take place before, after, and during instruction, which gives rise to diagnostic assessment, summative assessment, and formative assessment. **Diagnostic assessment** is conducted specifically to identify students' strengths and weaknesses on the intended learning objectives so that effective planning for instruction may take place. **Summative assessment** takes place at the conclusion of instruction in order to grade students for mastering instructional objectives and make decisions for student future learning. **Formative assessment** takes place as part of ongoing instruction in order to monitor and make adjustment to the ongoing instruction. Obviously, the above three types of assessments are relative to the instructional context. One unit of instruction can be a part of a larger program of study, and thus the summative assessment of one unit may become a diagnostic assessment for the next one or a formative assessment for the entire program of study. Please note, in the backward design approach, evidence for student mastery of unit learning outcomes must be decided before you plan for learning activities, which is why summative assessment is planned before formative assessment.

Diagnostic Assessment

Diagnostic assessment takes place when you plan for a new sequence of science instruction, such as a new unit. The purpose is to find out what preconceptions students have related to the learning standards and how they are different from the scientifically accepted conceptions. Although research in the past three decades has documented various students' alternative conceptions related to a large number of key science concepts (Baker, 2004; Wandersee, Mintzes, & Novak, 1994), and it is likely that many of those alternative conceptions documented in the research literature apply to your students, there are a number of benefits for science teachers to conduct their own diagnostic assessment. The important benefits are to

- identify different ideas that your students specifically have,

- convey to your students that you value their ideas and take their ideas into consideration in your planning,

- motivate students to learn as the learning activities are directly relevant to their ideas,

- develop in students a sense of self-control in their learning, and

- provide a baseline for both students and you to check for learning progression (Ebenezer & Connor, 1996).

There are many ways to conduct diagnostic assessment. For example, an elementary teacher may use drawing (e.g., drawing a scientist, drawing a diagram on the relationship between a producer and consumer), brainstorming, or journaling to find students' preconceptions when planning a science unit. A secondary science teacher may use a multiple-choice or an open-ended question survey to find out what students have already known and are still confused about the concepts to be taught in a new unit. Chapter 2 will introduce a variety of diagnostic assessment methods.

Summative Assessment

Summative assessment takes place when a sequence of science instruction, such as a unit, has been completed. The purpose is to find out how well students have mastered the intended learning outcomes. Summative assessment is usually the basis for grading but should not be the only basis. Summative assessment does not have to be paper and pencil based. Depending on the desired learning outcomes, summative assessment tasks can be in various forms. The multidimensional observations discussed earlier apply here. Given the current standards-based approach to science education and accountability, external tests can also become part of the summative assessment.

Summative assessment is the most commonly used assessment activity in science teaching. In elementary grades, teachers may use portfolios, homework, in-class participation, and tests to grade students; in secondary grades, teachers may use tests, projects, and even external tests (e.g., state tests) to grade students. Chapters 3, 4, and 5 will introduce various summative assessment methods and develop specific skills related to developing summative assessments, including using standardized tests.

Formative Assessment

Formative assessment takes place as components of ongoing science instructional activities. Its purpose is to obtain feedback on students' learning in terms of the desired learning outcomes so that ongoing adjustment to the learning activities may be made. Because of the seamless integration of formative assessment into ongoing instruction, there is no need for a clear distinction between formative assessment and learning activities.

Formative assessment can be done in many different ways, both formal and informal. For example, in elementary grades, a teacher may simply use homework as a way to obtain information about the ongoing instruction and make adjustments accordingly. A secondary science teacher may periodically give students a nongrading pop quiz to find out how students are making progress during the unit. Chapter 6 will develop some important formative assessment methods and specific skills for formative assessment. Methods of grading based on both summative and formative assessment information will be introduced in Chapter 7.

It needs to be pointed out that although three types of assessment are differentiated, in reality, the distinction among them is quite fuzzy. A diagnostic assessment may also be used as formative or summative assessment, and a formative assessment may also be used as a summative assessment. Therefore, the difference among the three types of assessment is mainly conceptual; in practice, one assessment activity may perform more than one function of the assessment. No matter what assessment is used, the process must be valid, reliable, and absent of bias. Chapter 8 will introduce techniques to examine science assessment as an inquiry process by establishing its validity, reliability, and absence of bias.

APPLICATION AND SELF-REFLECTION 1.3

It should be clear to you now that planning for science assessment should be concurrent with planning for science instruction. We have differentiated three types of science assessment: diagnostic assessment, summative assessment, and formative assessment. Can you think of two assessment methods, one for an elementary science grade and another for a secondary science grade, that can be used to serve all three forms of assessment? What are the advantages and disadvantages of using one method for multiple forms of assessments?

LEGAL CONSIDERATIONS PERTAINING TO SCIENCE ASSESSMENT

When planning and conducting science assessment, teachers need to be informed of pertinent federal laws. Here we review two public laws that are relevant to all assessment situations; specific laws pertaining to specific assessments (e.g., standardized tests) will be discussed later. One is related to privacy and the other to students with disabilities. Failing to follow the laws will result in court challenges with serious consequences, including academic discipline, teaching probation, and termination of teaching certification and contract. Becoming knowledgeable about pertinent laws related to the assessment of students is a part of a science teacher's professional competence.

Assessment Information and Student Records

The Family Education Rights to Privacy Act (FERPA), enacted in 1974, guarantees that students and their parents have the right to control the use of their personal information such as student academic records. Science teachers deal with all kinds of student personal information, such as test scores, course grades, report cards, and individualized education programs for students with disabilities. Student records, whether or not on a teacher's desk or in an official student file (including computer files), are confidential and may not be released without permission. Accordingly, all assessment data must be regarded as confidential by the teacher and the school. Before a student reaches age 18, the child's parents or the guardian must give consent before any of the student's personal data are released to a third party. After a child has reached 18, the child can grant permission regarding the release of his or her personal data. In addition, the child and the parents/guardians have the right to review and challenge the accuracy of the information kept in the child's file or record. This act also implies that assessment data can be collected only by the teacher. If a third party, such as an external agency or university researcher, would like to conduct an assessment, written consent must be obtained from parents before assessment is conducted.

Specific to assessment, peer grading is a common practice in science classrooms. The Supreme Court ruling suggests that peer grading is not part of student record and thus does not violate the privacy act despite the objection to the practice by some parents (Aquila, 2008). However, if students' grades are posted in the hallway, this would clearly violate the privacy act. There are exceptions to FERPA. Information about a student that can be released includes directory information, such as the student's name, address, telephone number, and date and place of birth; major field of study; dates of attendance; participation in officially recognized activities and sports; weight and height of members of athletic teams; date of graduation; and awards received. A school may also show or turn over student records without permission to (a) other officials of the same school system; (b) certain federal, state, and local authorities performing functions authorized by law; (c) the juvenile justice system under subpoena or a court order; (d) accrediting agencies; and (e) in emergencies to protect a student's health or safety (Carin & Bass, 1997).

Test Accommodation and Alternative Assessment

Another law pertaining to assessment is the Individuals with Disabilities Education Act (IDEA). The most recent version of IDEA was passed by Congress in December 2004, replacing the 1997 version of the act. According to IDEA 2004, disability refers to mental retardation, hearing impairments (including deafness), speech or language impairments, visual impairments (including blindness), serious emotional disturbance (referred to in this title as *emotional disturbance*), orthopedic impairments, autism, traumatic brain injury, other health impairments, or specific learning disabilities. It further defines that a child aged 3 through 9 may, at the discretion of the state and the local educational agency, be considered as having disability if a child is experiencing developmental delays, as defined by the state and as measured by appropriate diagnostic instruments and procedures, in one or more of the following areas: physical development, cognitive development, communication development, social or emotional development, or adaptive development. The law regards disability a natural part of the human experience and should in no way diminish the right of students to participate in learning.

Specific to science instruction, science teachers must follow the following six principles (Carin & Bass, 1997):

- Zero reject: No student with disabilities can be excluded from a free, appropriate education.

- Nondiscriminatory evaluation: Schools must evaluate students fairly (without bias) to determine if they have a disability, identify what kind of disability that student has, and identify how extensive it is.

- Appropriate education: Schools must tailor education for individual students (individualized education program) based on nondiscriminatory education. Schools are also required to augment that education with related support services and supplementary aids.

- Least restrictive environment: Schools must educate students with disabilities alongside students without disabilities to the maximum extent appropriate for the students with disabilities. The school may not remove a student from general education unless the student cannot be educated there successfully.

- Procedural due process: IDEA provides safeguards for students against schools' actions, including a right to sue in court.

- Parental and student participation: Schools must collaborate with parents and adolescent students in designing and carrying out special education programs.

Because science assessment is closely related to science instruction, the above six principles have important implications to science assessments. There are two types of assessment activities in which science teachers may be involved: (a) initial assessment to identify a student suspected of having disability and (b) assessment accommodations and alternative assessment. Before any assessment accommodation or alternative assessment is provided, a formal evaluation of a child is needed to determine if the child has a disability. A parent of a child, a state educational agency, another state agency, or a local educational agency may initiate a request for an initial evaluation to determine if the child has a disability. Evaluation should use a variety of assessment tools and strategies to gather relevant functional, developmental, and academic information, including information provided by the parent. At least one regular classroom teacher must be a member of the evaluation team. After a child has been determined to have a disability, an individualized education program or IEP must be developed. An IEP is a written statement for each child with a disability that includes, among other things, (a) a statement of the child's present levels of academic achievement and functional performance; (b) a statement of measurable annual goals, including academic and functional goals; and (c) a description of how the child's progress toward meeting the annual goals will be measured, including any individually appropriate assessment accommodations or alternative assessments on a particular state or district-wide assessment of student achievement. It can be seen that test accommodation and alternative assessment provision are not a spontaneous decision; they are planned as part of the IEP for the child with a disability.

Various accommodations are possible depending on the nature and degree of the disability. Sample accommodations are Braille, large prints, recorded tests, individually administered tests, oral dictation, extended time, separate rooms, and so on. Similarly, various alternative assessment forms may be provided depending on the nature and degree of disability. Sample alternative tests to paper-and-pencil tests are translation into another language, shorter version of the test, portfolio assessment, observations, performance test, and so forth.

APPLICATION AND SELF-REFLECTION 1.4

Imagine the following two cases. Decide if test accommodation, alternative assessment, or differentiated assessment is necessary for an end-of-unit test and, if yes, how and why.

Andy: a fifth-grade student identified as having a disability in reading. Andy receives science instruction together with the rest of the class. He participates in all activities, although he receives help from designated classmates or the teacher when an activity involves extensive reading. Andy does not seem to have any difficulty in understanding and mastering the science content.

Ruth: a 10th-grade student taking a biology course. She is the most advanced student in the class. It seems that she has already known and understood most of the curriculum materials; she is taking the course because this course is required by the state to graduate. Given her situation, the teacher often assigns different and more advanced homework for her to do. She is also regularly asked to help other students who are struggling in the course.

SCIENCE ASSESSMENT STANDARDS

Each of you may have different concerns related to various science assessment aspects described above. What are expectations of science teachers in terms of science assessment? The NRC (1996) developed a set of assessment standards as part of the National Science Education Standards. The NRC assessment standards contain five standards as follows:

1. Assessment Standard A: Assessment must be consistent with the decisions they are designed to inform. This standard is further elaborated into the following substandards:
   a. Assessments are designed deliberately.
   b. Assessments have explicitly stated purposes.
   c. The relationship between the decisions and the data is clear.
   d. Assessment procedures are internally consistent.

2. Assessment Standard B: Achievement and opportunity to learn science must be assessed. This standard is further elaborated into the following substandards:

    a. Achievement data collected focus on the science content that is most important for students to learn.

    b. Opportunity-to-learn data collected focus on the most powerful indicators of learning.

    c. Equal attention must be given to the assessment of opportunity to learn and to the assessment of student achievement.

3. Assessment Standard C: The technical quality of the data collected is well matched to the decisions and actions taken on the basis of their interpretation. This standard is further elaborated into the following substandards:

    a. The feature that is claimed to be measured is actually measured.

    b. An individual student's performance is similar on two or more tasks that claim to measure the same aspect of student achievement.

    c. Students have an adequate opportunity to demonstrate their achievements.

    d. Assessment tasks and methods for presenting them provide data that are sufficiently stable to lead to the same decisions if used at different times.

4. Assessment Standard D: Assessment practices must be fair. This standard is further elaborated into the following substandards:

    a. Assessment tasks must be reviewed for the use of stereotypes, for assumptions that reflect the perspectives or experiences of a particular group, for language that might be offensive to a particular group, and for other features that might distract students from the intended tasks.

    b. Large-scale assessments must use statistical techniques to identify potential bias among subgroups.

    c. Assessment tasks must be modified appropriately to accommodate the needs of students with physical disabilities, learning disabilities, or limited English proficiency.

    d. Assessment tasks must be set in a variety of contexts, be engaging to students with different interests and experiences, and must not assume the perspective or experience of a particular gender, racial, or ethnic group.

5. Assessment Standard E: The inferences made from assessments about student achievement and opportunity to learn must be sound. This standard is further elaborated into the following substandards:

    a. When making inferences from assessment data about student achievement and opportunity to learn science, explicit reference needs to be made to the assumptions on which the inferences are based.

The above science assessment standards are comprehensive and demanding; adequate and systematic preparation in knowledge and skills of science assessment is necessary. This book intends to just do that. This book will walk you through the needed assessment knowledge and skills to help you plan an effective learning unit. Those of you who are motivated to know more about current research on the assessment methods introduced in each chapter may pursue further readings suggested at the end of each chapter. Helping every teacher to meet the above assessment standards is the ultimate goal of this book.

APPLICATION AND SELF-REFLECTION 1.5

Let's take a closer look at the above assessment standards. For which standards do you think you understand the specific expectations? For which standards do you think you are not sure about the specific expectations? Place a √ to indicate "you understand" and a ? for "not sure."

Standard	Your Feeling
Aa. Deliberately design assessment.	
Ab. Use assessments for explicit purposes.	
Ac. Relate clearly decisions to data.	
Ad. Follow internally consistent assessment procedures.	
Ba. Collect achievement data on the science content that is most important for students to learn.	
Bb. Collect opportunity-to-learn data as the most powerful indicators of learning.	
Bc. Assess both opportunity to learn and student achievement.	
Ca. Ensure that the feature claimed to be measured is actually measured.	
Cb. Ensure that an individual student's performance is similar on two or more tasks that claim to measure the same aspect of student achievement.	
Cc. Ensure that students have adequate opportunity to demonstrate their achievements.	
Cd. Ensure that assessment tasks and methods for presenting them provide data that are sufficiently stable to lead to the same decisions if used at different times.	
Da. Review assessment tasks for the use of stereotypes, for assumptions that reflect the perspectives or experiences of a particular group, for language that might be offensive to a particular group, and for other features that might distract students from the intended tasks.	
Db. Use statistical techniques in large-scale assessments to identify potential bias among various subgroups.	

(Continued)

(Continued)

Standard		Your Feeling
Dc.	Appropriately modify assessment tasks to accommodate needs of students with physical disabilities, learning disabilities, or limited English proficiency.	
Dd.	Set assessment tasks in a variety of contexts, to engage students with different interests and experiences, and not to assume the perspective or experience of a particular gender or racial or ethnic group.	
Ea.	Make sound inferences based on assessment data about student achievement and the opportunity to learn science.	

You may find yourself unsure about many of the above standards. For example, what does it mean by "deliberately design assessment"? What does it mean by "make sound inferences based on assessment data about student achievement and opportunity to learn science"? One important reason that you are not sure about these standards is because you do not yet possess enough assessment knowledge and skills. Also, you may not know specific science teaching and learning contexts in which assessment takes place. There are no absolute assessment competences without referring to specific science teaching and learning contexts. Effective science assessment must be planned and conducted within a science teaching and learning framework. This book will help you in both of the above two regards; it will introduce not only a wide variety of assessment methods but also the science teaching and learning contexts to which various assessment methods apply. Each chapter will begin with a list of pertinent assessment standards the chapter will address, followed by a list of assessment skills the chapter will help develop in order for you to meet the assessment standards. At the end of each chapter, there will also be a mastery checklist of the essential skills.

HOW THIS BOOK IS ORGANIZED

There are seven chapters following this first chapter. The seven chapters are presented in the order of diagnostic assessment (Chapter 2), summative assessment (Chapters 3, 4, and 5), and formative assessment (Chapter 6). Chapter 7 deals with grading. The final chapter, Chapter 8, deals with a common element of all assessment—data—and discusses ways of using data to improve science teaching and learning. Chapter 8 also presents a rationale of science assessment as an inquiry to integrate all chapters in this book into a coherent conceptual framework. Please note that the above order is only one way to sequence the chapters. With the exceptions of Chapters 1 and 8, which should be used as the first and last chapters, the other six chapters are relatively independent from each other and thus can be used in any order.

Guiding all chapters in this book are the assessment standards within the National Science Education Standards (NRC, 1996) and the Understanding by Design (UbD) approach (Wiggins & McTighe, 2005). At the beginning of each chapter, a box will identify the NSES assessment standards the chapter addresses, and another box will list the essential assessment skills the chapter intends to develop. Because UbD is presently a common way to structure a science methods course, relations between individual chapters and the UbD scheme are shown in Figure 1.3. Similar relations can be identified between the book chapters and other conceptual frameworks of methods courses.

FIGURE 1.3   Organization of the Book

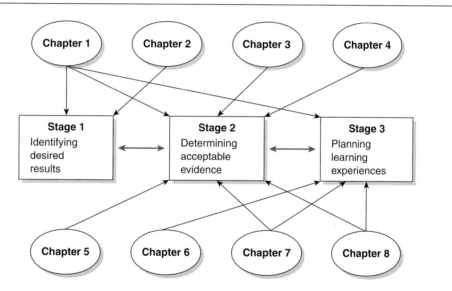

Within each chapter, an Application and Self-Reflection will be placed at the end of each major section. At the end of each chapter, a Chapter Summary will describe major ideas and skills presented in the chapter. A Mastery Checklist is then presented for you to check if you have mastered all the essential skills. Finally, you will be directed to a Web site where you will find useful resources such as research findings, sample assessment work, Web links, assessment instruments, worksheets, and statistical analysis templates. For those who are interested in knowing more about research pertaining to the topics presented in the chapter, the Further Readings section suggests some key references to study.

THE CASES OF ERIC AND ELISIA:
WHAT IS SCIENCE ASSESSMENT ALL ABOUT?

Eric and Elisia began this chapter without much expectation because they thought science assessment was more or less a commonsense practice. After finishing this first chapter, they now seem to realize that assessment may not be as simple as they initially thought at all. They can see how assessment is integral to instruction; thus, planning for science instruction and assessment must take place simultaneously. Furthermore, they understand that, besides grading students, assessment can play an important role in improving their teaching. They are somewhat familiar with different types of assessments (e.g., summative, formative, and diagnostic), but they did not realize how different assessment methods can form a coherent assessment system. The federal laws pertaining to assessment are new to them; they can now understand how handling student assessment information, assessment accommodation and alternative assessment provisions, and differentiated assessments can be serious and thus must be conducted within legal boundaries and with due care. The assessment standards specified in the National Science Education Standards are very comprehensive; most of them are quite vague to them. Given those assessment standards, they have now become anxious to know exactly what those standards require and how to become competent in them. Overall, this chapter seems to have opened their eyes, but they remain unclear how the following chapters will help them to become a science teacher in terms of assessment. Eric and Elisia's learning journey on science assessment continues. . . .

Do the experiences of Eric and Elisia sound familiar to your? What was your initial expectation of science assessment, and how it has changed as the result of this chapter?

Chapter Summary

- Science assessment is an integral component of science teaching and learning; it takes place within science teaching and learning contexts to support student learning. Science assessment is also distinct from science teaching and learning because one central aspect of science assessment involves data collection, analysis, and interpretation.

- Science assessment consists of three foundations: cognition, observation, and interpretation. Observation refers to assessment tasks through which students' attainment of learning outcomes is elicited, interpretation refers to measurement models through which the assessment data are interpreted, and cognition refers to theories on how students learn. Observation and interpretation are related to data collection, analysis, and validation, and cognition is related to science teaching and learning. Observation and interpretation and science teaching and learning must agree with each other.

- Planning for science assessment should take place concurrently with planning for science teaching and learning. Consistent with the backward design approach to planning for science teaching and learning, science assessment should include diagnostic assessment, summative assessment, and formative assessment.

- Applicable federal laws to assessment are the Family Education Rights to Privacy Act (FERPA) and Individuals with Disabilities Education Act (IDEA). Student assessment information is confidential and may not be released without permission. Students with disabilities have the right to assessment accommodation and alternative assessment. Assessment accommodation and alternative assessment must be planned as part of students' individualized education programs (IEPs). Students without disabilities may also need differentiated assessment. Differentiated assessment must match differentiated instruction.

- The 1996 National Science Education Standards include five science assessment standards. The science assessment standards cover purposes and uses of science assessment, scopes of science assessment, and technical qualities of science assessment.

√ Mastery Checklist

- ☐ Describe the three components of science assessment.
- ☐ Develop an assessment plan to support science teaching and learning.
- ☐ Know when test accommodation, alternative assessment, and differentiated assessment are needed.
- ☐ Know how to handle assessment information within the limit of the federal privacy act.
- ☐ State the assessment standards outlined in the National Science Education Standards.

Web-Based Student Study Site

The Companion Web site for *Essentials of Science Classroom Assessment* can be found at **www.sagepub.com/liustudy.**

The site includes a variety of materials to enhance your understanding of the chapter content. Visit the study site to complete an online self-assessment of essential knowledge and skills introduced in this chapter. The study materials also include flash cards, Web resources, and more.

Further Readings

National Research Council (NRC). (2005). *Knowing what students know: The science and design of educational assessment.* Washington, DC: National Academy Press.

This book presents a systematic review of current learning theories and the accompanying assessment approaches. It introduces the most promising measurement models, statistical methods, and technological advances supporting assessment. This book should be foundational reading for anyone who is interested in cognitive dimensions and psychometric models underlying educational assessment.

Wiggins, G., & McTighe, J. (2005). *Understanding by design*. Alexandria, VA: Association for Supervision and Curriculum Development.

This book provides an excellent discussion on the backward design approach to planning instruction for understanding. Assessment is an integral component of the backward design approach. Practical planning templates and many practical examples, with some of them in science, are available in the book.

References

Aquila, F. D. (2008). *School law for K–12 educators*. Thousand Oaks, CA: Sage.

Baker, V. (2004). *Beyond appearances: Students' misconceptions about basic chemical ideas* (2nd ed.). London: Royal Society of Chemistry. http://www.chemsoc.org/pdf/LearnNet/rsc/miscon.pdf

Bransford, J. D., Brown, A. L., & Cocking, R. R. (Eds.). (2000). *How people learn: Brain, mind, experience, and school*. Washington, DC: National Academy Press.

Carin, A. A., & Bass, J. E. (1997). *Teaching science as inquiry* (9th ed.). Upper Saddle River, NJ: Merrill.

Ebenezer, J. V., & Connor, S. (1996). *Learning to teach science: A model for the 21st century*. Upper Saddle River, NJ: Merrill.

National Research Council (NRC). (1996). *National science education standards*. Washington, DC: National Academy Press.

National Research Council (NRC). (2001). *Knowing what students know: The science and design of educational assessment*. Committee on the Foundations of Assessment. Washington, DC: National Academy Press.

Tobin, K., Tippins, D. J., & Gallard, A. J. (1994). Research on instructional strategies for teaching science. In D. L. Gabel (Ed.), *Handbook of research on science teaching and learning* (pp. 45–93). New York: Macmillan.

Wandersee, J. H., Mintzes, J. J., & Novak, J. D. (1994). Research on alternative conceptions in science. In D. L. Gabel (Ed.), *Handbook of research on science teaching and learning* (pp. 177–210). New York: Macmillan.

Wiggins, G., & McTighe, J. (2005). *Understanding by design*. Alexandria, VA: Association for Supervision and Curriculum Development.

CHAPTER 2

Assessment of Preconceptions

Chapter 1 has developed a conceptual framework of science assessment and explained how science assessment should be an integral part of science instruction. Specifically, Chapter 1 suggests that planning for science assessment should take place at the same time as planning for instruction. This chapter pertains to National Science Education Standards (NSES) Assessment Standard B because knowledge of student preconceptions helps define most appropriate learning outcomes for students to achieve, as well as plan most appropriate learning activities for students to experience. In addition, because student preconceptions are the most important factors affecting student learning, identification of student preconceptions helps create the most important opportunities for students to learn. This chapter develops assessment skills essential for identifying student preconceptions. These essential skills are (a) developing questions for specific understandings, (b) conducting group interviews, (c) conducting prediction-observation-explanation sessions, (d) developing conceptual surveys, and (e) locating and using published conceptual inventories. These assessment skills help identify students' preconceptions to inform planning a unit of instruction.

Following the Understanding by Design (UbD) approach defined by Wiggins and McTighe (2005), when you plan a unit of instruction, you need to decide specific learning outcomes students will achieve at the end of the unit. Many of you may simply copy pertinent statements from the state or national content standards and use them as the learning goals for the learning unit. If your intention of the unit is to develop students' in-depth understanding rather than simple factual knowledge, then the above practice is problematic for at least two reasons: (a) Statements in content standards are usually general and vague and do not indicate what understanding students are expected to develop and to what degree, and (b) they do not necessarily relate to students' current ideas of the topic. For these two reasons, statements from content standards when used as objectives of the learning unit may be meaningless for informing the planning of student leaning activities and may be irrelevant to students as they may see no connection between what they already know and what they are asked to learn. The backward design approach by Wiggins and McTighe (2005) addresses this problem. One essential component of the first stage of the backward design approach is to identify student preconceptions so that the desired learning results are directly relevant and meaningful to students. **Student preconceptions** are different ideas students bring with them before they learn the new unit. Student preconceptions provide valuable insight into what students' current understandings

ASSESSMENT STANDARDS ADDRESSED IN CHAPTER 2

NSES Assessment Standard B
    Achievement and opportunity to learn science must be assessed. This standard is further elaborated into the following substandards:

- Achievement data collected focus on the science content that is most important for students to learn.
- Opportunity-to-learn data collected focus on the most powerful indicators of learning.
- Equal attention must be given to the assessment of opportunity to learn and to the assessment of student achievement. (National Research Council [NRC], 1996, p. 79)

are, how they may have developed, and what new understandings need to be further developed for students to meet the learning standards.

Given that the essence of student preconceptions is understanding, and any instructional unit should emphasize understanding, before we introduce those specific skills, let's take a close examination of what understanding is and how to develop appropriate questions for assessing specific understating.

DEVELOPING QUESTIONS TO TARGET SPECIFIC UNDERSTANDING

Preconceptions are due to many sources, such as personal experiences in informal learning, formal science learning, and developmental maturation. Underlying student preconceptions is understanding. There are six facets of understanding: explanation, interpretation, application, perspective, empathy, and self-knowledge (Wiggins & McTighe, 2005). **Explanation** refers to a person's ability to provide knowledgeable and justifiable accounts of events, actions, and ideas. An example of explanation is that the earth's tilt on its axis causes the season changes on the earth. Interpretation refers to the narratives or translations that provide meaning to events or objects. For example, an elementary student interprets the earth's season changes by describing how hot the summer is and how cold the winter is. **Application** is the ability to use knowledge effectively in a new situation to solve a problem. For example, a middle school student uses his knowledge of simple circuits to find a faulty lightbulb in a device. **Perspectives** are the ability to appreciate different points of views. For example, a student can see how her classmate made a mistake in solving a problem in balancing a chemical reaction equation. **Empathy** is the ability to get inside another person's feelings and worldviews. You may not agree with another person, but you respect the person's views and can feel how the person strongly

---

ESSENTIAL SKILLS ADDRESSED IN CHAPTER 2

- Developing questions pertaining to specific understandings
- Conducting group interviews
- Conducting prediction-observation-explanation sessions
- Developing a conceptual survey
- Locating and using published conceptual inventories

holds the views. For example, you share the feeling that environmental activists have in their efforts in conserving the endangered animals but may not necessarily agree with some of their extreme actions. Finally, **self-knowledge** is a person's ability to identify his or her own weaknesses and to actively seek improvement. For example, some students are better than others in self-evaluating their own learning and more able to look for additional resources to improve their learning. Six facets of understanding can function independently, and the more facets a person's understanding involves, the better.

How may understanding be demonstrated? This question is directly relevant to methods for assessing student preconceptions. White and Gunstone (1992) identified six elements in which understanding of concepts may be stored and retrieved from long-term memory: proposition, string, image, episode, intellectual skill, and motor skill. **Propositions** are facts, opinions, and beliefs. For example, Earth is one of the planets of the solar system. Facts, opinions, and beliefs, although distinct, may not be necessarily differentiable in student alternative conceptions. For example, students may think that it is a fact that plants take food from the soil, but this statement is only a personal belief that is scientifically incorrect. **Strings** are fundamental statements or generalizations that do not vary from situation to situation. Strings are usually in the form of proverbs, laws, and rules. For example, that matter cannot be created or destroyed, and thus is conserved, is a string, but that water is matter is a proposition. **Images** are mental representations of sensory perceptions. For example, a clear lake is an image of water. **Episodes** are memories of events experienced directly or vicariously. For example, swimming in a lake is an episode of the buoyancy force. **Intellectual skills** are mental processes performed to solve a problem or conduct a task. For example, comparing the differences between physical change and chemical change involves an intellectual skill of differentiation. Finally, **motor skills** are procedures followed to conduct a physical task. An example of motor skills is performing a measurement. The six elements of understanding are located in different regions of the long-term memory; they operate independently. A person may understand something by describing an episode but not being able to state a proposition or string. The more elements used by a person, the better the person's understanding is.

Applying the above facets and elements, we can use the following matrix to plan questions to assess student preconceptions.

		Facets					
		Explanation	Interpretation	Application	Perspective	Empathy	Self-Knowledge
E	Proposition						
l	String						
e	Image						
m	Episode						
e n	Intellectual skill						
t	Motor skill						

In the above matrix, elements suggest how questions may be asked, and facets suggest what type of understanding may be assessed. Thus, a variety of questions may be asked depending on the concept, intended understanding, and grade level of students. For example, suppose you would like to find out what your fifth-grade students understand about matter. If one intended facet of understanding, according to the state science content standard, is interpretation, and the element of the intended understanding is episode, then sample interview questions can be the following: Can you describe an event in which matter is involved? What are some examples in which you have experienced matter?

APPLICATION AND SELF-REFLECTION 2.1

Write sample questions (e.g., open-ended questions, multiple-choice questions, and performance tasks) for the following instructional planning scenarios. Indicate the element(s) and facet(s) involved in the questions:

1. To find out what a Grade 3 class of students know about living things based on pictures of animals and plants

2. To find out what a Grade 8 class of students know about phases of the moon based on personal episodes

3. To find out if a Grade 10 biology class of students can apply the concept of evolution to explain the similarities and differences of various living things

4. To find out whether a Grade 11 physics class of students is able to evaluate some popular misconceptions commonly held by students

INTERVIEWS

Types of Interviews

Interviews are conversations on a specific topic between the science teacher and a student (i.e., individual interview) or between the science teacher and a whole class (i.e., group interview). Interviews are typically semi-structured by following a predetermined sequence of questions plus additional probing questions developed on the spot. Research has suggested that using either pictures or objects of instances and events can help elicit in-depth student understanding. Interviews using pictures or objects of instances are called *interviews about instances,* and interviews using pictures or objects of events are called *interviews about events* (Gilbert, Watts, & Osborne, 1985). An interview may involve both instances and events.

An example of an interview about instance/event using pictures for a middle school earth science topic is as follows:

> The following two pictures show the inactive Mount Saint Helens volcano, Vancouver, Washington, before and after its eruption.

Source: U.S. Geological Survey (http://vulcan.wr.usgs.gov/Volcanoes/MSH/Publications/MSHPPF/MSH_past_present_future.html).

> Interview questions:
>
> Can you tell me which picture shows the inactive volcano after its eruption? (intended facet and element of understanding: interpretation—intellectual skill)
>
> What do you think causes the volcano eruption? (intended facet and element of understanding: explanation—proposition)
>
> What potential impacts to the environment might a volcanic eruption have? (intended facet and element of understanding: empathy—proposition; perspective—episode)

An example of an interview about instance/event using real objects to probe Grade 3 to 12 students' understanding of matter is as follows:

Interview Guide/Questions	Intended Facet and Element
Let's look at what we have in front of us on the table today (baking soda, vinegar-[cider], and water, all in beakers with original container next to each). For each of these, ask, "What do you know about this?" Are you familiar with this?	Interpretation—proposition
Let's examine each one of these closely. For each of them: How would you describe this to someone so that they would know what it is?	Interpretation—image; interpretation—episode
You noticed that vinegar has a smell. How does the smell get from the vinegar to your nose? If they say it is in the air, ask how it gets in the air. Ask them to describe evaporation if it comes up.	Explanation—proposition; Explanation—episode
(For each substance) What is this made of? Try to get down to smallest aspect they can name. Ask them to define any terms they say. Ask: how do you know that (term)? What does it mean to you?	Explanation—proposition; Explanation—image
What do you think will happen when I add the vinegar to the water? What will that be? Is the vinegar still in there? How about the water? How do you know that?	Interpretation—proposition; explanation—proposition
What do you think will happen when I add the baking soda to the water and stir it? After doing it and stirring it up until it dissolves, ask them to describe and explain (why/how) what happened. Ask about where the baking soda is now. Repeat: how do you think that happened? For all students, if they mention dissolving, ask what they mean by that (how they understand that).	Interpretation—proposition; explanation—proposition
What do you think will happen when I add some baking soda to the vinegar? Why do you think that? After combining them, ask them to describe and explain (why/how) what happened. Ask what the fizzing means, and what is in the bubbles, and follow up their answers. If they mention chemical reaction, probe what that means to them. Ask about where the baking soda is now. Repeat: how do you think that happened?	Interpretation—proposition; explanation—proposition
Ask students to compare dissolving and reacting situations—if they are the same or different. Ask for elaboration of answers.	Explanation—intellectual skills; interpretation—intellectual skills
For the vinegar and baking soda combination, what can affect rate or speed of what you saw happen?	Application—episode; application—proposition

Source: Liu & Lesniak (2006). *Journal of Research in Science Teaching, 43*(3), 320–347. Copyright © 2006, John Wiley & Sons Inc. Reprinted with permission of Wiley-Liss, Inc., a subsidary of John Wiley & Sons, Inc.

APPLICATION AND SELF-REFLECTION **2.2**

Think about a topic and a target grade level (e.g., Grade 4 on living things, Grade 8 on force and motion). What are the desired understandings you would like your students to develop at the end of the learning unit? Gather a set of pictures or objects of instances/events related to the topic, and use the understanding matrix to develop a sequence of interview questions.

Conducting Group Interviews

Although individual interviews are desirable to probe student preconceptions, effective individual interviews require adequate training and practices. For example, a student may respond to questions without much thinking (i.e., answer at random) or provide an answer that he or she does not really believe. Detecting these types of responses requires specialized training and experiences that take much time and practice to learn. Also, individual interviews need to be audiotaped and subsequently transcribed for analysis, which is time-consuming. Interviewing a representative sample of students in a class is often unfeasible for most science teachers. Because of the above, group interviews are more practical. Group interviewing is similar to commonly used brainstorming. Typically, a 10- to 15-minute group interview can elicit sufficient information on student preconceptions for planning a learning unit.

Group interviews should take place in the regular classroom setting as part of an introductory lesson of a new unit or a review lesson of a just completed unit. A typical procedure to conduct the group interviews is as follows:

- Introduce the purpose for the group interview. Explain why this group interview is conducted. Emphasize that the information to be collected will help you as the teacher to plan better learning activities for the class.

- Introduce the materials and objects to be used in the interview. Explain briefly how the interview will be conducted and how long it will take (typically 10–15 minutes). Ensure that the students can ask questions at any time during the interview.

- Begin the interview by asking predetermined questions and follow up with probing questions. Make sure to give students adequate time to form answers to the questions. Pay special attention to those quiet students and encourage them to speak out. Repeat a student's response to double-check if that is what the student meant. Ask the same question using different phrases to cross-validate students' answers. Record student ideas on chart paper.

- Conclude the interview by asking students if they have further questions and thank the students for sharing their understanding.

- Write notes and reflections immediately to help later analysis.

Group dynamics is critical to a successful group interview. To create a group dynamic conducive to eliciting student alternative conceptions, you must tell the group that all ideas are encouraged and respected. Attention must be paid to prevent a few students from dominating group interviews and to encourage quieter students to speak out. Furthermore, you must adopt an appropriate way of recording group interview results. Although audiorecording would be ideal, it may not be feasible in many occasions due to the lack of equipment and the difficulty in setting up, recording, transcribing, and seeking permissions. Using chart paper to record student ideas, as typically done in a brainstorming session, is a reasonable alternative to consider. Giving students a sheet of paper with group interview questions on it to record their answers is another good alternative, although this alternative tends to lead the group interview more toward a structured interview and thus reduces group dynamics.

The following checklist was created for the interviewer (*card* in the table below refers to a flash card with a picture of an instance [i.e., interview about instances] or of an event [i.e., interview about events]).

Dos	Don'ts
1. Try to establish clearly how and what the *pupil* thinks. Emphasize it is the *pupil's* ideas that are important and are being explored.	Do not give any indication to the pupil of your meaning(s) for the word or appear to judge the pupil's response in terms of your meaning(s).
2. Provide a balance between open and closed questions and between simple and penetrating questions. In so doing, maintain and develop pupil confidence.	Do not ask leading questions. Do not ask the type of question where it is easy for the pupil to simply agree with whatever you say.
3. Listen carefully to the pupil's responses and follow up points which are not clear.	Do not rush on (e.g., to the next card) before thinking about the pupil's last response.
4. Where necessary to gain interviewer thinking time, or for the clarity of the audio-record, repeat the pupil response.	Do not respond with a modified version of the pupil response; repeat exactly what was said.
5. Give the pupil plenty of time to formulate a reply.	Do not rush but on the other hand do not exacerbate embarrassing silence.
6. Where pupils express doubt and hesitation, encourage them to share their thinking.	Do not allow pupils to think that this is a test situation and there is a right answer required.
7. Be sensitive to possible misinterpretations of, or misunderstanding about, the initial question. Where appropriate, explore this, and then clarify.	Do not make any assumptions about the way the pupil is thinking.
8. Be sensitive to the unanticipated response, and explore it carefully and with sensitivity.	Do not ignore responses you don't understand. Rather, follow them up until you do understand.

Dos	Don'ts
9. Be sensitive to self-contradictory statements by the pupil.	Try not to forget earlier responses in the same interview.
10. Be supportive of a pupil querying the question you have asked and, in this and other ways, develop an informal atmosphere.	Do not let the interview become an interrogation rather than a friendly chat.
11. Read the question out loud to pupils.	Do not rely on pupils' reading ability.
12. Where all efforts to develop pupil confidence fail, abort the interview.	Do not proceed with an interview where the pupil becomes irrevocably withdrawn.
13. Verbally identify for the audio-record the pupil's name, age, and each card as it is introduced into the discussion.	Do not return to earlier cards without verbal identification for the audio-record.
14. Be sensitive to the possibility that pupils will give an answer simply to fill a silence.	Do not accept an answer without exploring the reasoning behind it.
15. Appreciate that a card omitted will result in missing data.	Make no assumption about the way a pupil would respond to a particular card.

Source: Bell, Osborne, & Tasker (1985). Reproduced by permission.

Analyzing Interview Data

Analyzing student interview data does not have to be formal. One way to analyze data is to compile a list of propositions based on students' responses (White & Gunstone, 1992). Propositions are complete sentences that express relationships or patterns. For example, the following list of propositions is compiled from an interview with an eighth-grade student on matter:

Water is clear liquid

Water is made of hydrogen and oxygen

Water is a molecule

Atoms are the smallest form of matter

Vinegar smell is like air—travels through the atmosphere

Vinegar can mix with water to produce a homogeneous mixture

Homogeneous mixtures can be separated

Water will water down the vinegar but still will not have the same properties of vinegar

Water molecules absorb vinegar molecules

Further analysis of propositions may also be conducted. For example, the frequency of each proposition may be counted among all students interviewed, so that the propositions may be rank-ordered based on their popularities. Propositions may also be grouped into categories and then arranged from the most scientific to least scientific. For example, students' conceptions of matter may be grouped in the following categories from most scientific to least scientific: (a) Matter consists of small particles with distinct chemical properties, (b) matter consists of small particles with distinct physical properties, (c) matter is a pure substance, (d) matter is a mixture of various substances, and (e) matter is an object.

APPLICATION AND SELF-REFLECTION 2.3

Pair with a classmate and conduct a 3-minute one-on-one interview on a subject of mutual interest. Record the interview. Play back the interview and listen together. Discuss how the interview may be improved.

PREDICTION-OBSERVATION-EXPLANATION

Prediction-observation-explanation, or simply POE, is a specialized group interview aiming at probing students' understanding of a natural phenomenon. A POE session typically consists of three tasks: (a) predicting what will happen and justifying the prediction, (b) describing what is happening, and (c) reconciling any conflict between prediction and observation (White & Gunstone, 1992). POE as a diagnostic assessment method is unique in that it focuses on student understanding based on student predications and explanations of a phenomenon. Understanding probed by POE is related to Wiggins and McTighe's facets of explanation, interpretation, and application. This is because when students predict and justify what will happen, they have to apply their prior knowledge and understanding of relevant science theories; when they describe what is happening, they have to interpret their observations based on their knowledge and understanding of relevant science theories; and when they reconcile any conflict between prediction and observation, they once again have to explain the discrepancies by using what they know and understand. Because POE is a group event, when students are asked to share their predictions and explanations, there is also a potential for students to demonstrate their perspectives—an appreciation of different ideas of others—and self-knowledge—an appreciation of their own understanding.

One key to realizing the above potentials of POE in probing student understanding is the selection of the event or phenomenon. If the event is too simple to students, students will only need to recall their prior knowledge, which results in minimal understanding probed. If the phenomenon is too difficult and bears no connection to students' prior knowledge or experiences, students will simply resort to randomly guessing. Thus, a POE event must be somewhat familiar to students, yet not too straightforward or easy in terms of the targeted understanding. One such type of event is called a discrepant event. A **discrepant event** is a surprising, counterintuitive, unexpected, and paradoxical phenomenon. For example, everyone expects objects fall downward. However, if you place a smaller empty test tube into a half-filled bigger test tube and invert them, you will observe the smaller test tube actually moving upward instead of downward when water is dripping out of the larger test tube. The understanding involved in this phenomenon is that air exerts pressure. When water starts dripping from the bigger test tube, it creates a vacuum at the bottom of the bigger test tube, while the air pressure outside the test tubes remains the same. The created difference in air pressure between the vacuum and outside the test tubes results in a net upward force, pushing the smaller test tube upward. When you use this discrepant event to probe student understanding of air pressure, students have to interpret what is happening by analyzing the contextual variables involved in this phenomenon (i.e., air pressure, gravity, weight, and vacuum) and apply their understanding of those contextual variables to create a coherent explanation. Thus, the probed understanding is contextualized rather than static. It involves multiple levels of cognitive reasoning such as understanding, applying, and analyzing.

The following procedures are recommended for using POE to assess student preconceptions:

1. Select a discrepant event that involves the targeted understanding to be developed in the new curriculum unit.

EXAMPLE

Grade 5 target understanding: Plants absorb water through a process called *capillary action;* capillary action creates force called *osmotic pressure.*

Discrepant event: Arrange five half-broken toothpicks with the broken ends together. After placing one drop of water at the center, the toothpicks will move away from each other to form a star.

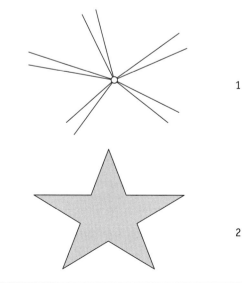

1

2

Grade 10 target understanding: The earth exerts the same gravitational force to all objects. As a result, the acceleration of falling is the same for all objects no matter what the mass is.

Discrepant event: Drop a sheet of paper and a book at the same time separately. The book will fall on the ground first, but the sheet of paper will float in the air and gradually fall on the ground. However, when the sheet of paper is placed on the top of the book and then dropped together, the sheet of paper will stick to the book and fall on the ground together at the same time.

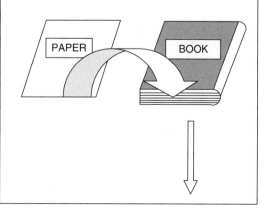

2. Introduce the event to students by stating the purpose of this event in terms of planning for the new unit of instruction, the materials involved, and the procedures to follow. During this introduction, it is important to emphasize that student responses will help plan better learning activities for the upcoming unit, and their responses will not be graded and thus they should feel free to express their ideas. A recording sheet can be very helpful and should be explained at this time. Important sections that should be included in the recording sheet are the following: Purpose, What Is Your Prediction, Bases for Your Prediction, What Has Happened, How Is Your Prediction Different From What Has Happened? How Can You Explain the Discrepancy If Any?

3. Ask students to make predictions and write them down on the recording sheet. During this stage, students should not share their predictions so that their predictions will truly reflect their understanding of the event. The purpose is to obtain a variety of predictions from students. For example, for the fifth-grade toothpick discrepant event described above, ask students what will happen to the toothpicks after you have placed a water drop at the center of the broken toothpicks. Some possible student predictions are as follows:

    a. Toothpicks will absorb water.
    b. Nothing will happen (e.g., toothpicks will not move).
    c. The toothpicks will become wet.
    d. The toothpicks will move away from each other.

For the 10th-grade book-dropping discrepant event described above, some possible student predictions are as follows:

    a. Paper will float in the air and then fall to the ground, while the book will fall to the ground immediately.
    b. Paper will fall straight down as the book does, but the book will fall to the ground faster.
    c. Paper and book will stay together and fall to the ground at the same time.

4. Ask students to justify their predications and write them down on the recording sheet. Once again, no discussion is allowed during this stage so that a variety of student reasoning is obtained through their writings. Some of the possible explanations for the above two discrepant events are as follows:

Prediction	Justification
Discrepant Event: Toothpicks	
a. Toothpicks will absorb water.	a. Toothpicks are dry.
b. Nothing will happen (e.g., toothpicks will not move).	b. Water will just evaporate; one water drop cannot move toothpicks.
c. The toothpicks will become wet.	c. Toothpicks can suck in water.
d. The toothpicks will move away from each other.	d. Toothpicks will expand due to water absorbed.

Prediction	Justification
Discrepant Event: Paper and Book Dropping	
a. Paper will float in the air and then fall to the ground, while the book will fall to the ground immediately.	a. Paper is light, but the book is heavy.
b. Paper will fall straight down as the book does, but the book will fall to the ground faster.	b. Heavier objects fall faster than lighter objects.
c. Paper and book will stay together and fall to the ground at the same time.	c. The book drags paper and keeps it on top.

5. Conduct the demonstration, and ask students to write down what is happening. Writing down what is happening is very important because even with the same phenomenon, different students may see different things due to their different understanding. Once again, the purpose of this step is to document students' variety of descriptions of the phenomenon.

6. Ask students to compare their predictions with what has happened, and write down their explanation if there is any discrepancy. As a result of a discrepant event, it is anticipated that students' predictions are different from what has happened. This can potentially create a cognitive dissonance, which provides an opportune and motivational moment for students to apply additional knowledge and understanding to reason about the phenomenon. One key characteristic of students' preconceptions is the deep commitment by students. Thus, whether students are able to change their preconceptions in the situation of cognitive conflict is a very important indication of the degree of students' commitment to their misconceptions.

The above process of POE focuses on students' reasoning about a phenomenon when making predictions, justifying predictions, describing the phenomenon, and reconciling any potential discrepancies between the prediction and the outcome. Because students' above reasoning is documented in their individual writings on the recording sheet, POE should result in a large amount of wealthy information about students' preconceptions on a given topic.

Analyzing students' writings obtained from POE can be done in a similar manner as analyzing interview data. Categories of students' predictions and justifications may be listed, and the frequencies of the categories among the students can then be tallied. The different frequencies of the categories indicate popularity of different preconceptions among students.

APPLICATION AND SELF-REFLECTION 2.4

Now let's put your knowledge and skills into practice. Design a POE sequence, including a student recording sheet to probe students' preconceptions on the following two topics: (a) air occupies space (5th grade) and (b) osmosis through semipermeable membranes of plants (11th-grade biology).

DEVELOPING CONCEPTUAL SURVEYS

A conceptual survey is based on paper-and-pencil tests. Different from a paper-and-pencil test, a conceptual survey is not graded. Because the purpose of a conceptual survey is to identify students' alternative conceptions or preconceptions, open-ended questions are normally used. To avoid responses from students that are too broad and diverse, you may place some restrictions on the open-ended questions. For example, you may limit student responses to specific aspects most relevant to the new unit of instruction. You may also limit the length of student responses. A sample conceptual survey on matter is as follows:

SURVEY OF PRECONCEPTIONS OF MATTER

List 10 words or phrases that you think describe the concept of matter:

Write one paragraph on how the above 10 words are related to matter and to each other:

Another form of conceptual survey is to use the selected-response question format that produces results for easy analysis and large-scale administration. The most commonly used selected-response question format is multiple choice (MC). Using MC questions for identifying student preconceptions suffers from a number of limitations, such as inability to assess the student reasoning process and guessing. The above limitations of MC questions for identifying student alternative conceptions can be addressed with two-tiered MC questions. **A two-tiered MC question** is a combination of two conventional multiple-choice questions, with the first one asking students to answer a question by selecting the best answer and the second one asking students to justify the given answer by selecting all applicable reasons. Here is an example of a two-tiered MC question:

EXAMPLE

After a large ice cube has melted in a beaker of water, how will the water level change?

   a. Higher

   b. Lower

   c. The same*

Why do you think so? Choose all that apply.

   a. The mass of water displaced is equal to the mass of the ice.*

   b. Ice has more volume than water.

   c. Water is denser than ice.

   d. The ice cube decreases the temperature of water.

   e. Water molecules in water occupy more space than in ice.

Note: The correct answer is marked with an asterisk.

As we can see from the above example, two-tiered MC questions provide information about a student's reasoning for selecting an MC choice. This format is particularly powerful when the reasons provided in the second tier are from students' common reasons or alternative conceptions identified through interviews, observations, or research literature. Variations to this format are also possible. For example, in addition to providing a few choices for reasons, the second tier can also be open-ended, such as using "Please justify," or give a few reasons and have the last choice as "Other (please list)."

Another variation of the two-tiered MC question format is to add a third tier: the confidence. The confidence scale can be added to both tiers of the question. For example:

WHICH CIRCUIT(S) WILL LIGHT THE BULB?

Circuit(s): _____

Circuit 1   Circuit 2   Circuit 3   Circuit 4

Please circle your level of confidence in your answer:

Highest Confidence   5   4   3   2   1   0   Lowest Confidence

Reason:

(a) Because the bulb needs to be connected to the battery by a single wire or two wires.

(b) Because there is a complete circuit from one end of the battery to the other.

(c) Because the bulb is placed directly on the battery.

(d) Because this connection enables the current to travel in two directions to meet at the lightbulb.

(e) Others (please specify): _____

Please circle your level of confidence in your reason:

Highest Confidence   5   4   3   2   1   0   Lowest Confidence

---

Source: Sabah (2007). Reproduced by permission.

The advantage of having a confidence scale is to find out how strongly students may hold alterative conceptions. Incorrect responses with high confidence are indications of strong misconceptions, which can have important implications for curriculum and instruction. Strongly held misconceptions may be difficult to change and thus require special attention during instruction.

Developing a standardized two-tiered conceptual survey is a time-consuming process and not as simple as it may appear. David Treagust (1988, 1995) suggests a three-phase process that consists of defining the content, obtaining information about students' misconceptions, and developing the two-tier test items. Each of the above phases may involve multiple procedures. For example, Phase 2 may involve (a) examining the related literature, (b) conducting unstructured student interviews, and (c) developing multiple-choice content items with free response. A well-developed standardized two-tiered conceptual survey, such as some published ones (described below), is typically the result of multicycles of developing, pilot testing, and revising.

APPLICATION AND SELF-REFLECTION 2.5

Now let's put your knowledge and skills on developing conceptual survey into practice. Working with a partner, choose a science topic from the content standard of a particular grade and develop a conceptual survey. Make sure you define your domain of understanding before you develop questions. Present the survey to the class.

STANDARDIZED CONCEPTUAL INVENTORIES

Over the past three decades, science educators have developed a wide variety of standardized conceptual inventories to identify students' alternative conceptions of various concepts. Different from a conceptual survey a teacher develops, standardized conceptual inventories have gone through a rigorous validation process to establish their validity and reliability. Another characteristic of standardized conceptual inventories is that they use primarily multiple choice, including two-tiered multiple-choice questions, and thus they are appropriate for whole-class and large-scale administration. Currently, most standardized conceptual inventories pertain to topics of high school and college introductory science courses. A partial list of standardized conceptual inventories, including sources, is available in Table 2.1; the course Web site contains links to a number of conceptual inventories accessible on the Web.

The following is a sample well-known conceptual inventory:

Hestenes, D., Wells, M., & Swackmaher, G. (1992). Force Concept Inventory. *The Physics Teacher, 30,* 141–158.

The Force Concept Inventory (FCI) is probably the most widely used physics diagnostic test. It contains 30 multiple-choice questions that "require a forced choice between Newtonian concepts and common-sense alternatives" (Hestenes, Wells, & Swackmaher, 1992, p. 142). The FCI was developed through analysis of interviews of students from ninth grade to university undergraduate and graduate physics with distracters derived from student-incorrect conceptions. Because most of the instrument's distracters are culled from student-incorrect reasoning, it is common for new students with no previous physics instruction to score much lower on the FCI than random chance alone would predict. Therefore, the "errors" on the inventory are more informative than the "correct" choices.

About half of the questions on the FCI come directly from another similar diagnostic test called the Mechanics Diagnostic test. Although no statistical results on validity and reliability are available on the FCI, the authors claimed that "considerable care was taken to establish the validity and reliability of the Diagnostic. Formal procedures to do the same for the Inventory are unnecessary." The authors interviewed 20 students and found that students gave very similar responses to FCI questions as to previous Diagnostic questions. A comprehensive set of pretest and posttest baseline data at various high schools and universities is available.

TABLE 2.1   A Partial List of Conceptual Inventories

Title	Applicable Grade/Subject	Source
Chemistry Concepts Inventory (CCI)	High school and college/chemistry	Mulford, D. R., & Robinson, W. R. (2002). An inventory for alternate conceptions among first-semester general chemistry students. *Journal of Chemical Education, 79*(6), 739–744.
Conceptual Inventory of Natural Selection	High school and college/biology	Andeson, D. L., & Fisher, K. M. (2002). Development and evaluation of the Conceptual Inventory of Natural Selection. *Journal of Research in Science Teaching, 39*(10), 952–978.
Conceptual Survey in Electricity and Magnetism (CSEM)	High school and college/physics	Maloney, D. P., & O'Kuma, T. L. (2001). Surveying students' conceptual knowledge of electricity and magnetism. *American Journal of Physics, 69*(7, Suppl.), S12–S23.
Determining and Interpreting Resistive Electric Circuits Concept Test (DIRECT)	High school and college/physics	Engelhardt, P. V., & Beichner, R. J. (2004). Students' understanding of direct current resistive electrical circuits. *American Journal of Physics, 72*(1), 98–115.
Diffusion and Osmosis Test (DOT)	High school and college/biology	Odom, A. L., & Barrow, L. H. (1995). Development and application of a two-tier diagnostic test measuring college biology students' understanding of diffusion and osmosis after a course of instruction. *Journal of Research in Science Teaching, 32*(1), 45–61.
Force Concept Inventory (FCI)	High school and college/physics	Hestenes, D., Wells, M., & Swackmaher, G. (1992). Force Concept Inventory. *The Physics Teacher, 30,* 141–158.
Geosciences Concept Inventory (GCI)	High school and college	Libarkin, J. C., & Anderson, S. W. (2006). The Geosciences Concept Inventory: Application of Rasch analysis to concept inventory development in higher education. In X. Liu & W. Boone (Eds.), *Applications of Rasch measurement in science education* (pp. 45–73). Maple Grove, MN: JAM Press.
Gravity and the Motion of Planets	High school/physics	Treagust, D., & Smith, C. (1989). Secondary students' understanding of gravity and the motion of planets. *School Science and Mathematics, 89*(5), 380–391.

Title	Applicable Grade/Subject	Source
Qualitative Analysis Diagnostic Instrument	High school/ chemistry	Tan, D., Goh, N. K., Chia, L. S., & Treagust, D. F. (2002). Development and application of a two-tier multiple choice diagnostic instrument to assess high school students' understanding of inorganic chemistry qualitative analysis. *Journal of Research in Science Teaching, 39*(4), 283–301.

The following is a sample question from the FCI:

A woman exerts a constant horizontal force on a large box. As a result, the box moves across a horizontal floor at a constant speed "v_0."
The constant horizontal force applied by the woman:

(A)   Has the same magnitude as the weight of the box.
(B)   Is greater than the weight of the box.
(C)   Has the same magnitude as the total force which resists the motion of the box.
(D)   Is greater than the total force which resists the motion of the box.
(E)   Is greater than either the weight of the box or the total force which resists its motion.

Source: Reprinted with permission from Hestenes, D. Wells, M., & Swackmaher, G. (1992), *The Physics Teacher, 30,* 141–158.

APPLICATION AND SELF-REFLECTION 2.6

What do you like about standardized conceptual inventories? Go to the Sage Web site, and review a variety of standardized conceptual inventories for a wide range of grade levels. Do you see some commonalities among the standardized conceptual inventories? Choose one standardized conceptual inventory and present it to the class by describing how it may be useful for planning a particular science unit.

THE CASES OF ERIC AND ELISIA: ASSESSMENT OF PRECONCEPTIONS

Eric and Elisia ended this chapter with mixed feelings. Initially, they thought that, like any other teachers, they would know their students well and did not really see a necessity to spend time to identify students' preconceptions to help them plan a new unit of instruction. Based on previous experiences as grade students, they knew which concepts were difficult and what were possible student misconceptions. The types of understanding by Wiggins and McTighe took them by surprise. They never thought that understanding could be demonstrated in so many different ways and how

(Continued)

(Continued)

developing good understanding in their students may not be such a simple task. They can now see how identifying specific types of students' preconceptions or understanding that students bring into a unit of instruction can be potentially helpful. They understand now that different techniques (e.g., interview techniques, POE, conceptual surveys, and standardized conceptual surveys) result in information on students' different types of understanding and how it is very important to use a method that is most appropriate for the target understanding they would like to develop in the new unit of instruction. For Eric, he can see interviews, POE, and conceptual surveys to be particularly useful given his students' young ages, while Elisia can see the relevance of all the techniques, including standardized conceptual surveys, to her high school students. Both Eric and Elisia are now eager to apply the techniques introduced in this chapter when they plan their next unit of instruction. However, they remain unsure about how much difference identifying student preconceptions will make in terms of developing students' understanding. With much anticipation and uncertainty, Eric and Elisia's learning journey on science assessment continues. . . .

Do the experiences of Eric and Elisia sound familiar to you? What were your initial ideas of assessment of preconceptions, and how have they changed as the result of this chapter?

Chapter Summary

- Interviews are conversations on a specific topic between the science teacher and a student (i.e., individual interview) or between the science teacher and a whole class (i.e., group interview). Interviews are typically semi-structured. Interview questions should be determined based on objectives of the learning module and may be guided by an element-by-facet of understanding matrix. Interviews can take place as interviews-about-instances or interviews-about-events. When conducting a whole-class interview (i.e., group interview), you need to pay special attention to group dynamics. Interviewing students requires thoughts and skills. Good interviews elicit student spontaneous convictions. Analyzing student interview data may take the form of compiling a list of propositions based on students' responses.

- POE is a specialized group interview aimed at probing students' understanding of and reasoning about a natural phenomenon. A POE session typically consists of three tasks: (a) predicting what will happen and justifying the prediction, (b) describing what is happening, and (c) reconciling any conflict between prediction and observation. POE usually uses a special type of demonstration called a *discrepant event*. A discrepant event is a surprising, counterintuitive, unexpected, and paradoxical phenomenon. Although POE is conducted in a whole group, students are asked to write down on a recording sheet their predictions, justifications, observations, and explanations of the discrepancy between the prediction and observation. Discussion among students takes place only after students have completed their individual writings.

- A conceptual survey is based on paper-and-pencil tests. Because the purpose of a conceptual survey is to identify students' alternative conceptions or preconceptions, open-ended questions are normally used. To avoid responses from students that are too broad and diverse, you may place some restrictions on the open-ended questions. Conceptual surveys may also use selected-response question formats, such as multiple choice (MC). A two-tiered MC question can address common limitations associated with MC questions. A two-tiered MC question is a combination of two conventional multiple-choice questions, with the first one asking students to answer a question by selecting the best answer and the second one asking students to justify the given answer by selecting all applicable reasons. One variation of the two-tiered MC question format is to add a third tier: the confidence. The confidence scale can be added to both tiers of the question.

- There are a wide variety of standardized conceptual inventories for identifying students' alternative conceptions of various specific concepts. Different from a conceptual survey a teacher develops, standardized conceptual inventories have gone through a rigorous validation process. Thus, their validity and reliability are already established.

√ Mastery Checklist

- ☐ Develop questions pertaining to specific understandings.
- ☐ Conduct group interviews.
- ☐ Conduct a prediction-observation-explanation session.
- ☐ Develop a conceptual survey.
- ☐ Locate and use a standardized conceptual inventory.

Web-Based Student Study Site

The Companion Web site for *Essentials of Science Classroom Assessment* can be found at **www.sagepub.com/liustudy**.

The site includes a variety of materials to enhance your understanding of the chapter content. Visit the study site to

- complete an online self-assessment of essential knowledge and skills introduced in this chapter
- find Web addresses that contain standardized conceptual inventories, as well as Web site addresses that contain resources on students' alternative conceptions of various science concepts
- find a list of students' alternative conceptions based on published studies; the list is organized by concepts commonly taught in elementary and secondary school science curriculums

Further Readings

Baker, V. (2004). *Beyond appearances: Students' misconceptions about basic chemical ideas* (2nd ed.). London: Royal Society of Chemistry. http://www.chemsoc.org/pdf/LearnNet/rsc/miscon.pdf

This book is a very comprehensive review of students' alternative conceptions of various chemical concepts. Each chapter provides a concise summary of research findings on student alternative conceptions of the concept and discusses implications for chemistry teaching and learning.

Liem, T. L. (1990). *Invitations to science inquiry* (2nd ed.). El Cajon, CA: Science Inquiry Enterprise.

This is a very popular resource book of discrepant events. The over 400 discrepant events contained in the book cover a wide variety of topics commonly taught in elementary and secondary science curricula. Each discrepant event is also accompanied by a scientific explanation of the involved phenomenon so that everyone can understand the concepts involved.

Taber, K. (2002). *Chemical misconceptions: Prevention, diagnosis and cure: Vol. II. Classroom resources.* London: Royal Society of Chemistry.

This resource book includes classroom activities and diagnostic instruments on various chemical concepts ready for chemistry teachers to use. Resources are organized into three age groups: ages 11 to 14, ages 14 to 16, and after age 16.

Wandersee, J. H., Mintzes, J. J., & Novak, J. D. (1994). Research on alternative conceptions in science. In D. Gabel (Ed.), *Handbook of research on science teaching and learning* (pp. 177–210). New York: Macmillan.

This book chapter provides a systematic review of research on student preconceptions. In addition to a summary of student preconceptions related to various concepts in biology, chemistry, earth science, and physics, the chapter also discusses the theoretical framework underlying research on student alternative conceptions research.

White, R., & Gunstone, R. (1992). *Probing understanding.* London: Falmer.

This is a very informative book on a wide variety of methods for probing students' understanding. The methods introduced in the book are concept mapping, prediction-observation-explanation, interviews, drawings, fortune lines, relational diagrams, word association, and question production. In addition, the book also provides a good review of theories on understanding and validity and reliability of probing student understanding.

References

Bell, B., Osborne, R., & Tasker, R. (1985). Finding out what children think. In R. Osborne & P. Freyberg (Eds.), *Learning in science: The implications of children's science* (pp. 160–161). Auckland, New Zealand: Heinemann Education.

Gilbert, J. K., Watts, D. M., & Osborne, R. J. (1985). Eliciting student views using an interview-about-instances technique. In L. H. T. West & A. L. Pine (Eds.), *Cognitive structure and conceptual change* (pp. 11–27). Orlando, FL: Academic Press.

Hestenes, D., Wells, M., & Swackmaher, G. (1992). Force Concept Inventory. *The Physics Teacher, 30,* 141–158.

Liu, X., & Lesniak, K. (2006). Progression in children's understanding of the matter concept from elementary to high school. *Journal of Research in Science Teaching, 43*(3), 320–347.

National Research Council (NRC). (1996). *National science education standards.* Washington, DC: National Academy Press.

Sabah, S. (2007). *Developing a two-tiered instrument with confidence levels for assessing students' conceptions of direct current circuits.* Unpublished doctoral dissertation, State University of New York at Buffalo.

Treagust, D. F. (1988). Development and use of diagnostic tests to evaluate students' misconceptions in science. *International Journal of Science Education, 10,* 159–169.

Treagust, D. F. (1995). Diagnostic assessment of students' science knowledge. In S. M. Glynn & R. Duit (Eds.), *Learning science in the schools: Research reforming practice* (pp. 327–346). Mahwah, NJ: Lawrence Erlbaum.

White, R., & Gunstone, R. (1992). *Probing understanding.* London: Falmer.

Wiggins, G., & McTighe, J. (2005). *Understanding by design.* Alexandria, VA: Association for Supervision and Curriculum Development.

Chapter 3

Summative Assessment

Chapter 2 has introduced various techniques for assessing student preconceptions. Following the Understanding by Design (UbD) approach (Wiggins & McTighe, 2005), the next stage in planning a unit of instruction is deciding what evidence at the end of the unit indicates student mastery of learning outcomes, which calls for the development of summative assessment. Planning summative assessment before planning learning activities is what makes the UbD's backward design approach unique and powerful because knowledge of what students should demonstrate at the end of the unit can inform what you should plan for students during the unit (i.e., opportunity to learn).

Summative assessment takes place at the end of a learning sequence to find out if students have mastered the learning outcomes. There are two important uses of summative assessment results in science teaching: (a) to decide if remedial instruction is necessary for some students to help them meet the learning expectations and (b) to grade students to create a record of their achievement and to communicate it to parents and interested others. Because the above two uses have serious implications in terms of allocation of learning resources, time, and future learning opportunities, summative assessment needs to be conducted with great care and thought. In this chapter, we will first develop skills in creating a test blueprint for summative assessment. We will then develop specific skills in writing high-quality multiple-choice, matching, and constructed-response questions and in providing differentiated assessment to students for their individual differences. We will also develop skills in reviewing and selecting external test questions for summative assessment.

CREATING TEST GRIDS

A very important first step in developing a summative assessment is to define the domain of assessment. The domain of assessment represents the scope and depth of test coverage; it is directly derived from the defined goals and objectives for the unit. One way to define the domain of assessment is to use a two-dimensional table commonly called a test grid or test blueprint. **A test grid** consists of a topic dimension and a cognitive reasoning dimension. Because there may be different emphases given to different topics and different cognitive

ESSENTIAL SKILLS ADDRESSED IN CHAPTER 3

- Create a summative assessment test grid.
- Write high-quality multiple-choice questions.
- Write high-quality matching questions.
- Write high-quality constructed-response questions.
- Conducted differentiated assessment.
- Evaluate external test questions.

reasoning skills, it is necessary to assign different weights to different combinations of topics and cognitive reasoning skill. The above three components—that is, topic, cognitive reasoning skills, and weight—form a test grid with values. In a test grid with values, topics are usually in rows and cognitive reasoning skills in columns. Table 3.1 shows a sample test grid with values.

A test grid with values like Table 3.1 indicates two important aspects about the assessment domain: (a) what to assess (the intersections between rows and columns) and (b) how much emphasis there is for each combination in the assessment (the cell values). In the example of Table 3.1, we see that the assessment will cover five topics: substances, mixture, conservation, physical change, and chemical change; the above topics of content involve three cognitive reasoning skills: remembering, understanding, and applying. The cell values are determined by the product between weights of the corresponding topic and skill and the total points of the summative assessment. The procedure for creating such a table is as follows: (a) Identify topics to be assessed and their relative emphases in percentages (defining the rows), (b) identify cognitive skills expected and their relative emphases in percentages (defining the columns), (c) decide the total points for the summative assessment,

TABLE 3.1   A Sample Test Grid With Values

Values		Remembering 50%	Understanding 30%	Applying 20%	Subtotal (Points)
Substances	20%	5	3	2	10
Mixture	30%	8	4	3	15
Conservation	15%	4	2	2	8
Physical change	20%	5	3	2	10
Chemical change	15%	4	2	1	7
Subtotal (points)		26	14	10	**50 points**

ASSESSMENT STANDARDS ADDRESSED IN CHAPTER 3

NSES Assessment Standard A

Assessment must be consistent with the decisions they are designed to inform. This standard is further elaborated into the following substandards:

- Assessments are deliberately designed.
- Assessments have explicitly stated purposes.
- The relation between the decisions and the data is clear.
- Assessment procedures are internally consistent. (National Research Council [NRC], 1996, p. 78)

NSES Assessment Standard C

The technical quality of the data collected is well matched to the decisions and actions taken on the basis of their interpretation. This standard is further elaborated into the following substandards:

- The feature that is claimed to be measured is actually measured.
- An individual student's performance is similar on two or more tasks that claim to measure the same aspect of student achievement.
- Students have adequate opportunity to demonstrate their achievements.
- Assessment tasks and methods for presenting them provide data that are sufficiently stable to lead to the same decisions if used at different times. (NRC, 1996, pp. 83–85)

NSES Assessment Standard D

Assessment practices must be fair. This standard is further elaborated into the following substandards:

- Assessment tasks must be reviewed for the use of stereotypes, for assumptions that reflect the perspectives or experiences of a particular group, for language that might be offensive to a particular group, and for other features that might distract students from the intended tasks.
- Large-scale assessments must use statistical techniques to identify potential bias among subgroups.
- Assessment tasks must be appropriately modified to accommodate the needs of students with physical disabilities, learning disabilities, or limited English proficiency.
- Assessment tasks must be set in a variety of contexts, be engaging to students with different interests and experiences, and must not assume the perspective or experience of a particular gender, racial, or ethnic group. (NRC, 1996, pp. 85–86)

(d) calculate the cell values by multiplying total points by combined relative emphases, and (e) make adjustment to cell values and ensure that the total of cell values is equal to the total summative assessment points. Deciding emphases of topics and cognitive reasoning is subjective; important factors determining relative emphases may include importance in the curriculum, amount of instructional time to spend, and students' ability level. The total summative assessment point is arbitrary and decided mainly for convenience.

Once the assessment domain is defined in the form of a test grid with values, the next step to plan the summative assessment is to decide the assessment format and question type. There is a wide variety of assessment formats and question types from which to choose. The most commonly used assessment formats are paper-and-pencil tests and performance assessments. Paper-and-pencil tests are good at assessing knowledge and simple understanding, while performance assessments are good at assessing science inquiry. Both formats of assessment are typically necessary because good understanding needs to be demonstrated in multiple ways and contexts. Question types can be many, such as multiple-choice, matching, short constructed-response, extended constructed-response, and essay questions.

Once you have decided on assessment formats and question types, you can then operationalize the test grid with values into a test grid with items. Table 3.2 shows a sample test grid with items based on the test grid in Table 3.1.

From Table 3.2, we see that the summative assessment will include two tests (i.e., paper-and-pencil and performance tests). The paper-and-pencil test will include multiple-choice questions for assessing remembering and constructed-response questions for assessing understanding. The performance assessment will test students' ability to apply their knowledge of all the topics to conduct two performance tasks. We also see from Table 3.2 that the summative assessment will include 35 questions, among which 26 are multiple-choice questions, 7 constructed-response questions, and 2 performance tasks. The distribution of the questions is also indicated in the cells of the table. Relating cells of Table 3.2 to those of Table 3.1, we see that each multiple-choice question will have 1 point, each constructed-response question will have 2 or 3 points, and each performance assessment will have more than 1 point (such as 5 points for each task).

Once a test grid with items is created, the next steps in developing a summative assessment are to write test questions and develop performance assessment by using the test grid

TABLE 3.2   A Sample Test Grid With Items

Number of Items (Points)	Remembering Multiple Choice	Understanding Constructed Response	Applying Performance	Subtotal
Substances	5 (5)	2 (3)	2 (10)	
Mixture	8 (8)	2 (4)		
Conservation	4 (4)	1 (2)		
Physical change	5 (5)	1 (3)		
Chemical change	4 (4)	1 (2)		
Subtotal	26 (26)	7 (14)	2 (10)	**35 (50)**

with items as a guide. This chapter will focus on paper-and-pencil test questions; Chapter 4 will focus on other types of test questions. But before we proceed, let's take a moment to reflect and apply what we have learned.

APPLICATION AND SELF-REFLECTION 3.1

An intermediate science teacher is planning a unit on energy transfer. The unit will take 4 weeks. The overall goal of the unit is to develop an overall understanding that energy exists in many different forms, and although energy can be transferred from one form to another, the total amount of energy is conserved. The overall objective of the unit is to help students describe the sources and identify the transformations of energy observed in everyday life. The specific objectives for the unit are as follows:

By the end of the unit, students will understand the following:

1. The sun is a major source of energy for the earth. Other sources of energy include nuclear and geothermal energy.

2. Fossil fuels contain stored solar energy and are considered nonrenewable resources. They are a major source of energy in the United States. Solar energy, wind, moving water, and biomass are some examples of renewable energy resources.

3. Most activities in everyday life involve one form of energy being transformed into another. For example, the chemical energy in gasoline is transformed into mechanical energy in an automobile engine. Energy, in the form of heat, is almost always one of the products of energy transformations.

4. Different forms of energy include heat, light, electrical, mechanical, sound, nuclear, and chemical. Energy is transformed in many ways.

5. Energy can be considered to be either kinetic energy, which is the energy of motion, or potential energy, which depends on relative position.

Develop a test grid with values and a test grid with items for a summative assessment of this unit. Share your test grids with the class and critique each other's.

WRITING MULTIPLE-CHOICE QUESTIONS

Multiple-choice (MC) questions are probably the most commonly used question type in science assessment. MC questions consist of two components: the stem and the choices. The stem is a statement asking a question, and the choices are possible answers, usually four or five, to the stated question. Choices must contain one best or correct answer; other choices are distracters or foils.

Guidelines for Writing Multiple-Choice Questions

1. The stem should be meaningful by itself and present a definite question.

Rationale: Presenting a question in the stem makes students understand the learning outcome you intend to assess. Otherwise, students have to read both the stem and all the choices to figure out what the question is asking for, which makes the question ambiguous and more likely for students to misunderstand your intention.

EXAMPLE   **The item should be meaningful**

Poor   A scientist . . .

   a. Consults the writing of Aristotle.
   b. Debates with fellow scientists.
   c. Makes a careful observation during experiments.
   d. Thinks about the probability.

Better   How does a scientist typically discover new facts?

   a. Consulting the writing of Aristotle.
   b. Debating with fellow scientists.
   c. Making careful observations during experiments.*
   d. Thinking about the probability.

---

2. Items should be clear and in simple language.

Rationale: Learning outcomes in science are distinct from that in reading. It is necessary to separate reading and language skills from science achievements to increase the relevance of test scores.

EXAMPLE   **The item should be clear and in simple language**

Poor   In which state do records indicate a maximum statistical occurrence of earthquakes?

   a. California*
   b. Iowa
   c. New York
   d. South Carolina

Better   Which state has most earthquakes on record?

   a. California*
   b. Iowa
   c. New York
   d. South Carolina

3. Make all choices plausible to uninformed students.

Rationale: Student understanding should be the only factor in determining whether the student will answer the question correctly. Implausible choices reduce the number of functional choices, thus increasing the probability for an uninformed student to answer the question correctly by guessing.

EXAMPLE   Make choices plausible

Poor   What are electrons?

    a. Mechanical tools
    b. Negative particles*
    c. Neutral particles
    d. Nuclei of atoms

Better   What are electrons?

    a. Negative particles*
    b. Neutral particles
    c. Nuclei of atoms
    d. Positive particles

There are a few ways to make choices plausible to uninformed students. One way is to use typical student misconceptions identified during teaching or from published research. For example, research has shown that students commonly have the following misconceptions about motion: (a) All objects fall but heavy objects fall faster; (b) constant motion requires a constant force; (c) if a body is not moving, there is no force on it; and (d) if a body is moving, there is a force acting on it in the direction of motion. Accordingly, choices based on those misconceptions for an item on forces can be plausible for those uninformed students on mechanics.

4. Arrange the responses in an apparent logical order.

Rationale: Logically ordered choices suggest to students that there is no intention to place the correct answer in a particular position, and thus they should not speculate on the correct answer based on the order of choices. Because students will respond to the question based only on their understanding, the question will more likely serve its intended purpose.

EXAMPLE

Poor   How many seasons in a year?

    a. 3
    b. 2
    c. 4*
    d. 1

(Continued)

(Continued)

Better How many seasons in a year?

    a. 1
    b. 2
    c. 3
    d. 4*

5. Avoid extraneous clues to the correct choice.

Rationale: Unnecessary information included in the choices may mislead a student to an incorrect answer or lead a student to the correct answer even though the student may not possess the required understanding. Extraneous clues can be a mismatch in grammar between the stem and the choice, suggesting the choice to be incorrect; unequal length in choices, misleading students to think the longer choice to be correct; or adverbs such as *absolutely* and *always* that are normally not correct.

EXAMPLE

Poor How do plants make their food?

    a. Fertilizer
    b. Photosynthesis*
    c. Seed
    d. Soil

Better What is necessary for plants to make their food?

    a. Fertilizer
    b. Photosynthesis*
    c. Seed
    d. Soil

6. Avoid using "none of the above" and "all of the above" alternatives.

Rationale: The use of "none of the above" and "all of the above" choices is usually due to exhaustion of adequate distracters or uncertainty on what the assessment objective of the item is. They are either redundant or misleading and thus need to be replaced by plausible choices. Even when "none of the above" or "all of the above" is the intended correct answer, the use of them is still unnecessary because these choices do not indicate exactly what students know or don't know.

EXAMPLE

Poor   According to Boyle's law, which of the following changes will occur to the pressure of a gas at a given temperature when the volume of the gas is increased?

    a. Increase
    b. Decrease*
    c. No change
    d. None of the above

Better   According to Boyle's law, which of the following changes will occur to the pressure of a gas at a given temperature when the volume of the gas is increased?

    a. Increase
    b. Decrease*
    c. Increase first, then decrease
    d. Decrease first, then increase
    e. No change

EXAMPLE

Poor   Which of the following is a fossil fuel?

    a. Coal
    b. Natural gas
    c. Oil
    d. All of the above*

Better   Which of the following is NOT a fossil fuel?

    a. Coal
    b. Hydro*
    c. Natural gas
    d. Oil

---

7. Avoid using the "I don't know" choice.

Rationale: One good intention for the "I don't know" choice may be to discourage guessing. However, guessing is a reality with multiple-choice questions; if guessing is a concern, then other question types are available. The "I don't know" choice does not provide teachers or researchers any information on what a student knows or doesn't know. Some students who indeed don't know may select the "I don't know" choice and rightfully expect it to be the correct answer.

EXAMPLE

Poor   Which of the following is a mammal?
   a. Mosquito
   b. Rat*
   c. Spider
   d. I don't know

Better   Which of the following is a mammal?
   a. Mosquito
   b. Rat*
   c. Spider

Techniques for Writing Multiple-Choice Questions for Assessing Higher Order Thinking

One common criticism of multiple-choice questions is that they assess lower order think-ing (LOT). This criticism is not without merits. Given the details multiple-choice questions attend to, they are best at assessing factual knowledge, concrete reasoning, and discrete skills—LOT. However, the above do not necessarily mean that multiple-choice questions cannot assess higher order thinking (HOT). Using multiple-choice questions to assess HOT requires much more thoughts and skills. Before we discuss some techniques for assess-ing HOT using multiple-choice questions, let's first clarify what is LOT and what is HOT. LOT usually refers to the first three levels of the revised Bloom's cognitive taxonomy (i.e., remembering, understanding, and applying), and HOT usually refers to the last three levels of the revised Bloom's taxonomy (i.e., analyzing, evaluating, and creating). The common operational verbs for each of the above cognitive levels are as follows:

- Remember: recognize (identify), recall (retrieve)

- Understand: interpret (clarify, paraphrase, represent, translate), exemplify (illustrate, instantiate), classify (categorize, instantiate), summarize (abstract, generalize), infer (con-clude, extrapolate, interpolate, predict), compare (contrast, map, match), explain (con-struct, model)

- Apply: execute (carry out), implement (use)

- Analyze: differentiate (discriminate, distinguish, focus, select), organize (find coherence, integrate, outline, parse, structure), attribute (deconstruct)

- Evaluate: check (coordinate, detect, monitor, test), critique (judge)

- Create: generate (hypothesize), plan (design), produce (construct)

Keeping in mind the above operational verbs, we now discuss some techniques for assessing HOT using multiple-choice questions.

Technique 1: Use Combinations of Question Formats

Example 1: MC + MC

Understand	Analyze

After a large ice cube has melted in a beaker of water, how will the water level change?
 	
  a. Higher
  b. Lower
  c. The same*
	After a large ice cube has melted in a beaker of water, how will the water level change?
	
	  a. Higher
	  b. Lower
	  c. The same*
	
	Why do you think so? Choose all that apply.
	
	  a. The mass of water displaced is equal to the mass of the ice.*
	  b. Ice has more volume than water.
	  c. Water is denser than ice.
	  d. Ice cube decreases the temperature of water.
	  e. Water molecules in water occupy more space than in ice.

Example 2: MC + Constructed Response

Understand	Analyze

After a large ice cube has melted in a beaker of water, how will the water level change?
 	
  a. Higher
  b. Lower
  c. The same*
	After a large ice cube has melted in a beaker of water, how will the water level change?
	
	  a. Higher
	  b. Lower
	  c. The same*
	
	Why do you think so? Please justify your choice:

Technique 2: Provide a Factual Statement and Ask Students to Analyze

Example

Analyze

The sun is the only body in our solar system that gives off large amounts of light and heat. Select from the following the best reason for which we can see the moon.
 	
  a. It is nearer to the earth than the sun.
  b. It is reflecting light from the sun.*
  c. It is the biggest object in the solar system.
  d. It is without an atmosphere.

Technique 3: Provide a Diagram and Ask Students to Identify Elements

EXAMPLE

<table>
<tr><td colspan="2">*Analyze*</td></tr>
<tr>
<td>
The diagrams show nine different trials Usman carried out using carts with wheels of two different sizes and different numbers of blocks of equal mass. He used the same ramp for all trials, starting the carts from different heights. He wants to test this idea: The higher the ramp is placed, the faster the cart will travel at the bottom of the ramp. Which three trials should he compare?

   a. G, H, and I

   b. I, W, and Z

   c. I, V, and X

   d. U, W, and X

   e. H, V, and Y*
</td>
<td>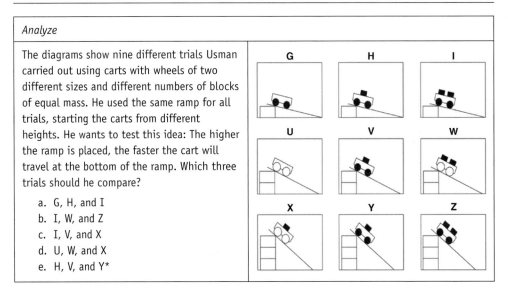</td>
</tr>
</table>

Source: © International Association for the Evaluation of Educational Achievement (IEA), TIMSS 2003 Released http://timss.bc.edu/. Reproduced by permission.

Technique 4: Provide Data and Ask Students to Develop a Hypothesis

EXAMPLE

<table>
<tr><td colspan="2">*Create*</td></tr>
<tr><td colspan="2">Amounts of oxygen produced in a pond at different depths are shown below:</td></tr>
<tr><td>Location</td><td>Oxygen</td></tr>
<tr><td>Top meter</td><td>4 g/m^3</td></tr>
<tr><td>Second meter</td><td>3 g/m^3</td></tr>
<tr><td>Third meter</td><td>1 g/m^3</td></tr>
<tr><td>Bottom meter</td><td>0 g/m^3</td></tr>
<tr><td colspan="2">Which statement is a reasonable hypothesis based on the data in the table?

   a. More oxygen production occurs near the surface because there is more light there.*

   b. More oxygen production occurs near the bottom because there are more plants there.

   c. The greater the water pressure, the more oxygen production occurs.

   d. The rate of oxygen production is not related to depth.</td></tr>
</table>

Technique 5: Provide a Statement and Ask Students to Evaluate Its Validity

EXAMPLE

Evaluate

You can hear a bell ringing in a vacuum chamber. How valid is this statement?

    a. Valid

    b. Partially valid

    c. Invalid*

    d. Not enough information to make a judgment

APPLICATION AND SELF-REFLECTION 3.2

Now let's try to practice what we have learned. For a topic on energy source (fifth grade), write one multiple-choice question for assessing each of the following cognitive reasoning skills: remembering, understanding, and evaluating. Present your questions to the class and evaluate each other's questions using the above guidelines.

WRITING MATCHING QUESTIONS

Matching questions typically assess students' understanding about relationships between concepts. A matching question consists of three components: (a) The *direction* poses a general problem, orients students to the question format, and instructs them on how to answer the question; (b) the *premises* elaborate on the general problem in the direction and pose a set of implicit questions; and (c) the *responses* provide potential answers as choices to the set of questions implied in the premises. Therefore, matching questions and MC questions share commonalities in requiring students to differentiate among choices and selecting the best ones to be matched. Different from MC questions, matching questions present a number of smaller questions of a general problem. The following is a sample matching question:

EXAMPLE

Different products involve different forms of energy. On the line at the left of each product, write the number of the energy form(s) from column B that the product involves. Energy forms in column B may be used once, more than once, or not at all.

(Continued)

(Continued)

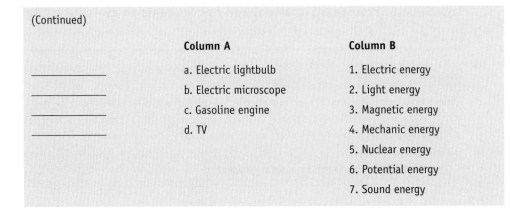

	Column A	Column B
_____	a. Electric lightbulb	1. Electric energy
_____	b. Electric microscope	2. Light energy
_____	c. Gasoline engine	3. Magnetic energy
_____	d. TV	4. Mechanic energy
		5. Nuclear energy
		6. Potential energy
		7. Sound energy

As can be seen from the above example, a matching question covers a wide range of aspects of a topic. The two lists, columns A and B, are uneven in number, which reduces the chance of guessing by using one-to-one correspondence. Instructing students to choose items from column B once or more than once further reduces the chance of guessing. Finally, the elements in each of the two columns are homogeneous, meaning that they belong to a same category. Making both columns homogeneous helps define the specific learning outcome the matching question intends to assess. Other features are also helpful. For example, we can see from the above example that elements in both columns are arranged in a logical order (i.e., alphabetically), reducing unnecessary speculation on correct answers. Column A is about products, and column B is about energy transfer. Column B logically follows column A. In summary, essential characteristics of matching questions are as follows: (a) Use only homogeneous materials in both the premises and responses; (b) include an unequal number of responses and premises; (c) instruct students that responses may be used once, more than once, or not at all; and (d) arrange the list of premises and responses in a logical order.

Compared with MC questions, however, matching questions have limitations. The most obvious one is that matching questions are less focused in the content to be assessed. Second, matching questions allow students to make multiple one-to-one connections, thus creating a high potential for examinees to make guesses, although the probability of answering the entire question correctly by guessing remains low.

WRITING CONSTRUCTED-RESPONSE QUESTIONS

Compared with selected-response questions, constructed-response questions are open-ended in that students have to generate words or sentences to answer questions; there is no chance for them to answer questions correctly by random guessing. However, because students' responses are not constrained, a same constructed-response question may solicit quite different responses. Thus, constructed-response questions are more appropriate for assessing learning outcomes that are divergent and more cognitively advanced, beyond knowledge and comprehension levels of the Bloom's taxonomy.

Depending on the extent of open-endedness, constructed-response questions can be (a) short constructed-response questions or (b) extended constructed-response questions.

Short Constructed-Response Questions

Short constructed-response questions require answers ranging from one word to a few sentences. Often, short constructed-response questions appear in a cluster following a brief introduction of a general problem, aspect, topic, concept, situation, and so on. Thus, like matching questions, a cluster of short constructed-response questions can cover a number of specific aspects of a concept or topic. Let's look at one example.

EXAMPLE

You will now finish a diagram of a food web in the pond. The food web shows what eats what in the pond system. Draw arrows in the diagram below from each living thing to the things that eat it. (The first arrow is drawn for you.)

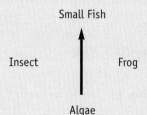

Scoring key:

Complete: Student demonstrates a thorough understanding of the relationships in the food web by drawing four correct arrows and no incorrect arrows. Credited responses include:

    a. Frog eats insect—arrow from insect to frog (1)

    b. Frog eats algae—arrow from algae to frog (a juvenile frog eats algae) (1)

    c. Insect eats algae—arrow from algae to insect (1)

    d. Small fish eats insect—arrow from insect to small fish (1)

Partial: Student demonstrates some understanding of the relationships in the food web by drawing one, two, or three correct arrows and no incorrect arrows.

Unsatisfactory/Incorrect: Student demonstrates little or no understanding of the relationships in the food web by drawing all incorrect arrows, or both correct and incorrect arrows.

Source: National Assessment of Education Progress (http://nces.ed.gov/nationsreportcard/itmrls/).

The number in a bracket is the credit for correctly answering the question. As we can see, short constructed-response questions are very specific. Although no choices are given, choices for correct answers are limited (often only one correct). Developing a complete and clear scoring rubric is critical to ensure that the questions assess the intended learning outcomes.

Extended Constructed-Response Questions

Compared with short constructed-response questions, extended constructed-response questions require more elaborate responses ranging from a few sentences to a short paragraph.

E X A M P L E   **Extended constructed-response questions should be more elaborate**

Air is colorless, odorless, and tasteless. Describe one way that air can be shown to exist.

Scoring rubric
Correct Response:

   1. Mentions that you can feel or see effects of air movement.
Examples: Wind, flags blowing, waving arms, and spreading smell.

   2. Mentions that (light) things may float in air.
Example: A piece of paper floats in air.

   3. Refers to the fact that air can be weighed.

   4. Mentions that balloons, tires, and so on can be filled with air.

   5. Refers to air pressure.
Example: Barometers show that air exists.

   6. Refers to being able to "see" air.
Example: You can see air bubbles in water.

   7. Other correct.

Incorrect Response:

1. We can breathe air. Refers only to the need of oxygen or air for life and other processes.
Examples: All living things need air/oxygen; candles extinguish without air; we would die if there was no air.

2. Refers to seeing water vapor.
Example: You can see water "vapor" when breathing out (on cold days or on a mirror or glass).

3. Merely repeats information in the stem.

4. Other incorrect.

Source: © International Association for the Evaluation of Educational Achievement (IEA), TIMSS 1995 Released http://timss.bc.edu/. Reproduced by permission.

As can be seen from the above example, an extended constructed-response question can be very brief, as short as one sentence. Because the expected answers are open-ended, the scoring scheme needs to be very detailed and comprehensive. Anticipation for all possible correct answers and incorrect answers is necessary for developing a good scoring rubric. In addition, it is a good idea to leave room for additional unexpected correct and incorrect answers.

Guidelines for Writing Constructed-Response Questions

1. Define the task completely and specifically.

E XAMPLE   Define the task completely and specifically

Poor   Describe whether you think pesticides should be used on farms.

Better   Describe the environmental effects of pesticide use on farms.

---

2. Give explicit directions such as the length, grading guideline, and time frame to complete.

E XAMPLE   Give explicit directions

Poor   State whether you think pesticide should be used on farms.

Better   State whether you think pesticide should be used on farms. Defend your position as follows:

   a. Identify any positive benefits associated with pesticide use.
   b. Identify any negative effects associated with pesticide use.
   c. Compare positive benefits against negative effects.
   d. Suggest if better alternatives than pesticides are available.

Your essay should be no more than two double-spaced pages. Two of the points will be used to evaluate the sentence structure, punctuation, and spelling (10 points).

---

3. Do not provide optional questions for students to choose.

This is because different questions may measure completely different learning outcomes, which makes comparisons among students difficult.

4. Define scoring clearly and appropriately.

A scoring rubric can be either analytic or holistic. Please refer to Chapter 4 for guidelines.

APPLICATION AND SELF-REFLECTION 3.3

Let's use the same topic—that is, energy sources (fifth grade). Write one short constructed-response question and one extended constructed-response question at the understanding cognitive reasoning level. Your questions should include scoring rubrics. Present your questions to the class and critique each other's questions.

DIFFERENTIATED SUMMATIVE ASSESSMENTS

One major challenge in today's science classroom is student individual differences. Given any class of students, it is easy to identify students with differences in their prior knowledge, motivation to learn, social-cultural values of science, and learning style, to name just a few. The National Science Education Standards (NRC, 1996) call for achieving science literacy by all students. While group differences in student achievements and opportunity to learn in terms of gender, ethnicity, socioeconomic status, and so on may require institutional efforts to address, student individual differences are an important part of classroom teachers' responsibilities. Effective science teachers teach students as individuals rather than as a group.

Student individual differences may exist in many ways. Postlethwaite (1993) classifies student individual differences into the following categories: (a) educational differences, (b) psychological differences, (c) physical differences, and (d) other differences. The educational differences may include knowledge, reasoning, reading, and problem solving. Psychological differences may include learning style, motivation, personality, locus of control, and IQ; physical differences may include differences related to the senses of vision, hearing, touching, and smelling. Other differences can be those related to socioeconomic status, gender, religious beliefs, and so on. Given the ubiquitous differences exhibited in any classroom, differentiated science instruction is a necessity.

Differentiated science instruction calls for differentiated assessment. **Differentiated assessment** is an approach to conducting assessment according to student individual differences. Differentiated assessment and differentiated instruction, although closely related, are distinct from each other based on their purposes. While differentiated instruction aims at providing ideal learning opportunities in order for every student to achieve his or her maximal learning potential, differentiated assessment aims at providing ideal conditions in order for every student to demonstrate his or her best science achievement.

Differentiated assessment has the following two basic principles:

Principle 1: Students should be assessed under conditions that best enable them to demonstrate their achievement.

Principle 2: Results from different assessment methods for different students should be related in order for a same scoring system to be used.

Principle 1 requires that assessment methods used match students' individual differences. For example, a more difficult and challenging test may be provided to those gifted and talented students. Students with visual impairment may be assessed using large prints or Braille. Principle 2 requires that different assessment methods for different students must assess related learning outcomes, and the scores resulting from different assessment methods must be comparable. This principle is particularly important in today's standards-based approach to science teaching and learning in which students are expected to achieve a common set of learning standards. Principle 2 also enables a common grading system (to be discussed in Chapter 7) to be used no matter what assessment methods students may have taken. To make scores from different assessment methods comparable, you must have a common ground, such as a common set of questions among different assessment methods. Principles 1 and 2 complement each other; together they form a valid differentiated assessment system.

Next we will discuss some common differentiated assessment methods applicable to common student individual differences. More severe differences formally identified under the Individuals with Disabilities Education Act (IDEA), such as physical handicaps, learning disabilities, and attention-deficit hyperactivity disorder (ADHD), require assessment accommodation, adaption, or alternative tests, which will be discussed in Chapter 5.

Differentiated Assessment for Educational Differences

Although educational differences can be in various forms, they can be classified into two types: science related and nonscience related. Science-related individual differences refer to different levels of science achievement by students, with some more advanced and others less advanced. Psychometric theories suggest that most valid and reliable tests are the ones that match students' abilities. That is, more advanced students should take more difficult tests, while less advanced students should take easier tests. Therefore, differentiated assessment for students of different science achievement levels requires alternative forms with different difficulties. For non-science-related individual differences such as different reading levels and different writing abilities, test difficulty may remain the same, but the test questions may be presented at different reading or writing levels. In this case, alternative forms of the same difficulty are necessary.

Developing Alternative Forms of Different Difficulties

After you have developed questions based on your test grid with items, you will arrange your test questions from easiest to most difficult based on your interpretation of the curriculum standards and students' capability. Divide the test questions into three groups: easier questions, average difficult questions, and difficult questions. An ideal distribution would be ½ of total questions in the average group and ¼ of total questions each in the easier and more difficult groups. However, whatever distribution results, stay with it; you should not modify or drop questions to obtain a preferred distribution because your test questions have been developed according to your test grids—the defined assessment domain. Changing questions at this time will result in changing your assessment domain. If there are not enough difficult questions for more advanced students, you may add additional difficult questions as bonus questions for students to receive extra credit. The above grouping may be represented in the following diagram:

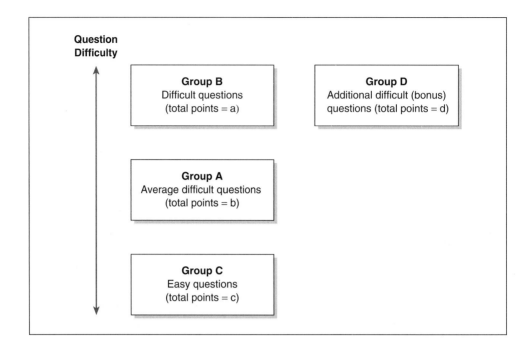

Once questions are grouped in the way described above, then three alternative forms of the same test may be created: Test Form A consists of Group A and a few Group B questions for average students; Test Form B consists of Group A and Group B questions, plus Group D (if available) questions for advanced students; and Test Form C consists of Group C and a few Group A questions for struggling students. The scoring of the above alternative forms is as follows:

Test Form A: total score = scores earned on questions of Groups A and B + c

Test Form B: total score = scores earned on questions of Groups A and B + c + bonus
(scores earned on Group D questions)

Test Form C: total score = scores earned on questions of Groups A and C

Developing Alternative Forms of a Same Difficulty

Differentiated assessment using alternative forms of a same difficulty requires that the alternative forms assess the same learning outcomes, although the formats of test questions may be different. This can be the case when some questions of a same test are presented at different reading levels. Although reading and science achievement may be related, since the focus of a science course is to improve student science achievement, not reading ability, a required high reading level may inhibit students of lower reading ability to demonstrate their best science achievement. In this case, developing an alternative test form at a lower reading level is necessary.

To develop an alternative test form at a lower reading level, you need first of all to understand factors affecting readability. Many measures of readability are available; two of them are the Flesch Reading Ease Test (FRET) and the Flesch-Kincaid Grade Level Test (FKGLT). FRET is a scale from 0 to 100; the higher the score, the easier it is to read. A FRET score of 60 to 70 is about the seventh- or eighth-grade reading level. The FRET formula is as follows:

$$FRET = 206.835 - (1.015 \times ASL) - (84.6 \times ASW),$$

where ASL = average sentence length (the number of words divided by the number of sentences), and ASW = average number of syllables per word (the number of syllables divided by the number of words).

Similar to FRET, FKGLT evaluates readability based on the average sentence length and average number of syllables per word. However, FKGLT produces a score that is equivalent to grade level. For example, a FKGLT score of 8 means that the reading level is about the eighth grade. FKGLT is calculated as follows:

$$FKGLT = (0.39 \times ASL) + (11.8 \times ASW) - 15.59,$$

where ASL and ASW are the same as in FRET.

MS Word 2007 produces both FRET and FKGLT scores automatically every time after you have completed a spelling check of your document. If you do not see a summary of readability statistics after the spelling check, you need to check the Show Readability Statistics option by taking the following procedures:

1. Click the **Microsoft Office Button** , and then click **Word Options.**

2. Click **Proofing.**

3. Make sure **Check grammar with spelling** is selected.

4. Under **When correcting grammar in Word,** select the **Show readability statistics.**

If you use older versions of MS Word, the readability statistics is shown by selecting **Properties** under the pull-down menu of **File.**

From the above readability statistics, you can see that using shorter sentences and shorter words is the effective way to reduce the overall reading level of a test. If you already know the range of your students' approximate reading levels, you may decide to develop two alternative test forms, with one aiming at the lower end of the reading level range and another at the average level. For example, if your students' reading levels range from Grades 4 to 8, then you may develop one test form at Grade 4 level and another test form at Grade 6 level. MS Word's readability statistics will help you to make the necessary adjustment of reading levels.

Developing alternative forms of a test of the same difficulty for different writing abilities pertains only to extended constructed-response questions, such as short and long essays. For these questions, the alternatives can ask students to use drawing or other media forms such as audiotaping. Once again, no matter what medium is provided as an alternative for students, the question and scoring must remain the same to ensure that the same learning outcome is assessed.

Differentiated Assessment for Psychological Differences

Various psychological differences may exist in a classroom as well. One of the most important psychological differences commonly encountered by science teachers is learning style. **Learning style** refers to the preferred approaches to the acquisition and organization of knowledge. Simply put, learning style is about how students learn best. For example, some students learn best through hands-on experience, while others learn best through reading. Learning style is closely related to cognitive style. **Cognitive style** refers to the organization and control of cognitive processes pertaining to information receiving, contexts, and information processing. For example, field-dependent individuals may be highly sensitive to contextual factors such as visual cues when solving a problem, while field-independent individuals may rely more on personal knowledge and self-appreciation when solving a problem. As another example, Howard Gardner (1983) differentiated seven distinct intelligences people may exhibit: linguistic intelligence, musical intelligence, logical-mathematical intelligence, spatial intelligence, bodily-kinesthetic intelligence, interpersonal intelligence, and intrapersonal intelligence. Cognitive styles shape learning styles.

When thinking about student individual differences in terms of learning styles, it is important to understand that learning styles are process variables; they do not equate to outcomes. Research has shown that the correlation between learning styles (i.e., field dependence/independence and locus of control) and science achievement is from modest to low for declarative knowledge (Baker & Piburn, 1997). Thus, for declarative knowledge in science, "styles are not better or worse. They are just different" (Baker & Piburn, 1997, p. 253). Thus, for the assessment of declarative knowledge, a question in favor of a particular learning style may place students of other learning styles at a disadvantage. However, for other types of knowledge, such as procedure knowledge, there is high correlation between learning style (i.e., field dependence/independence) and achievement. Thus, assessment of those types of knowledge needs to make sure if a particular learning style is indeed part of the assessment domain. If it is, differentiated assessment would actually undermine the validity of the assessment results and thus is not justified. For example, assessment of students' skills in performing an acid-base titration requires students to attend to contextual factors of burette, calibration solution, sample solution, indicators, and so on, which may match students with a learning style associated with field dependence. Differentiated assessment using paper-and-pencil tests to assess the acid-base titration lab skill would not be able to assess the same learning outcome as a hands-on manipulative test to assess the acid-base titration lab skill. Differentiated assessment is not an automatic option; it must be justified based on the consideration that alternative forms of assessment do not alter the intended assessment domain.

Various categorizations of student learning styles are available. One common categorization is in terms of preferred modality, which classifies learning styles to be visual, auditory, and hepatic. A student may demonstrate primarily one type of learning style or a combination of two or three. Table 3.3 summarizes characteristics of each learning style and the possible assessment differentiations.

Another common categorization is based on the preferred way of what and how information is acquired and processed during learning. There are two dimensions with each consisting of two bipolar modes, concrete versus abstract and sequential versus random. The

TABLE 3.3 Differentiated Assessment Methods for Learning Styles Based on Preferred Modality

Learning Style	Characteristics	Differentiated Assessment
Visual	1. Needs to see in order to understand 2. Strong sense of color 3. Artistic	1. Use graphical questions 2. Allow drawing and color pens to answer questions 3. Use flowchart to give directions
Auditory	1. Needs to hear in order to understand 2. Strong sense of sound 3. Good at oral communication	1. Use tape recording for instruction 2. Oral administration of tests 3. Audiotaping of responses to questions 4. Oral presentation
Haptic	1. Learns best by hands-on 2. Can assemble parts without reading directions 3. Enjoys physical activities 4. Shows good physical coordination and good in athletics	1. Performance assessment 2. Role-playing 3. Demonstration of responses to questions 4. Model creation

combination of the four poles results in four typical learning styles: concrete sequential (CS), abstract random (AR), concrete random (CR), and abstract sequential (AS). A student may demonstrate primarily one or a combination of the learning styles. Table 3.4 summarizes differentiated assessment methods for each of the four typical types of learning styles.

APPLICATION AND SELF-REFLECTION 3.4

1. Assume that you are going to create a test based on the test grid in Table 3.4. Describe a possible plan to develop two forms, with one for most students and another form for a few who are inclusion students with a lower academic performance level.

2. A fifth-grade teacher has just finished a unit on plants. The teacher's resource book has an end-of-unit test that consists of entirely multiple-choice questions. Discuss how you are going to create an alternative test form of the test with the same difficulty by attending to the following individual differences:

   a. Reading level at Grade 3
   b. Visual learners

TABLE 3.4 Differentiated Assessment Methods for Learning Styles Based on Preferred Information Acquisition and Processing

Learning Style	Characteristics	Differentiated Assessment
Concrete sequential (CS)	1. Ordered and structured 2. Detail and accuracy oriented 3. Hands-on 4. Prefers practical work with detailed directions	1. Selected response questions 2. Performance assessment 3. Data analysis 4. Structured problem solving 5. Interpreting or creating organization charts
Concrete random (CR)	1. Independent 2. Creative 3. Risk taker 4. Experimenter 5. Problem solver	1. Extended constructed-response questions 2. Open-ended problem solving 3. Project/long-term investigation 4. Model creation
Abstract random (AR)	1. Sensitive 2. Emotional 3. Imaginative 4. Personal 5. Flexible	1. Group project 2. Essay 3. Artistic expression 4. Model creation
Abstract sequential (AS)	1. Logical 2. Structured 3. Deep thinker 4. Evaluative	1. Selected response questions 2. Details instructions 3. Essay 4. Research project 5. Library research

EVALUATING EXTERNAL TEST QUESTIONS

Writing quality test questions requires time and skill. On the other hand, many assessment resources are available. For example, teacher resources accompanying a textbook may contain end-of-unit tests or exercises. Many states may also put previous years' state standardized tests online. Incorporating external test questions to develop summative assessment can not only save teachers' valuable time but also potentially enhance the quality of your summative assessment.

However, external test questions are not necessarily of high quality. Critically evaluating them is necessary. We will only discuss evaluation of individual test questions in this section; we will deal with the issue of using an entire external test in Chapter 5.

The first consideration when evaluating an external question is its relevance to the learning outcomes of your summative assessment. The relevance refers to the fit into your assessment domain as defined by your summative assessment test grid. If a test question fits into one of the cells of the test grid, the question is potentially useful. Otherwise, no further evaluation is needed. If a test question is relevant, its technical quality is the next focus of evaluation. The guidelines discussed above for writing various types of questions can be used as criteria to evaluate the quality of the assessment questions. For example, if the question is a multiple-choice question, the seven guidelines may be applied to evaluate the question. If a question meets all the guidelines, the question can be incorporated directly into your summative assessment. Often a question does not meet one or a few criteria. In this situation, you can either abandon the question or modify it to make it meet all the criteria.

The following checklist has been created to facilitate evaluation of test questions. Please note that true-false and fill-in-the-blank types of questions are not discussed in this chapter. This is because true-false questions involve too much guessing, and fill-in-the-blank questions encourage too much memorization. Since what true-false and fill-in-the-blank questions assess can also be assessed or even better assessed by multiple-choice questions, matching questions, or constructed-response questions, there is no need to use true-false and fill-in-the-blank question types.

Checklist for Evaluating External Test Questions

Multiple Choice		
1. The stem of an item is meaningful by itself and presents a definite question.	Yes	No
2. The item is written in clear and simple language.	Yes	No
3. All choices are plausible to uninformed students.	Yes	No
4. Choices are in a logical order.	Yes	No
5. There are no extraneous clues to the correct choice.	Yes	No
6. There are no "none of the above" and "all of the above" alternatives.	Yes	No
7. There is no "I don't know" choice.	Yes	No
8. The language including vocabulary is appropriate for the students.	Yes	No
Matching		
1. There are homogeneous elements in both premises and responses.	Yes	No
2. There are an unequal number of responses and premises.	Yes	No
3. Premises and responses are in a logical order.	Yes	No
4. Responses may be used once, more than once, or not at all.	Yes	No
5. The language including vocabulary is appropriate for the students.	Yes	No

(Continued)

(Continued)

Constructed Response		
1. The task is defined completely and specifically.	Yes	No
2. There are explicit directions such as the length, grading guideline, and time to complete.	Yes	No
3. There are no optional questions for students to choose.	Yes	No
4. Scoring is clear and appropriate.	Yes	No
5. The language including vocabulary is appropriate for the students.	Yes	No

APPLICATION AND SELF-REFLECTION 3.5

Locate some test questions from a teacher's resource book, a student textbook, or any other sources and evaluate the appropriateness of the test questions by using the above checklist.

THE CASES OF ERIC AND ELISIA: SUMMATIVE ASSESSMENT

Before beginning this chapter, Eric and Elisia thought themselves to be good at writing test questions. They took numerous tests from elementary school to university, and they knew what types of questions they would use to develop a test. The test grids introduced in this chapter opened their eyes about the test development process, and they began to appreciate that test questions by themselves may not be said to be good or bad; a more meaningful question to ask is whether those questions serve intended purposes. For end-of-unit summative assessment, a common purpose is to find out if students have mastered the stated unit objectives or learning standards. Eric and Elisia can see how test grids are valuable to them to ensure that each question they are going to write for the end-of-unit test serves a specific purpose. They feel that the guidelines for writing multiple-choice questions and constructed-response questions, although mostly common sense, can potentially help them write high-quality questions. However, using multiple-choice questions to assess higher order thinking skills is something they never thought of. For Eric, since he teaches elementary grades, he still thinks a paper-and-pencil test is of only limited use for him; he can see how differentiated assessment is important to his situation, given that the diversity among students in his class cannot be greater. For Elisia, given that state tests use primarily multiple-choice and constructed-response questions, she can see how she will be able to develop better end-of-unit tests by following the guidelines introduced in this chapter. She also sees the value of developing alternative forms of summative assessment because she has always struggled with the issue of accommodating student individual differences. For example, a few advanced students always complain that her tests are too easy. Overall, both Eric and Elisia feel that this chapter offers some practical suggestions for them to create an end-of-unit test, but they also feel that more variety of assessment question formats is needed. They look forward to subsequent chapters for more assessment ideas.

Do the experiences of Eric and Elisia sound familiar to you? What were your initial ideas of summative assessment, and how have they changed as the result of this chapter?

Chapter Summary

- Quality summative assessment depends on a systematic plan that matches intended learning outcomes. A test grid is a two-dimensional table defining the assessment domain in terms of topics and cognitive skills.

- Multiple-choice questions should contain a stem that poses a meaningful question and equally plausible choices, including a clearly correct answer. Choices should be arranged in a logical order; avoid extraneous clues and such choices as "none of the above," "all of the above," and "I don't know."

- Matching questions should contain two uneven numbers of homogeneous columns that are arranged in a logical order.

- Short and extended constructed-response questions should require clear and specific answers that can be scored either correctly or incorrectly. The analytic scoring scheme should be specific and comprehensive enough to encompass correct, partially correct, and incorrect responses.

- There is a wide variety of individual differences among students in a class. Differentiated assessment provides students with alternative assessment forms appropriate for educational, psychological, and other differences. Alternative assessment forms may be developed to accommodate different levels of science achievement or different learning styles. Alternative assessment forms can be with a same difficulty or different difficulties with common questions.

- There are many external sources for test questions. Not every external question is of high quality. When evaluating external test questions, you should first decide if they fit into the assessment domain defined by a test grid. Next it is necessary to review if test questions are properly written.

√ Mastery Checklist

- ☐ Create a summative assessment test grid.
- ☐ Write high-quality multiple-choice questions.
- ☐ Write multiple-choice questions to assess higher order thinking skills.
- ☐ Write high-quality matching questions.
- ☐ Write high-quality constructed-response questions.
- ☐ Develop alternative forms of tests of different difficulties for different achievement levels of students.
- ☐ Develop alternative forms of tests of a same difficulty for different learning styles.
- ☐ Evaluate external test questions.

Web-Based Student Study Site

The Companion Web site for *Essentials of Science Classroom Assessment* can be found at **www.sagepub.com/liustudy**.

The site includes a variety of materials to enhance your understanding of the chapter content. Visit the study site to complete an online self-assessment of essential knowledge and skills introduced in this chapter. The study materials also include flash cards, Web resources, and more.

Further Reading

Gallagher, J. D. (1998). *Classroom assessment for teachers*. Upper Saddle River, NJ: Merrill.

> Although not science specific, this popular assessment textbook contains chapters on developing all types of paper-and-pencil test questions and various alternative assessments such as portfolios and performance assessments. It also contains chapters related to planning for assessment, grading, and standardized testing.

References

Baker, D. R., & Piburn, M. D. (1997). *Constructing science in middle and secondary school classrooms*. Boston: Allyn & Bacon.

Gardner, H. (1983). *Frames of mind: The theory of multiple intelligences*. New York: Basic Books.

National Research Council (NRC). (1996). *National science education standards*. Washington, DC: National Academy Press.

Postlethwaite, K. (1993). *Differentiated science teaching*. Buckingham, UK: Open University Press.

Wiggins, G., & McTighe, J. (2005). *Understanding by design*. Alexandria, VA: Association for Supervision and Curriculum Development.

CHAPTER 4

Assessment of Science Inquiry

Chapter 3 has introduced an approach to developing an end-of-unit test. The approach starts with creating a test grid that represents the intended learning outcomes to be assessed and the required type and number of test questions. A test grid provides a test blueprint for developing a test. Chapter 3 has also introduced various guidelines for writing high-quality multiple-choice and constructed-response questions, as well as methods for developing differentiated assessment. However, summative assessment entails more than paper-and-pencil tests that consist of multiple-choice and constructed-response questions; other forms of tests are also needed to best assess other types of learning outcomes in science, such as science inquiry. This chapter introduces techniques for assessing student science achievement related to science inquiry.

The centrality of inquiry as both content and an approach to science teaching is well elaborated in the National Science Education Standards (NRC, 1996). Inquiry involves posing meaningful questions, designing appropriate procedures to collect data necessary for answering the questions, and analyzing and interpreting data to answer the research questions. Although inquiry does not take place in a step-by-step fashion, there are essential aspects underlying all inquiry activities. These aspects are hands-on skills pertaining to data collection and analysis, reasoning skills in relating data to theories, and abilities to perform inquiry tasks. Accordingly, this chapter will include three sections introducing assessment methods for science inquiry performances, laboratory skills, and reasoning about science inquiry.

ASSESSMENT OF SCIENCE INQUIRY PERFORMANCES

It is important to differentiate laboratory skills from science inquiry. Inquiry is not just a skill; it is a range of activities that involve cognitive, affective, and psychomotor domains. To conduct inquiry, students need to have access to tools, materials, media, and technological resources. During inquiry, students engage in posing questions; planning investigations; making observations; analyzing and interpreting data; proposing answers,

> ### ESSENTIAL SKILLS ADDRESSED IN CHAPTER 4
>
> • Develop a checklist to assess student mastery of laboratory skills.
> • Develop a rating scale to assess student mastery of laboratory skills.
> • Create a paper-and-pencil test to assess student mastery of laboratory skills.
> • Develop a performance assessment to assess student inquiry performances.
> • Use Vee diagramming to assess student reasoning in science inquiry.

explanations and predictions; and communicating the results. The National Science Education Standards state the following:

> Inquiry is a multifaceted activity that involves making observations; posing questions; examining books and other sources of information to see what is already known; planning investigations; reviewing what is already known in light of experimental evidence; using tools to gather, analyze, and interpret data; proposing answers, explanations, and predictions; and communicating the results. (NRC, 1996, p. 23)

Performance assessment is a hands-on test that requires students to perform a task by carrying out a scientific procedure, conducting a scientific investigation, or producing a useful product; it specifically assesses student science inquiry performances. Performance assessment usually takes place as an investigation, which can be both structured investigation and open-ended investigation. The expectation for students to investigate a problem in the curriculum standard is usually not apparent. Wiggins and McTighe (2005) argue for the necessity of performance tasks in assessing students' understanding. They differentiate authentic performance-based tasks from exercises or skills. Authentic performance tasks are best at assessing students' understanding related to essential questions or big ideas. Essential questions are integrated understanding of topics within a unit; they are about why students learn the topics, how the topics are related, what implications they have, and so on. In other words, essential questions are about the "forest" as compared with the "trees." Assessing student mastery of a unit must make sure that students develop such an integrated understanding of the unit using performance-based tasks.

Performance assessment in the forms of investigations and extended investigations consists of three components: performance task, response format, and scoring rubric (Brown & Shavelson, 1996). A performance task should be around a problem and meet the following requirements:

• The problem invites students to solve a problem or conduct an investigation. The problem can be well structured or ill structured (Shin, Jonassen, & McGee, 2003). Well-structured problems have all elements of the problem and a known solution. The procedures required to solve the problem are also routine and predicable. On the other hand, ill-structured problems do not necessarily have all elements of the problem presented. More important, ill-structured problems may possess multiple solutions, solution paths, or no solutions at all. Because ill-structured problems are open-ended, personal judgment is constantly needed

ASSESSMENT STANDARDS ADDRESSED IN CHAPTER 4

NSES Assessment Standard B

Achievement and opportunity to learn science must be assessed. This standard is further elaborated into the following substandards:

- Achievement data collected focus on the science content that is most important for students to learn.
- Opportunity-to-learn data collected focus on the most powerful indicators of learning.
- Equal attention must be given to the assessment of opportunity to learn and to the assessment of student achievement. (National Research Council [NRC], 1996, p. 79)

NSES Assessment Standard C

The technical quality of the data collected is well matched to the decisions and actions taken on the basis of their interpretation. This standard is further elaborated into the following substandards:

- The feature that is claimed to be measured is actually measured.
- An individual student's performance is similar on two or more tasks that claim to measure the same aspect of student achievement.
- Students have adequate opportunity to demonstrate their achievements.
- Assessment tasks and methods for presenting them provide data that are sufficiently stable to lead to the same decisions if used at different times. (NRC, 1996, pp. 83–85)

in the process of solving the problem. Well-structured problems are more appropriate for short investigations, and ill-structured problems are more appropriate for extended investigations.

- The problem requires the use of concrete materials. This requirement is to differentiate performance assessment tasks from paper-and-pencil-based problems. Performance tasks must involve hands-on operations.

- Provide a concrete contextualization of the problem or investigation. Context makes the problem authentic. Performance assessment tasks approximate real-world problems, and thus presenting the problem in a meaningful context is important.

Once a performance task is defined, the next component is to decide on the response format. The response format is to gather evidence of student performance for scoring. The response format must meet the following requirements: (a) provides opportunities for students to record processes and solutions, (b) prompts students for specific information, (c) allows students to decide how to summarize findings, and (d) asks students to justify solutions.

The last component of performance assessment is a scoring scheme or rubric. A **rubric** is a continuum along which different levels of competence in performing a task are differentiated. Given a task, there is always a variation in student performances; some are more novicelike while others more expertlike. The rubric must capture the "right" answer and reasonableness of procedures. It should also provide students useful feedback plus numerical scores. Given the number of students to be scored, the scoring rubric should also be easy and quick to use.

There are two essential aspects in a rubric: (a) a construct or competence underlying student performances and (b) qualitatively different levels of performance. The first aspect is also called a *trait,* and the second aspect is called a *quality category* that is ordinal in values. For example, students work collaboratively to construct a model of DNA. The construct underlying students' performance can be students' understanding of the double-helix structure of a DNA molecule. Additional constructs may also be considered, such as the appropriateness of the mathematical scale and artistic expression. The qualitatively different levels of performance, or proficiency, may be described as distinguished (3), average (2), and novice (1) or any other pertinent descriptions of varying proficiency.

There are two types of scoring rubrics: holistic and analytic. The **holistic scoring rubric** is a one-dimensional hierarchical differentiation that defines qualitatively different degrees of performances in terms of global characteristics. Global characteristics are an overall judgment or feeling about a product and/or process. Using the DNA model construction as an example, a holistic scoring rubric can be as follows:

Quality Category (Score)	Characteristics
Distinguished (3)	The model accurately represents the structure of a DNA molecule with attention to details (e.g., mathematical scale).
Average (2)	The model represents key features of a DNA molecule.
Novice (1)	The model is incomplete or inaccurately demonstrates a DNA molecule.

As can be seen from the above holistic rubric, the scorer has to be very knowledgeable about the intended learning outcomes of the task (i.e., the DNA structure). If that is the case, the scoring can be very efficient. However, the disadvantage is that the scores do not provide students with specific feedback on the strength and weakness of their models. Furthermore, the scoring subjectivity is potentially high, particularly if the scorer is not the creator of the task. Because of the above two major limitations, holistic scoring rubrics have only limited use in science classroom assessment.

Different from the holistic scoring rubric, an **analytic scoring rubric** is an elaborated scoring scheme that contains two dimensions: construct and proficiency. In an analytic scoring rubric, different aspects of the construct are identified, and different degrees of the proficiency of each aspect are specified. A sample analytic scoring rubric for the task of constructing a DNA model can be as follows:

Construct Proficiency	Understanding	Mathematical Scale	Artistic Expression
Distinguished (3)	Shows distinct components of the sugar-phosphate backbone, spiral strand, and attached bases Shows distinct pairs and hydrogen bonds between bases	Shows at least 10 nucleotide pairs per helical turn Shows accurate number of hydrogen bonds between different pairs of bases	Different colors and materials used to represent different components and connections
Average (2)	Shows an overall spiral structure with two connected strands Unclear or inaccurate representation of distinct components (sugar-phosphate backbone, bases, hydrogen bonds)	The distance between two strands is shorter than the overall height	Limited differentiation of different components and connections by color or choices of materials
Novice (1)	Apparent but unsuccessful attempt to build a spiral structure with two strands	Unclear differentiation between width and height	No variation in choices of materials and objects
Construct aspect score			
Weight (%)	50%	25%	25%
Total task score	Understanding × 50% + Mathematical Scale × 25% + Artistic Expression × 25%		
Total task score in percentages	Total Task Score/3 × 100		

As can be seen from the above rubric, an analytic rubric indicates both the underlying constructs expected of students to demonstrate and the degrees of meeting the expectations. Scores can be given to individual constructs and also to the entire task by applying appropriate weights. Scores may also be converted into percentages and given to students. Often students are provided with both individual construct scores and the total task score. Because of the above, an analytic scoring rubric is much more informative than a holistic scoring rubric for students on the current state of meeting the expected learning outcomes.

Developing a fine-grained description of the continuum of student competence in performing a task requires extensive observation and analysis of student performances. This type of continuum is needed for developing good rubrics. However, developing such a continuum takes time, which is why developing a good rubric should not be a one-shot deal; instead, it should be a cyclic process of development, trial, and revision. The following procedures may be followed to develop a scoring rubric:

Identify the constructs and decide the levels of competence related to the tasks according to a continuum of student competence in reaching learning standards.

State the expected characteristics in the student product and/or process of performing the task when a student has completely met the learning standards and the characteristics of the student product and/or process of performing the task when a student has very minimal competence.

Decide the number of intermediate levels of student performance between the full competence and minimal competence, and describe the characteristics based on anticipation.

After students have completed the task, gather student performance samples, and sort them into groups based on similarities and differences among the products/processes. Write down demonstrated qualities by each of the groups.

Combine the qualities into general categories and rank-order them into different competence levels. Some qualities may be closely related. The purpose is to reduce the total number of qualities to a manageable number.

Compare the competence levels with the competence levels initially defined and make revisions if necessary.

Assign a value to each of the final hierarchical levels. The numbers can be from 10 to 0 or from 5 to 1. This is arbitrary because the essence is the order, not the absolute value.

Find samples of student products/processes that illustrate each of the levels.

The above three components of performance assessment (i.e., performance task, response format, and scoring rubric) indicate that carrying out a performance assessment can be both time-consuming and resource intensive—both time and resources are limited in today's schools. Performance assessment in the form of investigation does not have to take place at the end of the unit; it may take place during the unit. Integrating performance assessment into ongoing instruction can serve both instructional and assessment purposes, which is very desirable.

The following is a sample performance assessment for an upper elementary school grade science unit on water.

PERFORMANCE TASK

You are a member of an environmental club in the school. You would like to propose a campaign on reducing household use of paper towels. Before you make such a proposal, you need to understand better how different brands of paper towels serve household needs such as water absorption. You have decided to conduct an investigation with a partner. You have three brands of paper towels in front of you. Your task is to find out which paper towel can hold, soak up, or absorb the most water and which paper towel can hold, soak up, or absorb the least water. There are some materials available in the room for you to use. You may use any other materials available in the room as well.

When you are finished, you are asked to write what you did so others can repeat the experiment exactly as you did it. You may want to keep notes on a sheet of paper to help you remember what you did and what you found out.

RESPONSE SHEET

Your conclusion:

The paper towel that holds, soaks up, or absorbs the most water is _____.

The paper towel that holds, soaks up, or absorbs the least water is _____.

Steps in Your Experiments (you may draw diagrams to help you explain):

Step	Activity
1.	
2.	
3.	
4.	
5.	

Paper Towel Performance Assessment Scoring Rubric

Outstanding: Rating = 4

Used containers and other relevant devices for measuring volume, weight, counting drops or time, and so on. Paper towels were completely saturated. Used controlled experimentation. Demonstrated care in manipulation and measuring. Both of the conclusions are correct.

(Continued)

(Continued)

Competent: Rating = 3

Used containers and other relevant devices for measuring volume, weight, counting drops or time, and so on. Paper towels were completely saturated. Controlled experimentation was not explicit or incomplete. Demonstrated some carelessness in manipulation and measuring. Both of the conclusions are correct.

Satisfactory: Rating = 2

Used containers and other relevant devices for measuring volume, weight, counting drops or time, and so on. Paper towels were not completely saturated. Controlled experimentation was not explicit or incomplete. Demonstrated some carelessness in manipulation and measuring. Only one of the two conclusions is correct.

Serious Flaws: Rating = 1

Inconsistent use of devices for measuring volume, weight, counting drops or time, and so on. Paper towels were not completely saturated. Controlled experimentation was not used. Failed to demonstrate care in manipulation and measuring. Only one or no conclusion is correct.

No Attempt: Rating = 0

No experiment was used. Did not make an effort to solve the problem. Random guess of final results.

Analytic Scoring Scheme

3	Very Good
2	Satisfactory
1	Needs improvement

Aspects	3	2	1	Score
1. What is controlled?	Paper and water	Paper or water	Time	
2. Procedures	Logical	Inconsistent logic	Trial and error	
3. What was measured?	Number of drops of water and volume or mass of water	Number of drops or volume or mass of water	Area, height, time	
4. Method of measurement	Using measurement instrument, such as scale, graduated cylinder	Counting drops	Estimating	

Aspects	3	2	1	Score
5. Outcome	Bounty-Scott-CVS	Bounty-CVS-Scott	CVS-Bounty-Scott	
6. Other aspects: collaboration	Equal sharing	Inconsistent collaboration	No collaboration	
			Total	

Source: Adapted from Erickson, Bartley, Carlisel, Meyer, & Stavy (1991).

The above investigation is structured in that it takes place during a given time period and uses a given set of materials. Performance assessment may also take place as an open-ended inquiry. Open-ended inquiry requires students to develop their own research questions; design their own data collection procedures, including selection of appropriate tools; analyze data; and make their own conclusions. Because different students may research different questions, different conclusions may be acceptable. Because open-ended inquiry takes place in an extended time period, it can assess both students' processes and outcomes of science inquiry.

The following excerpt shows the progression of a sixth-grade student's ongoing inquiry into light sources at home during a unit on light. Because the inquiry was open-ended, ongoing teacher guidance was also provided.

First entry by the student:

I think that the light is different in different rooms and at different times of the day because the rooms' windows might be in different spots and that would change the amount of light in the room. And as for quality of light it would depend on the weather that day. If it was a clear sky there would be a "heavy" amount of light and if it was cloudy there would be a "light" amount of light.

Teacher feedback to the first entry:

Great start! The position of the windows is an important variable to consider. As you begin to make observations, think about how you can relate the window position to the brightness. What is it about the location that allows more light to enter or exit? I also like that you are starting to develop descriptive terms for your observations. Once you've developed some words you will use to describe the brightness or quality, it might help to place them in a definite order so that you can keep your comparisons consistent. Nice work!

(Continued)

(Continued)

Second entry by the student:
"Option One" Observations:
*Day: Sunday, March 4th
*Average Time of Recording: 3:40 p.m.

Room #1: My bedroom

1. Time: 3:40 p.m. Weather: bright but cloudy

2. Moderate amount of light (52%)

3. Quality of light was very faint

4. Sources of light: 2 windows

5. Reflected light: mirror, laptop, desk, wood floors, and my keyboard

Room #2: My parents' room

1. Time: 3:41 p.m. Weather: bright but cloudy

2. Amount of light in the room was light (34%)

3. Quality of light is poor

4. Sources of light: 2 windows

5. Reflected light: lamp, dressers, mirror, and TV

Room #3: Living room

1. Time: 3:42 p.m. Weather: bright but partly cloudy

2. Amount of light in the room was high (72%)

3. Quality of light is great (bright)

4. Sources of light: 4 windows and a small window on my front door

5. Reflected light: desk, TV, entertainment center, mirror, clock, carpet, and the closet door

Room #4: The kitchen

1. Time: 3:45 p.m. Weather: sun was trying to peek through the clouds

2. A fair amount of light in the room (45%)

3. Quality of light was OK

4. Source of light was 1 fairly large window

5. Reflected light: cutting board, cupboards, refrigerator, garbage can, stove, dishwasher, floor, and microwave

Room #5: Family room

1. Time: 3:48 p.m. Weather: partly cloudy

2. High amount of light in the room (85%)

3. Quality of light is great

4. Sources of light: 7 windows

5. Reflected light: couch, dining table, 2 mirrors, 4 pictures on the wall, black lamp, rocking chair, coffee table, bench, black and green chairs, and the coats hanging on the wall

Student Conclusion:

1. I can explain quality of light by saying that the weather outside matters and where the room is positioned. As for the amount of light it would have to do with the positioning of the windows (where the light could get in the room) and also the weather.

The amount and quality of light are kind of related by the fact that they both have to do with how the weather is outside and where the light gets through.

Some things I learned in this project that helped me understand my observations were things like how light obviously travels in straight lines. And how light reflects off many different objects to make even more light.

A sample generic scoring rubric for student open-ended inquiry projects is as follows:

	3	*2*	*1*	*0*
Design of the individual experiment	One relevant independent variable is manipulated, while *all* other relevant independent variables are controlled.	One relevant independent variable is manipulated, while *some* other relevant independent variables are controlled.	More than one relevant independent variable is manipulated and some other relevant independent variables are controlled.	No variables are controlled in the design of the experiment.
Process of research in the experiment	All three research process elements (observations, analysis, and conclusions) are valid and internally consistent.	Two of three research process elements (observations, analysis, and conclusions) are valid and internally consistent.	One of three research process elements (observations, analysis, and conclusions) is valid and internally consistent.	Zero of three research process elements (observations, analysis, and conclusions) are valid and internally consistent.

(Continued)

(Continued)

	3	2	1	0
Research question progression	Strong: The new research questions directly address *all important* issues or outcomes of previous findings.	Weak: The new research questions directly address *some of the important* issues or outcomes of previous findings.	Trivial: The new research questions address *unimportant* issues or outcomes of previous findings.	None: The new research questions are *not* related to issues or outcomes of previous findings.
Conceptual change	Restructuring: New knowledge structures are created from the current ones.	Tuning: Constraints are placed to increase accuracy and applicability of the current knowledge structure.	Accretion: New knowledge is added or corrections are made to an already existing knowledge structure.	None: No apparent alternation in quantity or structure of knowledge.

Many performance assessment resources are available (please refer to the course Web site). When selecting a performance assessment from an external source, you first need to consider its fit with your test grid. In other words, your chosen performance assessment must assess the intended learning outcomes indicated in your test grid by the topic and cognitive skill. Once you have decided that there is a fit, you may proceed with evaluating the technical quality of the performance assessment. An evaluation checklist as follows may be used:

Performance Assessment Evaluation Checklist		
1. The problem invites students to solve a problem or conduct an investigation.	Yes	No
2. The problem requires the use of concrete materials.	Yes	No
3. The problem provides a concrete contextualization of the problem or investigation.	Yes	No
4. The response format provides opportunities for students to record processes and findings.	Yes	No
5. The response format prompts students for specific information.	Yes	No
6. The response format allows students to decide how to summarize findings.	Yes	No
7. The response format asks students to justify answers.	Yes	No
8. The scoring rubric captures "right" answers and reasonableness of procedures.	Yes	No
9. The scoring rubric provides students useful feedback plus numerical scores.	Yes	No
10. The scoring rubric is easy and quick to use.	Yes	No

APPLICATION AND SELF-REFLECTION 4.1

For the following learning outcomes, develop a performance assessment using a well-structured problem as a structured investigation and an ill-structured problem as an open-ended or extended investigation. Make sure to include in each performance assessment three components (i.e., the task, response format, and scoring rubric). Present your performance assessment to the class and discuss strengths and potential areas for improvement.

Learning outcomes:
Students should be able to describe the characteristics of and variations among living things, including the following:

a. *Animals need air, water, and food in order to live and thrive.*

b. *Plants require air, water, nutrients, and light in order to live and thrive.*

ASSESSMENT OF LABORATORY SKILLS

Although science inquiry takes place in many forms, contexts, and times, they commonly involve the use of standard science equipment and tools—the manipulative skills. In addition, students must also actively engage in mental activities related to observing, analyzing and interpreting, and concluding—the thinking skills. **Laboratory skills** refer to both the manipulative and thinking skills involved in laboratory activities; they are also called *process skills.*

Different states may require mastery of different laboratory tools. The following is an incomplete list:

Elementary and Middle School Science

- Use hand lens to view objects
- Use stopwatch to measure time
- Use ruler (metric) to measure length
- Use balances and spring scales to weigh objects
- Use thermometers to measure temperature (°C, °F)
- Use measuring cups to measure volumes of liquids
- Use graduated cylinders to measure volumes of liquids

High School Biology

- Count the growth of microorganisms
- Determine the size of a microscopic object, using a compound microscope
- Dissect a frog or a worm
- Germinate seeds
- Make a serial dilution
- Manipulate a compound microscope to view microscopic objects
- Prepare a wet mount slide

- Sketch an organism
- Slice a tissue for microscope examination
- Sterilize instruments
- Take a pulse
- Use appropriate staining techniques
- Use paper chromatography and electrophoresis to separate chemicals

High School Chemistry

- Boil liquid in beakers and test tubes
- Conduct an acid-base titration
- Cut, bend, and polish glass
- Dilute strong acids
- Pour liquid from a reagent bottle
- Prepare solutions of a given concentration
- Separate mixtures by filtration
- Smell a chemical
- Transfer powers and crystals from reagent bottles
- Weigh chemicals using an analytic balance

High School Earth Science

- Analyze soils
- Classify rocks
- Classify fossils
- Determine the volume of a regular- and an irregular-shaped solid
- Grow crystals
- Locate the epicenter of an earthquake
- Measure weather variables (e.g., barometer, anemometer, etc.)
- Orient a map with a compass
- Plot the sun's path
- Test the physical properties of minerals
- Use a stereoscope to view objects

High School Physics

- Connect electrical devices in parallel and series circuits
- Determine the focal length of mirrors and lenses
- Determine the electrical conductivity of a material using a simple circuit
- Determine the speed and acceleration of a moving object
- Locate images in mirrors
- Solder electrical connections
- Use electric meters

Assessment of student mastery of laboratory tools may be part of summative assessment—that is, including the laboratory skills as a topic and assigning appropriate weights or points in the test grid. Although student mastery of using tools may be assessed using paper-and-pencil test questions, the most effective assessment of using tools involves observation of students performing the skills. Because using laboratory tools is typically learned and practiced as part of labs, assessment of using laboratory tools may take place during student labs.

To assess student mastery of laboratory tools during labs, you must have a systematic plan in place. This plan outlines what laboratory skills need to be assessed and how and when they will be assessed. A checklist or rating scale is typically sufficient. A sample rating scale for a laboratory skill assessment related to using tools for an elementary grade is presented below; a sample checklist for assessing a biology laboratory skill (i.e., serial dilution) is presented after.

Elementary Laboratory Skill Assessment Involving Tools

Name _____

Date _____

Lab Skills	Developing	Mastery	Proficient
1. Use hand lens to view objects	_____	_____	_____
2. Use stopwatch to measure time	_____	_____	_____
3. Use ruler (metric) to measure length	_____	_____	_____
4. Use balances and spring scales to weigh objects	_____	_____	_____
5. Use thermometers to measure temperature (°C, °F)	_____	_____	_____
6. Use measuring cups to measure volumes of liquids	_____	_____	_____
7. Use graduated cylinders to measure volumes of liquids	_____	_____	_____

Biology Lab Skill Assessment: Making a Serial Dilution

Date_____

Student Name	Mastery	Not Mastery
A	_____	_____
B	_____	_____
C	_____	_____
D	_____	_____
. . . .	_____	_____

One benefit of a rating scale is to take into consideration that students may need time to develop competence in using a laboratory tool. If a laboratory tool is only taught and practiced once, then assessment of the laboratory tool may take place using a checklist. Both the checklist and rating scale need to list specific skills to be observed. For complex lab skills, such as using a microscope or conducting an acid-base titration, specific subskills may also be listed and observed during lab assessment.

Operation of laboratory tools is only one component of laboratory skills. Other laboratory skills involve more reasoning than manipulating tools, such as generating testable hypotheses, designing controlled experimentation, making accurate observations, analyzing and interpreting data, and making valid conclusions. Lunetta and Tamir (1979) identified the following laboratory skills involving extensive reasoning:

PLANNING AND DESIGNING

- Formulates a question or defines a problem to be investigated
- Predicts experimental result
- Formulates hypothesis to be tested
- Designs observation or measurement procedure
- Designs experiment

PERFORMANCE

- Carries out qualitative observation
- Carries out quantitative observation or measurement
- Records results, describes observation
- Performs numeric calculation
- Explains or makes a decision about experimental technique
- Works according to own design

ANALYSIS AND INTERPRETATION

- Transforms result into standard form (other than graphs)
- Graphs data
- Determines qualitative relationship
- Determines quantitative relationship
- Determines accuracy of experimental data
- Defines or discusses limitations and/or assumptions that underlie the experiment
- Formulates or proposes a generalization or model
- Explains a relationship
- Formulates new questions or defines problem based on result of investigation

APPLICATION

- Predicts, based on result of this investigation
- Formulates hypothesis based on results of this investigation
- Applies experimental techniques to new problem or variable

Assessment of the above laboratory skills can be conducted by observations or paper-and-pencil tests. Observations may take place during student labs or at the end of a unit of instruction as a laboratory skill assessment station. As an example, the Inquiry Skill Measure (ISM; Nelson & Abraham, 1973) is an observation-based test to measure upper elementary school students' laboratory skills. This test employs a sealed box with a number of different-colored sticks protruding from it. It is placed on a table in front of a child. The child examines the outside of the box using all five senses to tell as much about the outside of the box as possible. The teacher records verbatim the child's statements. This portion of the test is conducted to obtain a measure of a student's ability to observe. The child is then asked what he or she thinks the inside of the box is like based on his or her observations. This procedure provides a measure of the child's ability to draw inferences. For each inference made, the child is asked to give the reason on which each inference is based and how he or she would attempt to verify his or her inferences without opening the box. The child's ability to classify is measured by presenting nine transparent vials of varying sizes containing different amounts of colored liquids. The student tries to group the vials using different criteria. An accuracy and frequency score for each laboratory skill is obtained. Scoring is based on recorded student statements/utterances. The scoring rubrics are as follows:

OBSERVATIONS: STATEMENTS ABOUT THE OUTSIDE OF THE BOX

Scoring one point for each of the following:

a. Nouns and adjectives about the outside of the box (e.g., The box/is black = 2 points)

b. Demonstrative (e.g., *this, that, these*) or indefinite (e.g., *one, none, any*) pronouns (e.g., This/stick/is/green = 3 points)

c. Verbal phrases indicating actions done by the student (e.g., When I twist this stick/ = 1 point)

d. Prepositional phrases containing nouns, pronouns, and/or adjectives (e.g., between/ these/two/sticks = 4 points)

e. Prepositional phrases containing an impersonal pronoun (e.g., between them = 1 point)

f. Prepositional phrases starting with *like* and making a direct or indirect comparison of observables (e.g., The box is/like something I've seen before = 2 points)

g. Location words and phrases (e.g., on/this/stick = 3 points)

Score one error point for each of the following:

a. Inaccurate observations (e.g., There are five/red/sticks = 2 correct points and 1 error point because there are four red sticks, not five)

b. Verbal phrases indicating work not done or observed by the student (e.g., The paint ran here = 1 error point)

(Continued)

(Continued)

Inferences: Statements About the Inside of the Box

Score one point for each valid inference:

Examples:	Statement	Reason
	Object inside	I hear a noise when I shake it
	Something in it besides ball	When I move it back and forth, I hear something else

Score one error point for each inference based on another inference or error, or a guess:

Examples:	Statement	Reason
	Marble inside	Because it sounds like it
	It is hollow	Sticks are going through it

Verification: Determine If the Test as Stated Lends Experimental Support to the Inference

Score one point for each valid verification.
Score one error point for each of the following:

a. An inferential statement

b. A repeated observation

c. An impossible test

Classification: Group Objects Based on Observable Properties

Score one point for each valid classification.
Score one error point for each of the following:

a. No stated reason

b. An inferential rather than an observable property

c. A descriptive class

Paper-and-pencil tests using multiple-choice and constructed-response questions may also be used to assess laboratory skills involving reasoning. For example, the Test of the Integrated Process Skills (TIPS; Dillashaw & Okey, 1980) is a multiple-choice question test for measuring 7th- to 10th-grade students' laboratory skills associated with planning, conducting, and interpreting results from investigations. Questions are related to independent variables, dependent variables, controlled variables, hypotheses, experimental designs, graphing data, and pattern of relationships. Table 4.1 shows some sample questions from TIPS.

TABLE 4.1 Sample TIPS Questions

Assessment Objective	Sample Item
A. Given a description of an investigation, identify the independent, dependent, and controlled variables and the hypothesis being tested.	Sarah wanted to find out if temperature has an effect on the growth of bread mold. She grew the mold in nine containers containing the same amount and type of nutrients. Three containers were kept at 0°C, three were kept at 90°C, and three were kept at room temperature (about 27°C). The containers were examined and the growth of the bread mold was recorded at the end of 4 days. The dependent or responding variable is: 1. Growth of bread mold 2. Amount of nutrients in each container 3. Temperature of the containers 4. Number of containers at each temperature
B. Given a description of an investigation, identify how the variables are operationally defined.	The superintendent is concerned about the accidents in schools. He makes the hypothesis that safety advertising will reduce school accidents. He decides to test the hypothesis in four middle schools. Each school will use a different number of safety posters to see if the number of accidents is reduced. Each school nurse will keep a record of students who come to the office because of an accident. How is safety advertising measured in this study? 1. Number of accidents reported to the nurse 2. Number of middle schools involved 3. Number of safety posters in each school 4. Number of accidents in the school
C. Given a problem with a dependent variable specified, identify variables that may affect it.	Sue wants to find out what might affect the length of bean seedlings. She places a bean wrapped in moist tissue paper in each of 10 identical test tubes. She puts 5 tubes in a rack in a sunny window. She puts the other 5 tubes on a rack in a dark refrigerator. She measures the lengths of the bean seedlings in each group after each week. Which of the following variables might affect the length of the bean seedlings? 1. Temperature and moisture 2. Moisture and length of test tubes 3. Light and temperature 4. Light and amount of time

(Continued)

TABLE 4.1 (Continued)

Assessment Objective	Sample Item
D. Given a problem with dependent variables specified and a list of possible independent variables, identify a testable hypothesis.	A student has been playing with a water rocket. He can change the amount of water in the rocket and the angle at which he releases the rocket. He can also change the weight of the rocket by adding sand in the nose cone. He wants to see what might affect the height to which the rocket will rise. Which of the following is a hypothesis he could test? 1. Rockets with warm water will rise higher than rockets with cold water. 2. Rockets with four tail fins will rise higher than rockets with two tail fins. 3. Rockets with pointed nose cones will rise higher than rockets with rounded nose cones. 4. Rockets with more water will rise higher than rockets with less water.
E. Given a verbally described variable, select a suitable operational definition for it.	The effect of exercise on pulse rate is studied by a science class. Students do different numbers of jumping jacks and then measure the pulse rate. One group does jumping jacks for 1 minute. A second group does these for 2 minutes. A third group jumps for 3 minutes. A fourth group does not jump. How would you measure the pulse rate in this study? 1. By counting the number of jumping jacks for 1 minute 2. By counting the number of heartbeats in 1 minute 3. By counting the number of jumping jacks done by each group 4. By counting the number of exercises for each group
F. Given a problem with a dependent variable specified, identify a testable hypothesis.	Some chickens lay an egg almost every day. Other chickens produce few eggs. A study is planned to examine factors that might affect the number of eggs produced by chickens. Which of the following is NOT a suitable hypothesis for the study? 1. More eggs are produced by chickens that receive more hours of light. 2. The more eggs produced by chickens, the more weight they lose. 3. The larger the cage for chickens, the more eggs they will produce. 4. The more proteins there is in the feed, the more eggs they will produce.

APPLICATION AND SELF-REFLECTION 4.2

1. A fifth-grade science teacher would like to include an assessment of laboratory skills in her summative assessment for a unit on plants. Devise an observation sheet to be used during student activities for assessment of pertinent laboratory skills related to manipulation of tools.

2. An eighth-grade science teacher would like to include a few questions to assess students' laboratory skills to analyze and interpret data for an end-of-unit test on motion and forces. Please write one multiple-choice and one constructed-response question (including the scoring rubric) to be included in the end-of-unit test.

ASSESSMENT OF REASONING IN SCIENCE INQUIRY

Inquiry is both reasoning and performing. The relationship between reasoning and performing may be demonstrated by an essay. Another way to assess understanding of this relationship is by a Vee diagram. The Vee diagram was first developed by Bob Gowin at Cornell University (Novak & Gowin, 1984). A sample student Vee diagram is as follows:

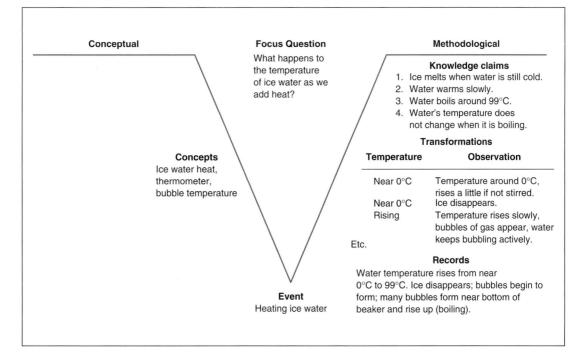

Source: Novak & Gowin (1984). Reproduced by permission.

From the above Vee diagram, we can see that a Vee diagram demonstrates understanding of the relationships among various components of an inquiry process; that is, posing questions—the center, data collection, observation, data analysis, and making conclusions—on the right-hand side and making use of a conceptual knowledge base on the left-hand side. The left-hand and right-hand sides can become more elaborated depending on the grade level of students. For example, the left-hand side can also include principles, which are statements of qualitative and quantitative relationships. An example principle is that as water boils, more and more water will evaporate. Theories, which provide explanations of a phenomenon, may also be incorporated. For example, the kinetic molecular theory may be included in the above Vee diagram to explain the water evaporation phenomenon. Similar to a concept map that highlights relationships between and among concepts, a Vee diagram highlights relationships between and among key components of science inquiry. Students often consider inquiry as isolated steps to be followed; they do not often see how various inquiry components are interrelated. Using Vee diagrams can help students to see such a relationship so that their understanding of inquiry will be enhanced.

Vee diagrams as a summative assessment include three components: (a) elicitation task, (b) response format, and (c) scoring scheme. The elicitation task is usually an inquiry task asking students to follow a process of inquiry to answer a question. When using a Vee diagram as an assessment, inquiry may take the format of a lab, an outside-school project, or an examination of a historically important experiment (e.g., Rutherford's golden sheet experiment). A sample elicitation task is as follows:

> The problem: Enzymes in human saliva play an important role in the process of food digestion. Design and conduct a laboratory investigation on the function of enzymes using a starch indicator, maltose, starch, and a heating source.
>
> You will complete the above investigation in groups of three. You will then present the results in a Vee diagram.

The response format can vary in similar ways to the case of performance assessment. For example, students may develop their own Vee diagram or work on a teacher-provided Vee diagram template. Vee diagrams may also be done individually or in groups, on paper, or on computers.

Finally, the scoring scheme needs to state the expected performances on the Vee diagram and the intermediate levels of student performances. As is the case for performance assessment, scoring schemes for Vee diagrams can be holistic or analytic. The following are sample holistic and analytic scoring schemes:

Holistic Scoring Scheme for Vee Diagrams

Points Aspect	0 (Missing)	1 (Rudimentary)	2 (Good)	3 (Excellent)
Focus question				
Object/events				
Principles/concepts				
Records/transformation				
Knowledge claim				

Analytic Scoring Scheme for Vee Diagrams

Focus Question	Points
No focus question is identified.	0
A question is identified, but does not focus on the concepts identified on the left side of the Vee.	1
A focus question is identified; includes concepts but does not suggest objects or the major event; or the wrong objects and events are identified in relation to the rest of the laboratory investigation.	2
A meaningful focus question is identified; includes concepts to be used and suggests the major event and accompanying objects.	3
Object/Event	Points
No objects or events are identified.	0
The major event or objects are identified and are consistent with the focus question, or an event and objects are identified but are inconsistent with the focus question.	1
The major event and the accompanying objects are identified and are consistent with the focus question.	2
Same as above, but also suggests what observations and data will be collected.	3
Principles and Concepts	Points
No information is presented on the conceptual side.	0
A few concepts are identified, but without principles and theory; or a principle written is the knowledge claim sought in the investigation.	1
Concepts and at least one type of principle (conceptual or methodological) or concept and relevant theory are identified.	2
Concepts, at least two types of principles, and relevant theories are identified.	3
Records/Transformation	Points
No records or transformations are identified.	0
Records are identified but are inconsistent with the focus question of the major event.	1
Either records or transformation are identified but not both.	2
Records are identified for the major event; transformations are consistent with both the focus question and the abilities and grade level of the student.	3

(Continued)

(Continued)

Knowledge Claim	Points
No conclusions are made.	0
Conclusions are made but are wrong.	1
Conclusions are partially correct.	2
Conclusions are made based on data and are correct.	3

Source: Adapted from Doran, Chan, Tamir, & Lenhardt (2002).

Note: Higher number indicates better quality.

THE CASES OF ERIC AND ELISIA: ASSESSMENT OF SCIENCE INQUIRY

This is an interesting chapter for Eric and Elisia. For Eric, he initially thought that since he teaches science in the regular classroom instead of a specialized science lab, laboratory skill assessment was not relevant to him. Now he understands that both manipulative and thinking skills are laboratory skills. For Elisia, while laboratory skills are routinely involved in her teaching, she did not differentiate between laboratory skills and science inquiry. Both Eric and Elisia can see how assessment of laboratory skills may be conducted by observations and paper-and-pencil tests. Eric likes the performance assessment idea but is not sure if his students are capable of conducting extended inquiry. He also thinks that Vee diagramming is too advanced for his elementary students, although he finds it helpful for him to understand science inquiry. Elisia now can see how performance assessment and Vee diagramming may become an important component of her end-of-unit summative assessment. Both Eric and Elisia found examples of assessment questions and tasks as well as scoring rubrics to be useful; they can see the possibility for them to model those assessment questions and tasks in their own assessment. Given that a variety of assessment methods may be used in their summative assessment based on the previous chapter and this chapter, both Eric and Elisia are still not sure how they will be able to combine scores from all the different assessment methods into a grade. They are also not quite sure how external assessment may play a role in their summative assessment. With much anticipation, Eric and Elisia continue their assessment learning journeys to the next chapters. . . .

Do the experiences of Eric and Elisia sound familiar to you? What were your initial ideas of assessment of science inquiry, and how have they changed as the result of this chapter?

APPLICATION AND SELF-REFLECTION 4.3

Using the holistic and analytic scoring rubrics, score the following Vee diagram produced by a group of students. How large is the difference between the two scores? Discuss how the scoring schemes and the scoring process may be improved to reduce the difference of scores to be obtained from the two scoring schemes.

Conceptual

Focus Question

Does enzyme in saliva facilitate breaking down of starch at the body temperature?

Methodological

Theories

1. *Human saliva contains an organism called enzymes*
2. *Enzyme reacts with starch (in food) to produce simple sugars (e.g., maltose, glucose)*
3. *Enzyme reaction takes place at a certain temperature*

Principles

1. *Starch turns Lugol's solution from brown to dark blue*
2. *Simple sugar turns Benedict's solution from blue to orange*

Concepts

1. *enzyme*
2. *suspension*
3. *starch*
4. *sugar*
5. *indicators*

Knowledge Claims

Enzyme in saliva helps break starch into simple sugar at the body temperature.

Record/Transformation

1. starch suspension + Lugol's: dark blue
2. at 37°C, starch suspension + Lugol's: color change from dark blue to light blue to clear
3. clear solution at end of procedure 4 + Benedict's: orange
4. maltose solution + Benedict's: orange

Event

1. one test tube containing 5 ml 1% starch suspension
2. add one drop Lugol's solution
3. heat test tube in a water bath at 37°C
4. at 10 seconds' interval, remove test tube and observe the color change
5. repeat step 4 until dark blue changes to clear. Add one drop Benedict's solution
6. one test tube containing 5 ml 1% maltose solution and add one drop of Benedict's solution

Chapter Summary

- Laboratory skills include both the manipulative and thinking skills involved in laboratory activities. Manipulative skills pertain to operation of laboratory tools such as using a microscope and conducting an acid-base titration. Thinking skills are mental processes related to making observations, designing and testing hypotheses, analyzing and interpreting data, and making conclusions. Assessment of manipulative skills can take place when they are taught and practiced using observations, and assessment of thinking skills can be assessed using paper-and-pencil tests.

- Performance assessment assesses student science inquiry performances. Science inquiry is a comprehensive ability involving not only laboratory skills but also conceptual understanding of scientific theories and concepts, as well as affective variables such as attitude and collaboration. Performance assessment presents a comprehensive problem in an authentic context. It consists of a task, a response format, and a scoring scheme.

- A Vee diagram demonstrates understanding of the relationships among various components of an inquiry process. Vee diagrams, as a summative assessment, include three components: (a) elicitation task, (b) response format, and (c) scoring scheme. The elicitation task is usually an inquiry task asking students to follow a process of inquiry in order to answer a question. The response format can vary from structured fill-in-the-blank type diagramming to open-ended diagramming. Finally, the scoring scheme is to state the expected and intermediate levels of student performances on the diagram. Either holistic or analytic scoring rubrics may be used.

√ Mastery Checklist

- ☐ Develop a checklist to assess student mastery of laboratory skills.
- ☐ Develop a rating scale to assess student mastery of laboratory skills.
- ☐ Create a paper-and-pencil test to assess student mastery of laboratory skills.
- ☐ Develop a performance assessment to assess student inquiry performances.
- ☐ Use Vee diagramming to assess student reasoning in science inquiry.

Web-Based Student Study Site

The Companion Web site for *Essentials of Science Classroom Assessment* can be found at **www.sagepub.com/liustudy**.

The site includes a variety of materials to enhance your understanding of the chapter content. Visit the study site to

- complete an online self-assessment of essential knowledge and skills introduced in this chapter
- find a Word file of a Vee diagram template
- find Web resources pertaining to performance assessments and to Web resources on rubrics
- find a collection of laboratory assessment tasks with scoring rubrics developed at the State University of New York at buffalo for Grade 8 science, biology, and earth science

Further Readings

Doran, R., Tamir, P., & Lenhardt, C. (2002). *Science educator's guide to laboratory assessment.* Arlington, VA: NSTA Press.

This is a research-based yet practical resource book for strategies and ample examples of alternative assessments, particularly performance assessments. It also contains chapters on performance assessment tasks and scoring rubrics in individual science subjects (i.e., biology, chemistry, earth science, and physics).

Mintzes, J. J., Wandersee, J., & Novak, J. D. (Eds.). (2000). *Assessing science understanding: A human constructivist view.* San Diego, CA: Academic Press.

This edited book is a collection of research articles by various authors summarizing current research on science assessment. Chapters on concept maps, Vee diagrams, structured interviews, dialogue, portfolios, and writing are particularly relevant to this chapter and provide excellent theoretical backgrounds for them to be used for understanding in general.

References

Brown, J. H., & Shavelson, R. J. (1996). *Assessing hands-on science: A teacher's guide to performance assessment.* Thousand Oaks, CA: Corwin.

Dillashaw, F. G., & Okey, J. R. (1980). Test of the Integrated Science Process Skills for secondary science students. *Science Education, 64*(5), 601–608.

Doran, R., Chan, F., Tamir, P., & Lenhardt, C. (2002). *Science educator's guide to laboratory assessment.* Arlington, VA: NSTA Press.

Erickson, G., Bartley, A., Carlisel, R., Meyer, K., & Stavy, R. (1991). *British Columbia assessment of science.* Victoria, BC: Ministry of Education.

Lunetta, V. N., & Tamir, P. (1979). Matching lab activities with teaching goals. *The Science Teacher, 46*(5), 22–24.

National Research Council (NRC). (1996). *National science education standards.* Washington, DC: National Academy Press.

Nelson, M., & Abraham, E. C. (1973). Inquiry Skill Measures. *Journal of Research in Science Teaching, 10*(4), 291–297.

Novak, J., & Gowin, B. D. (1984). *Learning how to learn.* New York: Cambridge University Press.

Shin, N., Jonassen, D. H., & McGee, S. (2003). Predictors of well-structured and ill-structured problem solving in an astronomy simulation. *Journal of Research in Science Teaching, 40*(1), 6–33.

Wiggins, G., & McTighe, J. (2005). *Understanding by design.* Alexandria, VA: Association for Supervision and Curriculum Development.

Chapter 5

Standardized Tests

Chapter 4 has introduced techniques for assessing laboratory skills, science inquiry performances, and reasoning about science inquiry. The techniques are part of summative assessment to find out if students have mastered learning standards. State standardized tests, as part of the accountability system, are now a requirement of the No Child Left Behind federal law. Other standardized tests, although not mandatory, are potentially useful for science teachers to plan for science teaching and learning. Whether you like it or not, standardized testing is here to stay. This chapter discusses three types of standardized testing that science teachers encounter: state standardized tests, national standardized tests, and international standardized tests.

STATE STANDARDIZED TESTS

A **standardized test** is a measurement tool that requires uniform administration, scoring, and interpretation. It is developed by external assessment experts through pilot testing and subsequent revisions until it has reached a certain degree of technical qualities.

The No Child Left Behind (NCLB) Act passed in 2001 requires every state to implement annual standardized assessment, beginning the school year of 2007–2008, to measure students' achievement in science. Even before NCLB, many states such as New York already had a state standardized test in place. Because of the accountability purpose, state standardized tests are associated with high stakes. For example, in Texas, state standardized tests have been used for student retention or denying graduation, school resources allocation and closure, and even teacher merit pay (Horn & Kincheloe, 2001). As a science teacher, you need to understand the stakes associated with state standardized tests and act accordingly for the interest of students, others, and yourself. Two extreme approaches can only do disservice to student learning. One is to totally ignore the state test and solely rely on your own assessment as a means for measuring student achievement. The other is to teach to the state test and use nothing else but the state test to measure student achievement. The first approach puts your students at a disadvantage by making them unprepared for a high-stakes test and ultimately paying a price for it; the second approach short-changes students by denying them other learning opportunities that maximize their learning potentials. Responsible science teachers take a more rational approach by adequately preparing

> ### ESSENTIAL SKILLS ADDRESSED IN CHAPTER 5
>
> - Prepare students to take state standardized tests.
> - Conduct alignment analysis among the instruction, standardized test, and content standard.
> - Use national science assessments for benchmarking.
> - Use international science assessments for benchmarking.

students for the state test and, at the same time, providing students with a variety of learning experiences expected in the curriculum and necessary to maximize student learning potentials. Science teachers need to become knowledgeable about three essential issues related to state standardized tests: legal requirements, test preparation, and alignment among the instruction, standardized test, and curriculum content standard.

Legal Requirements of State Standardized Tests

The NCLB requires that state standardized tests

1. be fully aligned with state content standards;

2. meet accepted professional standards with validity, reliability, and fairness for each purpose for which it will be used;

3. be reported to parents, teachers, and administrators in ways that are diagnostic, interpretive, and descriptive so that the results can be used to address individual students' academic needs; and

4. be reported in ways that provide evidence that all students in the state, regardless of race, ethnicity, economic status, or proficiency in English, are meeting the state's challenging academic standards (NRC, 2006).

The first requirement suggests that state content standards determine what the state test should assess. However, it does not say that every year's state test has to assess all learning outcomes in a state's content standard. Given the enormous number of learning outcomes in any state's content standards, it is unrealistic for any single state test to assess all the learning outcomes. The reality is that each year's state test may assess only a representative sample of learning outcomes, and over the years, state tests should have assessed all learning outcomes. Therefore, teaching to a single test is not going to be effective; the best approach is following the state content standards and teaching them well.

The second requirement implies that science teachers should follow the exact procedures stated by the state in administering and scoring state tests. In addition, because of the high technical qualities of state tests, teachers should make full use of them. One such use is to incorporate the state test into your grading system by giving it a certain percentage such as 15% or 20%; Chapter 7 will discuss this issue in more detail.

The third requirement implies that the state test can potentially provide rich information about student strengths and weaknesses of learning. Spending time to make sense of

ASSESSMENT STANDARDS ADDRESSED IN CHAPTER 5

NSES Assessment Standard A
Assessment must be consistent with the decisions they are designed to inform. This standard is further elaborated into the following substandards:

- Assessments are deliberately designed.
- Assessments have explicitly stated purposes.
- The relation between the decisions and the data is clear.
- Assessment procedures are internally consistent. (National Research Council [NRC], 1996, p. 78)

NSES Assessment Standard B
Achievement and opportunity to learn science must be assessed. This standard is further elaborated into the following substandards:

- Achievement data collected focus on the science content that is most important for students to learn.
- Opportunity-to-learn data collected focus on the most powerful indicators of learning.
- Equal attention must be given to the assessment of opportunity to learn and to the assessment of student achievement. (NRC, 1996, p. 79)

student performance on the state test can inform your planning of science teaching, a topic to be discussed fully in Chapter 8.

The fourth requirement implies that all students, including those who have physical and cognitive disabilities and limited English language proficiency, have to participate in the state tests. However, reasonable adaptations and accommodations for these students shall be made available in a valid and reliable manner (i.e., administering assessments in the language or form most likely to yield accurate data on what such students know and can do in academic content areas).

Different states have different guidelines as to test accommodation; it is always necessary to consult your state's official documents. For example, the California guideline "Testing Variations, Accommodations, and Modifications" provides the following test accommodation for students with disabilities within the federal Individuals with Disabilities Education Act (IDEA) to take the California High School Exit Exam (CHSEE):

- Test administration directions are simplified or clarified (not applicable to test questions).
- Allow the student to mark in the test booklet (other than responses), including highlighting.
- Test students in a small group setting.
- Give extra time on a test within a testing day.
- Allow the student the following additional accommodation and adaptation if they are used regularly in the classroom:
    ○ Test the student individually, provided that a test examiner directly supervises the student.

○ Allow using visual magnifying equipment.

○ Allow using audio amplification equipment.

○ Allow using noise buffers (e.g., individual carrel or study enclosure).

○ Allow special lighting, acoustics, and special or adaptive furniture.

○ Allow colored overlay, marks, or other means to maintain visual attention.

○ Use manually coded English or American Sign Language to present directions for administration (not applicable to test questions).

- Allow the student the following additional accommodations if they are specified in the individualized education program (IEP):

  ○ Student marks responses in the test booklet, and responses are then transferred to a scorable answer document by an employee of the school, district, or nonpublic school.

  ○ Responses are dictated orally or in manually coded English or American Sign Language to a scribe for selected-response items (multiple-choice questions).

  ○ Word-processing software is used with spell and grammar check tools turned off for the essay responses (writing portion of the test).

  ○ Essay responses are dictated orally or in manually coded English to a scribe, audio recorder, or speech-to-text converter, and the student provides all spelling and language conventions.

  ○ Assistive devices can be used that do not interfere with the independent work of the student on the multiple-choice and/or essay responses (writing portion of the test).

  ○ Braille transcriptions can be provided by the test contractor.

  ○ Large-print versions can be used or test items can be enlarged if a larger font is required on large-print versions.

  ○ Testing can be done over more than one day for a test, or a test part can be administered in a single sitting.

  ○ Supervised breaks are given within a section of the test.

  ○ Test is administered at the most beneficial time of day to the student.

  ○ Test is administered at home or in the hospital by a test examiner.

  ○ A dictionary can be used.

Similarly, different states have different guidelines regarding test accommodation for students who are identified with limited English proficiency (LEP). The following test accommodations are available for the New York state eighth-grade science test for LEP students:

- *Time extension:* Schools may extend the test time for LEP students. Principals may use any reasonable extensions, such as "time and a half" (the required testing time plus half that amount of time), in accordance with their best judgment about the needs of the LEP students. Principals should consult with each student's classroom teacher in making these determinations.

- *Separate location:* Schools are encouraged to provide optimal testing environments and facilities for all students. They may administer state tests to LEP students individually or in small groups in a separate location.

- *Bilingual dictionaries and glossaries:* LEP students may use bilingual dictionaries and glossaries when taking the test. The bilingual dictionaries and glossaries may provide *only* direct translations of words. Bilingual dictionaries or glossaries that provide definitions or explanations are *not* permitted.

- *Simultaneous use of English and alternative language editions:* LEP students may use both an English and an alternative language edition of the test simultaneously. However, they should be carefully instructed to record all of their responses in only one of the two editions. The alternative language edition used by the student should be so indicated on the student's answer sheet.

- *Oral translation for lower incidence languages:* Schools may provide LEP students with an oral translation of this test when there is no translated edition provided by the state. All translations must be oral, direct translations of the English editions; written translations are not allowed. No clarifications or explanations may be provided. Translators should receive copies of the English edition of the tests one hour prior to administration.

- *Writing responses in the native language:* LEP students may write their responses to the open-ended questions in their native language.

In addition to test accommodation and adaptation required by the IDEA, the NCLB further requires that each state provide alternative assessments for students with disabilities whose IEP teams have determined that they cannot participate in the state's regular assessments with appropriate accommodations and adaptation. Examples of alternative assessments are student-written work/products, videotaping, audiotaping, or observation of the student demonstrating a performance task. For example, New York state recommends that multiple pieces of student "work" (3–5 pieces of evidence) are collected and scored with a rubric as an alternative assessment.

Preparing Students for State Standardized Tests

Because state standardized tests are high stakes, it is important to ensure that scores on the tests reflect students' best abilities. However, nonessential factors such as test-taking skills, if missing, may hinder students in performing their best. Other factors, such as test anxiety, may seriously reduce students' performances. Thus, to ensure equal opportunities for students to perform well on tests, you must prepare students to take state standardized tests. A National Research Council committee recommends that "all students are entitled to sufficient test preparation so their performance will not be adversely affected by unfamiliarity with item format or by ignorance of appropriate test-taking strategies. Test users should balance efforts to prepare students for a particular test format against the possibility that excessively narrow preparation will invalidate test outcomes" (NRC, 1999, p. 280).

To prepare students for the state test, you should first check if the state has available any study guides (such as the *Texas Knowledge and Skills Study Guides* for fifth grade, eighth grade, and exit level) or test samplers (such as the *New York State Science Assessment Test Samplers* for fourth and eighth grades). If they are available, you should incorporate them into your test preparation. The following are general guidelines for preparing students for state standardized tests:

1. *Inform students about the purpose and the nature of the state test.* State standardized tests are for accountability purposes. Students' scores on the state tests may determine their promotion to the next grade or if they can graduate from high school. Their scores may also have an impact on the school and even the teacher. Thus, it is important that students take

the state test seriously and perform their best. It should also be emphasized to the students that state tests do not replace classroom assessments, although the two may overlap to some degree. Explain to the students why state test scores may account for a portion of their course grade if your grading system includes a component of the state test. Clearly informing students on the importance and possible consequences of the state standardized test helps students prepare accordingly. Uninformed students as well as parents can be penalized potentially for insufficient preparation, efforts, or motivation. Equally important is informing students and parents about their rights and obligations in order for them to recognize any possible misuse or misinterpretation of standardized test scores.

2. *Provide quality instruction during the school year.* A key science assessment standard is to ensure that students have the opportunity to learn so that they are well prepared and are likely to succeed. A key indicator of the opportunity to learn is the curriculum coverage. Unlearned topics will put students at a disadvantaged position, which makes the test potentially unfair. Keep in mind that the state test is expected to be aligned with the state content standards per the NCLB, although a given state test may not necessarily assess all the learning outcomes in the content standard. It is a common misconception that preparing students to take the state standardized test means spending weeks practicing previous test questions. Because a given state test may assess only a sample of the content standard, teaching to single tests is risky and may be counterproductive. The most effective preparation for the state test is in fact adequate instruction during the school year so that students are getting ready over the entire school year rather than in a few weeks.

3. *Familiarize students with the types of questions.* Familiarizing students with the types of questions and the length of the test can greatly increase students' confidence and reduce their test anxiety. Previous tests, if made public by the state, should only be used at limited times because intensive use of previous tests amounts to drills and practices, which is pedagogically unsound and psychometrically undermines test validity. Unreleased previous tests should remain secured, and it is unethical to use any of the questions for practice. Teachers should prepare practice tests that may include some sample questions from previously released tests. Practice tests should be aligned with the curriculum you have been following.

4. *Provide adequate content review before the test.* In addition to adequate curriculum coverage and instruction, adequate review before the standardized test is also necessary. However, review before the test should not be just practicing test questions; rather, it should focus on helping students to conceptualize all the learned topics so that they can develop a better understanding about the connections among the topics. This is particularly important because a state test, such as the eighth-grade test, typically assesses all learning outcomes expected by the end of the grade level, and preparing students for the state test needs to cover multiple years of learning. Reviewing only the topics taught in one year will likely miss many other important topics taught in other years covered by the state test. Review should aim at enhancing previous learning and developing new integrated understanding.

5. *Help students approach the test positively.* Although state tests are high stakes and it is always desirable to perform well, overemphasizing the importance and consequences of failing it is counterproductive. Students should be informed that alternative opportunities do exist, and each standardized test is nothing but one opportunity. Even a failed test can be a valuable learning experience and can increase potential to succeed next time.

6. *Help students manage their test anxiety and stress.* Given the high stakes of the state standardized tests, some students will always have anxiety and stress about the tests. Some procedures may be helpful for students to deal with the anxiety and stress during the test. For example, deep breathing and mental imagining exercises can momentarily restore calm and confidence. Sufficient sleep and adequate nutrition and exercise the day before the test are also essential.

7. *Teach students to use time wisely during tests.* State standardized tests are within a time limit; it is important that students finish all the questions before the allotted time for the test is over. Appropriately budgeting time for answering all questions is necessary. The following tips may be helpful: (a) Quickly scan the entire test before beginning, (b) answer easy questions first and difficult questions last, (c) never be stuck at one question (do skip to next one after you have spent enough time on the question), (d) mark uncertain answers for later revision, and (e) budget adequate time for final checking before time is over.

8. *Teach students to pay attention to the mechanism of the test.* Students should not overlook the importance of the test mechanism. For example, if answers are to be optically scanned, it is important to use the right type of pencil (e.g., HB or #2) and record the answers on the scanning sheets completely and neatly. If changes are made to previous answers, make sure that previous answers are erased completely. When answering multiple-choice questions, students should try to guess if they don't know the correct answer.

Many states such as California, New York, and Texas release previous test items or even the entire tests. These released test items and tests are typically available on the Web. Unfortunately, most states do not have an explicit guideline regarding uses of released items and tests, leaving individual teachers to decide how to use them. Gallagher (1998) stated two guiding principles for preparing students to take standardized tests: (a) the ethical principle, in which test preparation should conform to ethical standards of the education profession, and (b) the educational principle, in which test preparation should not aim at increasing student scores without simultaneously increasing students' mastery of the subject matter assessed. The ethical principle advises against practices such as encouraging cheating, copying, breach of test security, and so on. The implications of the education principle are not as clear as those of the ethical principle. In general, the education principle suggests that any test preparation, such as the practices suggested above, should be expected to increase student understanding in addition to increasing student test scores. For example, test preparation integrated with regular and ongoing instruction is an educationally sound practice. As another example, spending 4 weeks before the state test for students to practice questions on released state tests would not be in agreement with the education principle. A few states such as California have clear guidelines regarding preparing students for state tests. For example, the California Code of Regulations, Title 5, Section 854a (http://www.cde.ca.gov/ta/tg/sa/documents/academicprep.pdf), states, "Except for materials specifically included within the designated achievement test, no program or materials shall be used by any school district or employee of a school district that are specifically formulated or intended to prepare pupils for the designated achievement test. No administration or use of an alternate or parallel form of the designated test for any stated purpose shall be permitted for any pupils in grades 2 through 11, inclusive." The California regulation further suggests five questions to be answered to decide if a test preparation practice is appropriate:

1. Are all students in my school/district being provided with a standards-based instructional program employing the instructional principles and practices set forth in the content area frameworks?

2. Are the preparation materials and/or practices being provided to students meant to improve student learning rather than to achieve a score on a particular test?

3. Are students in my school/district being taught test-taking skills designed to assist them in taking any type of test rather than a particular state test?

4. Are the released test items and other materials used in academic preparation being embedded within our school's/district's standards-based instructional program?

5. Are the released test items and other materials used in academic preparation in my school/district included for the limited purpose of familiarizing students with the structure and format of the items and with strategies for taking multiple-choice tests?

Educationally sound preparation of students for the state standardized test should be based on a yes answer to all the above five questions. In summary, test preparation is not a 1-week or 2-week practice; instead, it should be an ongoing practice during the school year that is an integral part of the curriculum.

APPLICATION AND SELF-REFLECTION 5.1

Are the following practices professionally ethical and educationally defensible? State reasons for your choice to the class.

Practice	Professionally Ethical?	Educationally Defensible?
1. Choose a random sample of items from the latest edition of the test, administer them as a pretest, and then use them to identify the areas students need to drill on before the formal administration of the test.	Yes/No/ Depends	Yes/No/ Depends
2. Use separate answer sheets with some of your classroom tests so that your elementary students get exposure to manipulating them, tracking item numbers with answer numbers, and bubbling in identification information and answers appropriately.	Yes/No/ Depends	Yes/No/ Depends

Practice	Professionally Ethical?	Educationally Defensible?
3. Administer the state's practice test for the edition of the standardized tests used in your state. Discuss the answers and the test-taking process afterward with your students.	Yes/No/ Depends	Yes/No/ Depends
4. Use leftover copies of an older edition of the state test as practice tests for the new edition that will be administered under formal conditions.	Yes/No/ Depends	Yes/No/ Depends
5. Read through the items of the current edition of the test, and then construct your own items that mirror their content and format for use as a practice test.	Yes/No/ Depends	Yes/No/ Depends
6. Create a test-taking skills unit that focuses on the specific assessment approach and content of the upcoming standardized test. Time the unit so that students finish it just before the formal administration of the standardized test.	Yes/No/ Depends	Yes/No/ Depends
7. Instruct your students in how to read (or listen to) directions, interpret them accurately, and follow them carefully using practice test directions as one example among others.	Yes/No/ Depends	Yes/No/ Depends

Source: Adapted from Gallagher (1998, pp. 452–453).

Alignment Among Instruction, Standardized Test, and Content Standard

From the above discussion, we see that the best preparation for students to take the state standardized test is to teach students well. One important indication of quality instruction is the content coverage (i.e., the alignment between instruction and the state content standard). Given that the state test is expected to align with the state content standard, if instruction is aligned with the content standard, then the instruction will be aligned with the standardized test as well. One way to analyze the alignment is to represent the standard, instruction, and standardized test in three columns of a table. A checkmark is placed in the cell if a standard has been taught and/or if it is present in the test. Table 5.1 is a sample alignment table.

In the above example, Learning Standards 1a and 1b have been both taught, but only Standard 1a is present on the test. Standards 1c and 1d are gaps in instruction because neither standard has been taught, although only 1c is on the test. A simple percentage of checked standards out of the total number of standards for the second and third columns can be calculated as a rough measure of alignment between instruction and the content

TABLE 5.1   Sample Alignment Table

Learning Standards	Instruction	Standardized Test
1a. Living things are composed of cells. Cells provide structure and carry on major functions to sustain life. Cells are usually microscopic in size.	√	√
1b. The way in which cells function is similar in all living things. Cells grow and divide, producing more cells. Cells take in nutrients, which they use to provide energy for the work that cells do and to make the materials that a cell or an organism needs.	√	
1c. Most cells have cell membranes, genetic material, and cytoplasm. Some cells have a cell wall and/or chloroplasts. Many cells have a nucleus.		√
1d. Some organisms are single cells; others, including humans, are multicellular.		
. . .		

standard (e.g., $\frac{2}{4}$ or 50% in Table 5.1) and between the standardized test and the content standard (e.g., $\frac{2}{4}$ or 50% in Table 5.1). As for the alignment between instruction and test coverage, a percentage of standards checked in both columns out of the total number of standards can be calculated as a measure for alignment (e.g., $\frac{1}{4}$ or 25%). Alternatively, a correlation between instructional coverage and test coverage of the learning standards may be calculated by assigning a value of 1 to each cell with a checkmark and 0 without. A high positive correlation coefficient indicates a better alignment.

The above analysis is obviously crude because not all content standards are equally important. It is common that teachers spend more time on some standards than on others, and the state standardized test emphasizes some standards over others. To take the issue of relative emphasis into consideration, we may modify the above analysis procedure to include measures of relative importance. For example, instead of checking yes or no for each content standard, the amount of instructional time may be entered under the column of Instruction, and actual points of items on the test can be entered under the column of Standardized Test. If the state content standard specifies an expected amount of times spent, then a correlation coefficient can be calculated as an alignment index. Similarly, the correlation coefficient can be calculated for the alignment between the content standard and the standardized test, as well as between the instruction and the standardized test. If the content standard does not specify an expected amount of time spent, then an estimate of the expected amount of time may be decided for each standard. Another way to calculate relative importance is to calculate the percentage of total time spent on each content standard. Similarly, a percentage of total test points devoted to each content standard may also be computed to indicate the relative importance among the content standards on the standardized test.

APPLICATION AND SELF-REFLECTION 5.2

Locate two previous state tests used from different years released for public use, make a list of the topics covered by each test, and compare the topics between the two tests. Are they the same? Compare the topics with the state content standard. Is there an alignment? Can you make a generalization based on results about what a state test assesses? Why?

NATIONAL STANDARDIZED TESTS

Known as the "Nation's Report Card," the National Assessment of Educational Progress (NAEP) is the only national and continuing assessment of what American students know and can do in various subject areas, including science. Since 1969, the NAEP science assessment has been given every 4 years. The most recent NAEP science assessment was conducted in 2005. Since 1990, NAEP assessments have also included a state assessment component, which is called NAEP-State, so that those states that choose to participate can receive assessment results on the performance of students in their states in the national context.

The NAEP science assessment is developed by a committee of science and measurement experts to capture the goals of the NAEP Science Framework. At Grades 4, 8, and 12, the assessment tests the following learning outcomes using various types of test questions:

- *multiple-choice questions* that assess students' knowledge of important facts and concepts and that probe students' analytical reasoning skills;

- *constructed-response questions* that explore students' abilities to explain, integrate, apply, reason about, plan, design, evaluate, and communicate science information; and

- *hands-on tasks* that probe students' abilities to use materials to make observations, perform investigations, evaluate experimental results, and apply problem-solving skills.

NAEP science assessment reports student group performance by region, state, and the nation as a whole on a scale ranging from 0 to 300. Students' performances are defined by the following three levels:

Basic	**Partial mastery** of prerequisite knowledge and skills that are fundamental for proficient work at each grade.
Proficient	**Solid academic performance** for each grade assessed. Students reaching this level have demonstrated competency over challenging subject matter, including subject matter knowledge, application of such knowledge to real-world situations, and analytical skills appropriate to the subject matter.
Advanced	**Superior performance.**

Unlike state tests, NAEP tests are not high stakes (i.e., test results have no consequences to individual students, teachers, or schools). Not every student participates in the NAEP; only randomly selected, nationally representative schools and students take part. Because the NAEP is mandated by Congress, all school districts, schools, and teachers must cooperate by providing pertinent information about classes and students for sampling and participating if they are randomly selected. Primary uses of the NAEP assessment results are science education policy making at the national and, to some extent, state levels because the NAEP collects not only student achievement data but also data on variables potentially affecting student achievements, such as science classroom teaching practices, teacher characteristics, science curriculums, school resources, community and family environments, and so on.

Per federal IDEA requirements, students selected to participate in the NAEP are also entitled to test accommodation. The following test accommodations are available for the NAEP:

1. Presentation format:
   a. Directions only signed
   b. Test questions signed
   c. Occasional words or phrases read aloud
   d. All or most of the test materials read aloud
   e. Large-print version of the test
   f. Magnifying equipment

2. Setting format:
   a. In a small group
   b. In a study carrel
   c. Preferential seating, special lighting, or furniture
   d. Administered by a familiar person

3. Timing/scheduling:
   a. Extend testing time (same day)
   b. More breaks

4. Response format:
   a. Braille typewriter
   b. Sign language
   c. Word processors or similar assistive device (no spell/grammar check allowed)
   d. Writes directly in test booklet
   e. Large marking pen or special writing tool
   f. Answer orally, point to answer to a scribe
   g. Template

5. Accommodation for English learners: direct linguistic support
   a. Directions only read aloud in native language
   b. Bilingual version of booklet (Spanish/English only)
   c. Bilingual word-for-word dictionary (without definitions)
   d. Occasional words or phrases read aloud in English
   e. All or most of the test materials read aloud in English

6. Accommodation for English learners: indirect linguistic support
   a. In a small group
   b. One on one
   c. Preferential seating
   d. Administered by a familiar person
   e. Extend testing time (same day)
   f. More breaks

Although the NAEP does not have a direct impact on individual students and science teachers, NAEP results can inform science teachers on how students do in general nationally and statewide—for example, the percentage of students who are at the *basic* level (partial mastery), the *proficient* level (solid academic performance), and the *advanced* level (superior performance). Given that education is a state responsibility in the United States, and each state has its own curricula and assessment, it is beneficial to know where students in your state stand compared with students in other states. Teachers tend to think that their students are doing above average due to the Lake Wobegon effect. The **Lake Wobegon effect** refers to people's tendency to overestimate themselves in relation to others. It is named for the fictional town of Lake Wobegon from the radio series *A Prairie Home Companion,* where, according to the presenter, Garrison Keillor, "all the children are above average." Science teachers need to break the Lake Wobegon effect and take a realistic look at how their students are doing in comparison to others.

One specific way science teachers can benefit from the NAEP is to use released items to find out how their students are doing in comparison to students in the country and in the state. Although entire NAEP assessment instruments are secured and are not available for public use, sample NAEP questions and student performance results are available at the NAEP Web site (http://nces.ed.gov/nationsreportcard/science/). Those sample questions along with the national and state student performance results can provide important benchmarking for a class of students. **Benchmarking** refers to comparing one group of students' performance to the state, national, or international average. In addition, released items can also help initiate classroom discussions around certain ideas targeted by the questions, discuss common error patterns, and prepare students in general on test-taking strategies.

The following is a sample question from the eighth-grade year 2000 NAEP science assessment.

Which of the following is designed to convert energy into mechanical work?

A. Electric fan*
B. Kerosene heater
C. Flashlight
D. Baking oven

2000 National Performance Results: Percentage correct: 53%, incorrect 46%, and omitted 1%

The above question assesses students' understanding of energy forms and their transfer. This question appears to be quite basic as any teacher who has taught a middle school unit on energy should have introduced various forms of energy and their common sources. In this question, students need to analyze what forms of energy are involved in each of the household devices. However, nationally, only 53% of students answered this question correctly. Is this performance level acceptable? Can your students do better than this? Give this question to your students as part of your regular instruction of the topic, or include this question as part of your end-of-unit test. If your students do not do any better than the national average, then you have been doing only an average job. If your students' performance is below your expectation, you need to identify areas of instructional improvement, such as using more everyday life examples to help students apply and analyze how science concepts are involved. Discussing why some students chose distracters and why some students omitted the question may also be helpful.

INTERNATIONAL STANDARDIZED TESTS

Similar to the approach to the NAEP, science teachers can make good use of international standardized tests for improving student learning. There are currently two ongoing international science assessments: the Trend in International Math and Science Study (TIMSS) and the Programme for International Student Assessment (PISA). TIMSS began in 1994; it is the largest and most comprehensive assessment of student achievement in science. In its first study taking place during the school year of 1994–1995, TIMSS was conducted at five grade levels (the third, fourth, seventh, eighth, and the final year of secondary school) in more than 40 countries. For the final secondary school year, students who were taking advanced physics were also assessed. In the United States, over 33,000 students and more than 500 schools participated in TIMSS. TIMSS assessment takes place in a 4-year cycle. Since 1998, TIMSS has been assessing only fourth and eighth graders.

The TIMSS science assessment domain is not tied to any country's curriculum; instead, a common set of learning outcomes deemed essential for science learning in all countries is assessed. The science content covered includes earth science, life science, physical sciences, environmental issues, science, technology and mathematics, nature of science, and science and other disciplines. The assessment questions fall into one of the following cognitive categories: (a) understanding; (b) theorizing, analyzing, and solving problems; (c) using tools and routine procedures; (d) investigating the natural world; and (e) communicating. TIMSS test items include both selected-response questions and constructed-response questions. Students' scores are reported on a scale with a mean of 500 and a standard deviation of 100.

TIMSS national and international student performance results of individual items allow for a class of students to be compared with those in the country and in the world—national and international benchmarking. A large number of items used in previous TIMSS assessments have been made available on the TIMSS Web site (http://www.timss.bc.edu); science teachers can select pertinent items to be part of their formative assessment or summative assessments for benchmarking. The following is a sample item from the TIMSS 1995 assessment for seventh- and eighth-grade students.

Animals are made up of many atoms. What happens to the atoms after an animal had died?

A. The atoms stop moving.

B. The atoms recycle back into environment.*

C. The atoms split into simpler parts and then combine to form other atoms.

D. The atoms no longer exist once the animal has decomposed.

Source: © International Association for the Evaluation of Educational Achievement (IEA), TIMSS 1995 Released http://timss.bc.edu/. Reproduced by permission.

The above question assesses seventh- and eighth-grade students' understanding of the conservation of matter. Internationally, only 26% of eighth-grade students and 22% of seventh-grade students answered the question correctly. Find out how your students would perform on this question in comparison to students internationally. If your students perform no better or even worse, then your instruction needs improvement. No matter how your students may perform on this question, or even if your students perform better than the international average, you may engage your students in a discussion as part of your instruction about why some students find the distracters appealing.

PISA is a student assessment conducted by the Organisation for Economic Co-operation and Development (OECD). It assesses how well students near the end of compulsory education (~ 15 years old) have acquired some of the knowledge and skills that are essential for full participation in society. Science is one of three subjects assessed (the other two are math and reading). Different from TIMSS, PISA assesses students' levels of scientific literacy, which is defined as "the capacity to use scientific knowledge, to identify questions and to draw evidence-based conclusions in order to understand and help make decisions about the natural world and the changes made to it through human activity." Sample test questions are available at the PISA Web site at http://www.pisa.oecd.org/. Here is a sample question from the 2000 PISA:

S126: BIODIVERSITY

Biodiversity Text 1

Read the following newspaper article and answer the questions which follow.

BIODIVERSITY IS THE KEY TO MANAGING ENVIRONMENT

An ecosystem that retains a high biodiversity (that is, a wide variety of living things) is much more likely to adapt to human-caused environment change than is one that has little.

Consider the two food webs shown in the diagram. The arrows point from the organism that gets eaten to the one that eats it. These food webs are highly simplified compared with food webs in real ecosystems, but they still illustrate a key difference between more diverse and less diverse ecosystems.

Food web B represents a situation with very low biodiversity, where at some levels the food path involves only a single type of organism. Food web A represents a more diverse ecosystem with, as a result, many more alternative feeding pathways.

Generally, loss of biodiversity should be regarded seriously, not only because the organisms that have become extinct represent a big loss for both ethical and utilitarian (useful benefit) reasons, but also because the organisms that remain have become more vulnerable (exposed) to extinction in the future.

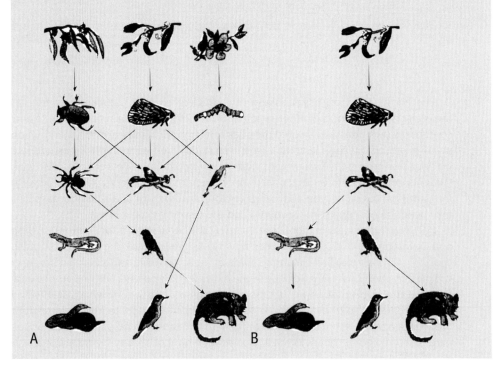

QUESTION 3: BIODIVERSITY S126Q03

In lines 9 and 10 it is stated that "Food web A represents a more diverse ecosystem with, as a result, many more alternative feeding pathways."

Look at FOOD WEB A. Only two animals in this food web have three direct (immediate) food sources. Which two animals are they?

A. Native Cat and Parasitic Wasp
B. Native Cat and Butcher Bird
C. Parasitic Wasp and Leaf Hopper
D. Parasitic Wasp and Spider
E. Native Cat and Honeyeater

BIODIVERSITY SCORING 3

QUESTION INTENT:
Process: Demonstrating knowledge and understanding
Theme: Ecosystems
Area: Science in life and health

Full credit

Code 1: A. Native Cat and Parasitic Wasp

No credit
Code 0: Other responses
Code 9: Missing

QUESTION 3: BIODIVERSITY S126Q04

Food webs A and B are in different locations. Imagine if Leaf Hoppers died out in both locations. Which one of these is the best prediction and explanation for the effect this would have on the food webs?

A. The effect would be greater in food web A because the Parasitic Wasp has only one food source in web A.
B. The effect would be greater in food web A because the Parasitic Wasp has several food sources in web A.
C. The effect would be greater in food web B because the Parasitic Wasp has only one food source in web B.
D. The effect would be greater in food web B because the Parasitic Wasp has several food sources in web B.

BIODIVERSITY SCORING 4
QUESTION INTENT:
Process: Drawing/evaluating conclusions
Theme: Biodiversity
Area: Science in life and health

Full credit
Code 1: C. The effect would be greater in food web B because the Parasitic Wasp has only one food source in web B.

No credit
Code 0: Other responses
Code 9: Missing

As can be seen from the above sample item, PISA test questions are more complex and authentic than TIMSS questions. TIMSS is more about science taught in schools, but PISA is more about students' ability to apply what they have learned in school science. Thus, TIMSS and PISA are complementary to each other.

In addition to the use of international tests for benchmarking, international tests also provide important contextual information about curriculum and instruction in different countries. Although country ranking is often the focus of media coverage, science teachers should focus more on identified factors contributing to different performances by students in different countries. For example, one important finding from the 1995 TIMSS study was that U.S. science curriculums simply covered too many topics at a superficial manner, a phenomenon called "mile-wide inch-deep" (Schmidt, McKnight, & Raizen, 1997). The implication for improving instruction is that we need to focus on a few major ideas and spend more time and develop in-depth understanding of them. Many research reports usually accompany a given international test, freely accessible on the Web. Science teachers should spend time on studying those reports and identifying pertinent recommendations to implement. The U.S. student population is extremely diverse, and not all recommendations may be pertinent to your students. You need to critically review the recommendations and adopt those that are relevant to your situation.

APPLICATION AND SELF-REFLECTION 5.3

Select one item each from the NAEP, TIMSS, and PISA and predict how students of a given class (e.g., a class of your practice teaching; a class of your former elementary school) may perform on the items. Compare the predicted levels to the national or international averages; explain the discrepancies between your predictions and the averages. Discuss what instructional improvement may take place to increase students' performance levels.

THE CASES OF ERIC AND ELISIA: STANDARDIZED TESTS

Before beginning this chapter, Eric and Elisia had only a vague idea about the importance of state standardized tests. They have heard the requirement of the NCLB Act and that many schools place a major emphasis on preparing students to pass the state standardized test. Although the stakes of state tests are different for students in elementary schools than they are in high schools, they both wanted their students to do well on the state tests. During their student teaching, Eric and Elisia witnessed that many teachers spent quite a few weeks to prepare students for the state tests by engaging them in intensive drills and practices. Many teachers also gave students entire tests from previous years to practice. After finishing this chapter, Eric and Elisia begin to question many common practices of teachers in preparing students for state tests. They can understand why the best preparation for state tests is to teach students well according to the state content standards during the school year. However, they are not sure if state tests are fully aligned with the content standard because the content standard seems so comprehensive that they don't think it is possible for any single test to assess all the learning outcomes in the standard. They are anxious to conduct some analysis using the technique introduced in this chapter to find out the alignment between a test and the content standard. Still, they don't quite understand why it may not be educationally sound to use the entire previous test for test preparation because their state, unlike California, does not have such specific guideline against this practice. Besides the state test, Eric and Elisia both did not have much knowledge of the NAEP, TIMSS, and PISA. They have heard some media reports about them but thought they were mainly for research. The suggested use of national and international tests for benchmarking opened both Eric's and Elisia's eyes. They are eager to find out how their future students will be compared with the national and international averages. Overall, this chapter has made Eric and Elisia think more seriously about many issues associated with standardized tests. They feel better informed about various uses and misuses of standardized tests. But a remaining major question puzzling them is grading—how a science teacher can make a grade for a student based on information from so many different forms of assessment, including standardized tests. Also, they wonder if assessment only takes place at the end of a unit or course, as discussed in previous chapters.

Do the experiences of Eric and Elisia sound familiar to you? What were your initial ideas of standardized tests, and how have they changed as the result of this chapter?

Chapter Summary

- State standardized tests measure student mastery of state content standards. Because of the high stakes of state tests, it is necessary to adequately prepare students to take the state standardized tests. The best approach to preparing students is to teach them well during the school year according to the state content standard. Brief preparation before the test should focus on test-taking skills and reviews aimed at helping students to make connections among individual topics learned over the years.

- The NCLB requires that students with learning disabilities be provided with test accommodation and adaptations. If students still cannot adequately demonstrate their achievements even with accommodation and adaptation, then schools and teachers need to provide those students with alternative assessments that may include observations, portfolios, performance assessment, and so on.

- The NAEP is the only national assessment of student science achievement in the United States. It is conducted every 4 years to students in Grades 4, 8, and 12. Only a random sample of students participates, and scores are reported by state, region, and the whole country.

- There are two ongoing international student achievement tests in science: TIMSS and PISA. TIMSS assesses fourth- and eighth-grade students' knowledge and understanding of fundamental science concepts and skills commonly taught in elementary and junior high schools. PISA assesses 15-year-old students' ability to apply what they have learned in school science to reason on and solve everyday problems.

- One important use of national and international assessments is to administer publicly released items to a class of students and compare students' performance with the state, national, or international performance averages. This use is called *benchmarking*.

√ Mastery Checklist

☐ Prepare students to take state standardized tests.

☐ Conduct alignment analysis among the instruction, standardized test, and content standard.

☐ Use national science assessments for benchmarking.

☐ Use international science assessments for benchmarking.

Web-Based Student Study Site

The Companion Web site for *Essentials of Science Classroom Assessment* can be found at **www.sagepub.com/liustudy.**

The site includes a variety of materials to enhance your understanding of the chapter content. Visit the study site to

- complete an online self-assessment of essential knowledge and skills introduced in this chapter

- find Web addresses for publicly released science assessment items from NAEP, IMSS, and PISA

Further Readings

National Research Council. (2003). *Assessment in support of instruction and learning: Bridging the gap between large-scale and classroom assessment—workshop report.* Washington, DC: National Academy Press.

    This book is a report by a committee on the relationship between classroom and large-scale standardized science assessments. It explains how classroom and large-scale assessments are supplementary to each other and thus should be considered at the same time by science teachers.

National Research Council. (2006). *Systems for state science assessment.* Washington, DC: National Academy Press.

    This is another report by a different committee reviewing the requirements of the NCLB for states to implement an accountability system. It argues that no single test is likely to fulfill the mandate of the NCLB; instead, a system of assessments that include teacher-made classroom assessments and state-implemented standardized tests is needed for a sound accountability system.

References

Gallagher, J. D. (1998). *Classroom assessment for teachers.* Upper Saddle River, NJ: Merrill.

Horn, R. A., & Kincheloe, J. L. (Eds.). (2001). *American standards: Quality education in a complex world: The Texas case.* New York: Peter Lange.

National Research Council (NRC). (1996). *National science education standards.* Washington, DC: National Academy Press.

National Research Council (NRC). (1999). *High stakes: Testing for tracking, promotion, and graduation.* Washington, DC: National Academy Press.

National Research Council (NRC). (2006). *Systems for state science assessment.* Washington, DC: National Academy Press.

Schmidt, W. H., McKnight, C. C., & Raizen, S. A. (1997). *A splintered vision: An investigation of U.S. science and mathematics education.* Dordrecht, the Netherlands: Kluwer.

CHAPTER 6

Assessment of Ongoing Learning

Chapter 3 to 5 have introduced various types of assessment methods aimed at providing evidence of student learning at the end of a unit as well as of that by standardized tests. Also, Chapter 2 has introduced a few techniques to identify student preconceptions to inform planning of a new unit. Planning a unit of science instruction involves making many decisions, such as defining learning objectives, sequencing and designing learning activities, and assessing students both during and at the end of the unit. This chapter focuses on assessment during the unit of instruction.

Assessment is always an integral component of instruction. Assessment conducted during instruction is called formative assessment. The purpose of formative assessment is to monitor ongoing instruction by collecting pertinent information to inform decisions for adjusting ongoing instruction. No instruction can proceed exactly as initially planned, no matter how thorough the planning is; ongoing adjustment to the instructional plan is always necessary to ensure that the instructional plan will achieve its objectives. Teachers need to make adjustment to their instructional plans whenever necessary; it is inconceivable, for example, for a teacher still to proceed with the lab when students are not performing the task because of unclear instructions. Of course, adjustment to instruction may take place spontaneously. However, formative assessment is more than spontaneous adjustment to instruction; it is an intentional and systematic effort on the part of the teacher to collect information, analyze it, and then take actions according to the analysis result (Gallagher, 2007). Formative assessment follows a continuous cycle of data collection, analysis, and action during instruction.

Teaching Standard C, of the National Science Education Standards, best summarizes the integration of assessment and instruction. It states that

Teachers of science engage in ongoing assessment for their teaching and of student learning. In doing this, teachers

- Use multiple methods and systematically gather data about student understanding and ability.

- Analyze assessment data to guide teaching.

- Use student data, observations of teaching, and interactions with colleagues to reflect on and improve teaching practice.

ESSENTIAL SKILLS ADDRESSED IN CHAPTER 6

- Using journaling to assess student conceptual change
- Using portfolios to assess student learning progression
- Using concept mapping to assess student structural knowledge
- Using the Likert scale and standardized instruments to assess student affective learning variables and classroom environments

---

- Use student data, observations of teaching, and interactions with colleagues to report student achievement and opportunities to learn to students, teachers, parents, policy makers, and the general public. (NRC, 1996, pp. 37–38)

Because of the close relationship between formative assessment and instruction, there is not a clear distinction between formative assessment methods and instructional methods. Assessment is learning, and learning is assessment. Opportunity to learn is another concept that reflects the mutual dependence between assessment and learning.

Opportunity to learn (OTL) refers to the provision of conditions, resources, and practices that maximize students' likelihood to achieve the expected learning competence. Specific to science classroom teaching and learning, OTL refers to best teaching practices to enable student learning. The most common OTL variables are (a) content coverage—whether there is a match between the curriculum taught and the content tested, (b) content exposure—whether there is enough time spent on the content tested, (c) content emphasis—whether the teacher provides sufficient emphasis on the content tested, and (d) quality of instruction—whether the teacher has taught the content adequately (Stevens, 1997). To ensure OTL implied by the above variables during science teaching and learning, you must have ongoing assessment.

This chapter focuses on assessment of the following types of opportunities to learn: conceptual change, learning trajectory, structural knowledge, and affective learning variables and classroom environments. Accordingly, the following assessment methods will be introduced: journaling, portfolios, concept mapping, and Likert scales. Given that formative assessment is to monitor student learning progression toward achieving learning standards, scoring of student work can be done either formally or informally.

USING JOURNALING TO MONITOR CONCEPTUAL CHANGE

The importance of writing in science is well recognized. First of all, writing is an essential part of scientific literacy. Norris and Phillips argue that, because Western science is primarily print medium based, it would be impossible to develop scientific literacy without writing, no matter how intelligent a person may be (Norris & Phillips, 2003). Yore, Hand, and Florence (2004) show how scientists are also writers. When scientists write an article, they are developing a form of reasoning comprising theoretical framework, data collection and analysis methods,

ASSESSMENT STANDARDS ADDRESSED IN CHAPTER 6

NSES Assessment Standard B
   Achievement and opportunity to learn science must be assessed. This standard is further elaborated into the following substandards:

- Achievement data collected focus on the science content that is most important for students to learn.
- Opportunity-to-learn data collected focus on the most powerful indicators of learning.
- Equal attention must be given to the assessment of opportunity to learn and to the assessment of student achievement. (National Research Council [NRC], 1996, p. 79)

results, and conclusions. This form of reasoning is empirical and usually deductive. Scientific writing is nonfiction writing, and thus technical accuracy and logical rigor are ultimately important. Champagne and Kouba (1999) argue that writing is also a part of scientific inquiry and thus reflects scientific understanding. Given the above importance of writing in science, engaging students in writing during science teaching and learning is natural.

One form of writing is journaling. One major advantage of journaling as assessment is the potential to assess students' conceptual change in developing understanding of a major science concept. For students to compose a journal entry on a science concept, they need to possess not only a certain amount of knowledge about the concept but also certain cognitive skills such as analyzing, synthesizing, and evaluating to apply the knowledge, which represents understanding.

Journaling to monitor student conceptual change can take place in three general forms: open-ended journaling, responsive journaling, and dialogic journaling. **Open-ended journaling** is when students can decide on a specific focus, format, and length to write about a given concept. Basic rules of writing are given, but specific topic choices are general enough to let the students control the composition of the entry. In **responsive journaling,** students answer questions posed by the teacher. While both the open-ended journaling and responsive journaling take place individually, **dialogic journaling** involves two persons (i.e., a student and the teacher). In dialogic journaling, the teacher and the student engage in an ongoing conversation about the concept. During the conversation, either the teacher or the student may post questions. With today's technology such as e-mail, dialogic journaling does not have to be done in a paper-and-pencil format; the teacher and the student can exchange questions and responses electronically. Both synchronous (i.e., real-time) and asynchronous (i.e., delayed) conversation may take place using today's Internet technologies.

Open-Ended Journaling

Because of its open-endedness, much responsibility of open-ended journaling rests on individual students. The main purpose of open-ended journaling as formative assessment is to gather information on students' ongoing learning to inform subsequent instruction. It is important that a specific topic or concept is provided to students so that what they write is relevant for formative assessment. A topic can be a general question related to the unit of study. For example, the question "how do different organ systems interact with each other to maintain life?" can be posed to students as a journaling topic during the study of a unit on the human body. You may ask students to make one entry each week and submit it for review. Although no grading may be given, an analysis of students' progressive writings by using a holistic rubric or analytic rubric can reveal important strengths and misconceptions students are developing, which can greatly inform the subsequent instruction.

Given that current reform in science education promotes inquiry, particularly the open-ended extended inquiry, open-ended journaling can be a very powerful tool for students to learn to become reflective thinkers. Regardless, if you assign the same inquiry project to all students or let students select their own inquiry projects, students can always maintain a weekly journal documenting and reflecting on what they have done, how they have done it, and what they plan to do next in carrying out the inquiry project. Students should submit their progressive journals to the teacher, so that the teacher can get a sense of the progress of their inquiry projects. Again, using a rubric to evaluate student journals can reveal both common and individual issues among students so that appropriate intervention/instruction may be introduced to facilitate student projects.

An excerpt of an eighth-grade student's ongoing journal during a long-term inquiry project on investigating human's reaction time is as follows:

10/15/05

I haven't seen anything new lately that interests me for the project. I do remember a little reaction activity at the National Air and Space Museum. I went there last summer and had a great time. There was a large ruler suspended by the magnet. When a button is pressed, the ruler falls, however the time between the button being pressed and the ruler falling is not constant. The point you grab the ruler is the distance travelled and determines your reaction time. I could probably collect data by measuring people's reaction times. I could look for relationships between gender and reaction time, or age and reaction time.

10/20/05

I started to collect data and try out my method. I held a ruler vertically over subjects' open first finger and thumb. I dropped the ruler without telling them when. I found that the method worked really well. More importantly, however, I figured out what the other variable will be. In talking to my subjects one person wondered if people who played video games would be quicker with their reactions. I developed a set of choices on hours spent per week playing video games, for subjects to choose from. So I have developed my small questionnaire to use when collecting data.

10/27/05

I collected data from students who were in my class. It worked fairly well, however, not many of them play video games. I need to find more people who play video games to complete the questionnaire and to do the test. I am going to ask my friends to help me out.

11/5/02

I received the data, it looked really good at first. The only problem was that it was recorded in inches rather than centimeters. I had to convert them all. They should be good enough, however, I am sure that my friends rounded to the nearest half inch rather than nearest centimeter.

. . . .

The above excerpt shows how the student's inquiry project evolved and how his thinking progressed. This journal should give the teacher valuable information on the student's ongoing inquiry. A rubric such as the one introduced in Chapter 4 for investigation-type performance assessment may also be used to assess student journals so that both quantitative and qualitative feedback may be provided to students.

Responsive Journaling

Responsive journaling is a structured question-response writing process. Although it is structured, responsive journaling can also be very flexible. The topic of journaling should be related to the topic of ongoing instruction, so that information from student journals can inform continuing instructional planning. One specific method of responsive journal is to use the KLW structure, described as follows:

Unit Topic

Name _____   Date _____

What did you <u>know</u> before today's class?

What did you <u>learn</u> today? How is it useful?

What do you <u>want</u> to learn next?

The above KLW structured journaling can be done at the beginning and the end of a science class. It should take no more than 5 minutes. Student journal responses may be collected at the end of the class and returned to students at the beginning of the next class. Grading based on a scoring rubric may be used by the teacher when reviewing student journals, but the scores do not need to be shared with students. One potential issue with KLW is that students recite the textbook or teacher language through recall without demonstrating real understanding. To avoid rote memorization and to direct students to write more on their ideas, you may include more specific questions in KLW. For example, in the above sample, one additional question, "how is it useful?" asks students to think how to apply what they have learned to other situations—an important type of understanding (i.e., application).

Dialogic Journaling

Different from the above two types of journaling, dialogic journaling is one-to-one communication between the teacher and the student. Dialogic journaling using paper and pencil can be very time-consuming; you may not be able to respond to every student's journal in a timely manner. Given the wide availability of telecommunication technology, using the Internet (e.g., e-mail) to conduct dialogic journaling (i.e., electronic dialogic journaling) is possible. Even with telecommunication, due to the intensity, it is still impossible for the teacher to engage in dialogic journaling with a large number of students simultaneously. However, dialogic journaling may be conducted with a few representative students whose learning abilities represent the whole class. Students engaged in dialogic journaling may change from unit to unit; thus, over a year, most students, if not everyone, should have been involved in dialogic journaling with the teacher.

The following is an excerpt from an ongoing dialogic journal between a chemistry teacher and a student during the unit on chemical bonding:

The teacher (11/01/2004) 9:39 pm

Based on your understanding of ionic and covalent compounds, what do you think will happen when the two groups test their solutions? Which solution (if any) will conduct electricity and why? Which solution (if any) will not conduct electricity and why?

The student (11/02/2004) 7:48 pm

I think I understand your questions. The table sugar will conduct because the covalent bonds have high electronegativities and want to gain electrons. The more electrons the better chance it has to conduct energy. The magnesium chloride should also conduct because the Mg and Cl have different electronegativities (Mg is low, Cl is high) and the sharing of electrons will be a good conductor.

Source: English (2005). Reproduced by permission.

Reading over the student's response, the teacher realized that the just completed instruction on conductivity of solutions was not quite effective because serious misconceptions were demonstrated by the student. The teacher initially thought that the student's understanding of ionic and covalent bonding concepts was solid, but the student's response to the most recent posting demonstrated otherwise, and her level of understanding was in question.

The teacher decided to spend some time in class the next day going over the solubility process of ionic and covalent compounds. Continuing with the journaling, the teacher then asked the student to think about the situation where a nonmetal atom bonds to a nonmetal atom and whether the difference in electronegativities would be large or small. After reading the student's answer, the teacher realized that the student was not thinking of bonding at the atomic level, and there was a need to review the bonding process when two atoms of different electronegativities approach each other.

The student (11/03/2004) 8:31 pm

Because there are 2 nonmetals the electronegativities should be close. A small difference . . . which means one non-metal can not fully gain electrons from another. This is why the covalent bond is shared electrons.

Source: English (2005). Reproduced by permission.

As can be seen from the above excerpt, dialogic journaling can be very effective in finding out where students may have misconceptions or need help in clarifying understanding. The teacher's probing questions are critical. Using specific examples where students are required to apply what they have learned to explain or interpret is more effective than asking simple factual information questions.

APPLICATION AND SELF-REFLECTION 6.1

Comparing the three types of journaling described above, what are the advantages and disadvantages of each? Choose a unit of instruction at a certain grade. What type of journaling do you think would be effective and efficient to monitor students' conceptual change?

USING PORTFOLIOS TO DOCUMENT STUDENT LEARNING PROGRESSION

Portfolio assessment is a purposeful, collaborative, and self-reflective collection of student work generated during the process of instruction. Portfolio assessment is consistent with current theories of instruction and philosophy of schools that promote involvement of students in their learning (Gallagher, 1998). Specifically, portfolio assessment is consistent with the principles of social constructivism. The social constructivist approach to science teaching calls for students to play a major role in the learning process. Because students are different in their prior knowledge, language and cultural background, socioeconomic status, learning style, and so on, they follow different pathways to achieve the same science learning standards. There is a call for an assessment approach that accommodates individual student differences and at the same time maintains the same learning standards for all students. Portfolio assessment is such an approach.

Portfolios are particularly effective as a formative assessment. They can be used to document student progress and achievement. Portfolios also contribute to a supportive learning environment. Portfolios particularly promote productive dialogues between teachers and students, as well as between teachers and parents. Vitale and Romance developed a knowledge-based portfolio assessment framework in which science curriculum, instruction, and assessment are integrated (Vitale & Romance, 2000). According to this framework, portfolio assessment is planned and implemented in the context of overall curriculum objectives and student learning activities. The portfolio assessment domains may include various forms of data collection that support curriculum development and student learning. Additional advantages of portfolio assessments are that portfolio assessment (a) is an excellent way to document student learning progress and strength rather than weakness and deficiency; (b) promotes student ownership, reflection, and decision making of their learning; (c) is comprehensive in gathering evidence of students' learning through multiple forms and products; and (d) accommodates student learning differences (Vitale & Romance, 2000).

Portfolio assessment can potentially assess all domains of science learning outcomes, which makes it authentic. Portfolio assessment can include a wide variety of entries; some of them may be related to documenting students' learning outcomes in the cognitive domain, some in the psychomotor domain, some in the affective domain, and some in metacognitive domain. For example, some entries may show how students understand Newton's laws and apply the laws to explain everyday phenomena. Some may document the process of a scientific investigation to solve a meaningful everyday problem. Some entries may be creative writings that show how students appreciate the beauty in the natural world. Because students need to document their learning progress, they will also demonstrate how self-reflective they are during science learning.

Characteristics of Portfolio Assessment

Portfolio assessment has the following characteristics:

Portfolio assessment is based on a purposefully organized multisource collection of student work. Before deciding to use portfolio assessment, you need to ask questions such as what learning outcomes the portfolio assessment intends to assess, what assessment methods are best to assess them, and how portfolio assessment may supplement other methods of assessment. Answers to the above questions ensure that portfolio assessment is the right choice for the right purposes. Portfolios are not a fashion; they serve unique assessment needs and require unique commitment from teachers and students. One such commitment is to accept multiple sources of student work as evidence for demonstrating ongoing learning outcomes.

Portfolio assessment involves students in selection of sample work. Portfolio assessment requires a shift in philosophy of assessment from teacher control to student control in content. You must be willing to give students freedom in deciding pieces of evidence to demonstrate their progress in the mastery of learning objectives. This does not mean you are completely hands-off. Your role becomes mainly consulting and facilitating. Students differ in their abilities to make good judgments on most appropriate pieces of work, and it is your responsibility to provide necessary help and bring students to an equal playing level.

Portfolio assessment involves student self-reflection and self-evaluation. Although students will be autonomous in selecting entries, they are doing so with a sound rationale and mindfulness. Students must justify their decisions on portfolio entries. To demonstrate the above, students must be self-reflective and able to analyze strength and weakness in their own learning.

Portfolio assessment documents both mastery of learning outcomes and ongoing progress along with instruction. In addition to demonstrating students' mastery of learning outcomes, portfolio assessment must also demonstrate student learning progress. To achieve this, portfolio assessment must be an integral part of the ongoing instruction. This means portfolio assessment must be a long-term project. No matter what a student's initial achievement level is, every student has to demonstrate that progress has been made and new learning outcomes have been achieved.

Portfolio assessment is a tool for communication. Portfolio assessment not only demonstrates students' mastery of learning outcomes and the progress toward the mastery of the learning outcomes, but it is also a tool for you to engage in communication with students and parents. Each portfolio only provides snapshots of a student's learning; it is through dialogue that you, the student, and the parents can develop a more complete and common understanding about the student as a learner. The communication can serve as a platform for planning further learning as well.

Procedures for Portfolio Assessment

Successful portfolio assessment requires careful planning; close collaboration among the teacher, students and the parents; and diligent implementation of specified format and scoring. The following procedures are typical steps to follow in order to conduct an appropriate portfolio assessment:

1. *Clearly articulate the purpose of the portfolio assessment.* Portfolio assessment never intends to act independently from other assessments. Developing a portfolio assessment always begins with a strategic planning of assessments for the entire unit or course. It is essential from the very beginning to develop an overall assessment plan for the entire unit or course, so that the learning outcomes to be assessed by the portfolio assessment are unique. A decision on a portfolio assessment comes with clear answers for the following: (a) which learning standards or outcomes need to be assessed, (b) what learning growth and effort need to be demonstrated, and (c) what cognitive processes must be demonstrated by student portfolios.

2. *Develop a portfolio product specification that is congruent with the articulated purposes.* Once portfolio assessment objectives are in place, the next step is to decide what portfolio products or entries are necessary to meet the objectives. This step requires decisions on (a) the number of products or entries, (b) the types of products or entries, (c) the organization format for the products and entries, and (d) the time frame for the products or entries to be completed.

3. *Develop scoring rubrics for evaluating portfolio products.* One scoring rubric should accompany each portfolio product. Scoring rubrics make explicit the agreement between the portfolio assessment purpose and the portfolio product or entry specification in Steps 1 and 2. Scoring rubrics can be analytic or holistic. If the role for portfolio assessment is both formative and summative evaluation, two sets of scoring rubrics—one analytic for formative evaluation and one holistic for summative evaluation—may be necessary.

4. *Communicate the articulated purpose, content selection criteria, and evaluation criteria to students and parents.* Portfolio assessment is a collaborative project among the teacher, students, and parents. Clear understanding of the roles for each party is essential for the successful development of student portfolios. Clarification with students on the expectations of the portfolio assessment should take place in class before students begin to develop portfolio entries, and a limited degree of negotiation should be allowed so that students are committed to the development of the portfolios once they have agreed. Communication with parents usually takes the form of a letter to the parents. Simply informing parents about the portfolio assessment is not enough; parents should also know how they may facilitate their children in the development of the portfolios.

5. *Monitor and guide student portfolio development.* During the portfolio development, the teacher needs to closely monitor students' progress. Regular checks should be made so that necessary help may be provided to students who need it. Sometimes, adjustment to the portfolio product specification and time frame may be necessary based on student progress. An analytic scoring scheme may be used to provide students with relevant and ongoing feedback. One major task during student portfolio development is the storage of student interim portfolios. It is usually better for the teacher to provide an accessible storage space for students to store their incomplete portfolios so that no pieces may go missing during the process.

6. *Score portfolios.* Scoring portfolios begins after students have completed all required portfolio products or entries. Scoring rubrics should already be in place at this stage. Because applying the scoring rubrics involves a certain degree of subjectivity, whenever feasible, ask another colleague or knowledgeable person to score student portfolios and compare the scores with yours. If the discrepancy is too big, scoring rubrics may need revision, and portfolios may need to be rescored.

7. *Conduct portfolio conferences with students and parents.* The last stage in portfolio assessment is the conference with students and parents. A student's portfolio tells stories about the student's learning, and it is extremely useful to help parents and students understand the strengths and weaknesses in learning with scored portfolios. Intended uses of the portfolio scores should also be explained to the students and parents.

As an example of portfolio assessment in science, the California Golden State Exam Science Portfolio specifies the Growth Through Writing portfolio as follows:

GROWTH THROUGH WRITING

The writing component should show progress in understanding a particular scientific concept over time. Information should be presented conceptually, not as isolated or unrelated facts. There must be clear connections among the parts of the student work and the identified scientific concept. The writings are to be arranged from earliest to latest, and dated. The thoughtful completion of the Growth Through Writing Self-Reflection Sheet is an essential part of the evaluation of the entry (see below). The entry will be evaluated by how well it meets or surpasses the following requirements:

Evidence of progress toward mastery of a concept:

1. Original work and improved versions are included and dated;

2. Revisions which show deeper understanding of science, not merely a neater appearance.

Relationships to other scientific concepts: Relates the scientific concept to other scientific concepts, subjects, or real-world situations;

Clear and coherent communication:

1. Relevant and appropriate terms;

2. Language and writing which promote effective communication;

3. Grammar and spelling which do not interfere with the presentation of ideas.

GSE Self-Reflection Sheet

Growth Through Writing

1. Thoroughly explain the scientific concept you are presenting in your writing selection(s). Give specific examples that show how this concept relates to your Growth Through Writing entry.

2. Explain how you decided what to revise and improve in this entry. Be specific about what you learned that led you to make the revisions.

3. Give specific examples from your revised pieces of work that provide evidence that you now understand the concept better.

(Continued)

(Continued)

4. Describe, in detail, the relationship that exists between the scientific concept you are presenting in this entry and other subjects, scientific concepts, or real-world situations.

Source: Joe Mahood, Access Excellence @ the National Health Museum, http://www.accessexcellence.org/LC/TL/CGSE/growth.html. Reproduced by permission.

As can be seen from the Golden State Exam Science Portfolio, Growth Through Writing, a clear description of the requirement and structure of the portfolio entry is necessary for students to demonstrate their learning progression. The description and structure also ensure that students have equal opportunities to demonstrate their learning progression.

One major determent for teachers to implement portfolio assessment is time and management required to help students develop portfolios. Classroom storage can also be a challenge. The above challenges can now be addressed using technology, such as the Internet. Commercial portfolio management systems, such as TaskStream (http://taskstream.com), are also available.

APPLICATION AND SELF-REFLECTION 6.2

The following learning outcomes are for a fourth-grade learning unit based on a state's science content standard:

Describe the characteristics of and variations between living and nonliving things. Major understandings:

1.1a Animals need air, water, and food in order to live and thrive.
1.1b Plants require air, water, nutrients, and light in order to live and thrive.
1.1c Nonliving things do not live and thrive.
1.1d Nonliving things can be human created or naturally occurring.

Develop a specification of a portfolio assessment that includes (a) the assessment purpose, (b) portfolio entries and content selection, and (c) scoring rubrics.

USING CONCEPT MAPPING TO ASSESS STRUCTURAL KNOWLEDGE

Concept mapping is credited to the work by Joseph Novak at Cornell University; it is a process of creating a graphical representation of a relationship between and among concepts. The graphical representation is also called a *concept map*. A concept map consists of nodes and labeled lines. The nodes correspond to science concepts, and the lines denote relations between pairs of concepts. Each link is a proposition. Links may be directional (i.e., with arrows). Figure 6.1 is a sample concept map.

From the above sample concept map, we can see the following characteristics of a concept map:

Concepts: words or short phrases, not sentences.

Links: predicates relating two concepts within a same branch to indicate the type of relationship between the two, such as type of, part of, causal effect, characteristics, quantification, and so on. Each link forms a proposition.

Cross-links: predicates relating two branches to indicate the type of relationship among concepts in the two branches. Each cross-link also forms a proposition.

FIGURE 6.1   A Sample Concept Map

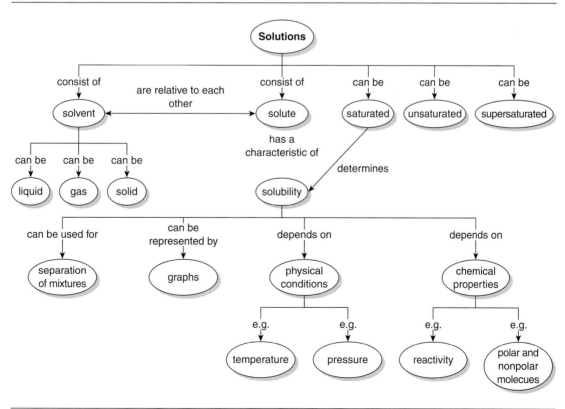

Hierarchy: concepts are arranged from general to specific. Examples may also be included and usually are placed at the bottom.

The above characteristics of concepts are not arbitrary; they are based on how human long-term memory is structured (Novak & Gowin, 1984). This type of knowledge structure is also called *structure knowledge* (Jonassen, 1996). **Structure knowledge** is the knowledge of how concepts within a domain are interrelated. Structure knowledge claims to mediate the translation of declarative knowledge and procedure knowledge. For example, a student's understanding of acids and bases does not necessarily guarantee that the student will be able to perform a titration experiment if he or she does not know how acids and bases are different and how other concepts (i.e., concentration, solutions, ions, indicators, etc.) are related to acids and bases.

Using concept mapping as a formative assessment to assess student structural knowledge requires the concept mapping task to include three components: an elicitation task, a response format, and a scoring scheme. An elicitation task is a specification on what concepts are to be used to create a concept map. Concepts can come from two sources: teacher provided or student generated. If the teacher is to provide a list of important concepts, then the concept mapping is called *closed concept mapping.* If the student is to generate his or her own concepts to be used for concept maps, then the process is called *open-ended concept mapping.* In both closed and open-ended concept mapping situations, it is preferable to specify the total number of concepts to be used, typically 10 to 20. The range of 10 to 20 concepts provides adequate flexibility for students to demonstrate their structure knowledge, yet makes the variation and size of concept maps to be developed manageable.

Response format is the process to be followed by students to construct concept maps. Response format can vary in many ways. First, concept mapping can be constructed individually or in groups. Group concept mapping provides an excellent opportunity for students to construct meanings collectively. It can also provide students an opportunity to critically evaluate each other's ideas. Second, concept mapping can be done on paper (e.g., chart paper) or on computers. There are many commercial programs specializing in concept mappings. One such example is Inspiration (http://inspiration.com). The advantage of using a computer program to develop concept maps is the ease of revising. Some concept mapping programs such as Inspiration also provide a wealth of pictures on various topics such as plants and animals.

Scoring should be based on important characteristics of concept maps. These characteristics are concepts, links, cross-links, and hierarchy. Although concept maps usually contain many examples at the bottom, research has shown that including examples into a scoring scheme does not contribute to validity (Liu & Hinchey, 1996). Concept maps can be scored holistically or analytically. No matter what scoring scheme is to be used, a criterion concept map is needed. Scoring a concept map involves comparing student concept maps with the criterion concept map. Criterion concept maps represent the expected learning outcomes.

The following are two sample scoring schemes:

HOLISTIC SCORING SCHEME

After comparing concepts, links, cross-links, and hierarchies in the student map with the concepts, links, cross-links, and hierarchies in the criterion map, rate each of them as poor (1), fair (2), good (3), very good (4), and excellent (5). Enter the scores into the following formula to obtain a total score for the concept map:

Total score (%) = [(concept + link + cross-link * 10 + hierarchy * 5)/85] * 100.

ANALYTIC SCORING SCHEME

Find out the percentage of valid concepts, links, cross-links, and hierarchies in the student map out of the concepts, links, cross-links, and hierarchies in the criterion map, and enter them into the following formula to obtain a total score for the concept map:

Total score (%) = [(concept% + link% + cross-link% * 10 + hierarchy% * 5)/17] * 100.

Both of the above scoring schemes will produce a score in percentage. Scores given for the same concept map using the above two scoring schemes should be close, although variation is expected depending on the scorer's knowledge on the topic. Figure 6.2 is a sample student concept map.

Because concept maps can be revised continuously during a unit of instruction, if the assigned concept mapping is related to the topic of the unit instruction, then student concept maps should be able to provide teachers with important indications of students' development of structure knowledge on the topic. Necessary adjustment to ongoing instruction can be made based on students' misconceptions demonstrated in their concept maps.

APPLICATION AND SELF-REFLECTION 6.3

Using the concept map in Figure 6.1 as the criterion map, score the sample student concept map in Figure 6.2 using both the holistic and analytic scoring schemes. Compare the two scores for the concept map. Are they different? How much? Why is there a difference between the two scores? Which one do you like better and why?

FIGURE 6.2 A Sample Student Concept Map

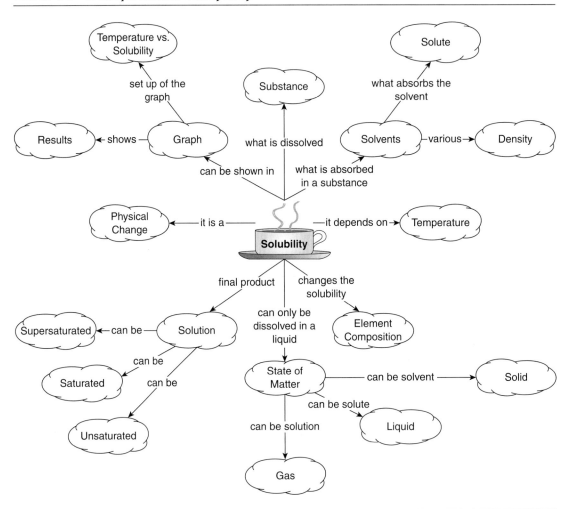

ASSESSING AFFECTIVE AND LEARNING ENVIRONMENT VARIABLES

Effective science teaching requires positive individual student disposition and a conducive learning environment. No learning is purely cognitive; learning takes place under a certain affective disposition and within a social-cultural community. The affective disposition may include such variables as attitude toward science, motivation to learn science, perceptions of science, and so on. A social-cultural community may consist of multiple nested communities that include classroom, school, and society (Bransford, Brown, & Cocking, 2000). It is important that attention is paid to variables related not only to individuals but also to the classroom, school, and society. Different from assessing cognitive learning variables, assessing affective and learning environment variables requires types of questions with no right or wrong answers and involving perceptions and preferences. Two types of questions are commonly used: the Likert scale and the checklist.

A **Likert scale** question is a statement followed by different degrees of agreement. It was first proposed by Rensis Likert in 1932. A set of statements about the same construct (e.g., attitude toward science) is presented to students. The agreement to the statement is presented as three to five choices phrased from strongly agree to strongly disagree. Because the choices are ordered and may be given a numerical value, student responses to a set of the questions can be totaled as one score, the Likert scale score. The set of questions is thus called a Likert scale.

A sample attitude toward science Likert scale is as follows:

STUDENT ATTITUDES TOWARD SCIENCE

For statements 1 through 18, circle the letter that best indicates your view. Use the following rating scale: a = always, b = frequently, c = sometimes, d = rarely, and e = never.

	Always	Frequently	Sometimes	Rarely	Never
1. Science classes are fun.	a	b	c	d	e
2. Science classes increase my curiosity.	a	b	c	d	e
3. The things studied in science classes are useful to me in daily living.	a	b	c	d	e
4. Science classes help me test ideas I have.	a	b	c	d	e
5. My science teacher frequently admits to not having answers to my questions.	a	b	c	d	e
6. Science classes provide me with skills to use outside of school.	a	b	c	d	e
7. My science class deals with the information produced by scientists.	a	b	c	d	e
8. Science classes are exciting.	a	b	c	d	e
9. Science classes provide a chance for me to follow up on questions I have.	a	b	c	d	e

(Continued)

(Continued)

	Always	Frequently	Sometimes	Rarely	Never
10. Science teachers encourage me to question.	a	b	c	d	e
11. All people can do and practice basic science.	a	b	c	d	e
12. Being a scientist would be fun.	a	b	c	d	e
13. Being a scientist would make a person feel important.	a	b	c	d	e
14. Science classes are boring.	a	b	c	d	e
15. Being a scientist would be lonely.	a	b	c	d	e
16. Being a scientist would make a person rich.	a	b	c	d	e
17. Being a scientist would mean giving up some things of interest.	a	b	c	d	e
18. Scientists discover information that is difficult to understand.	a	b	c	d	e

Source: Enger & Yager (2001).

From the above instrument, we can see that a Likert scale contains a number of questions related to the same construct. This is important because only when all the questions are concerned about the same construct (e.g., attitude toward science) can scores on individual questions be summed into a total scale score. To ensure the consistency among responses by students to the questions, a Likert scale needs to contain at least 5 questions; 10 or more are preferred.

Although there are standardized instruments available to assess student affective learning variables, there is always a need for science teachers to develop a Likert scale specifically for a particular purpose. The following guideline should be followed to develop a Likert scale:

1. Statements should be expressions of desired behaviors or values, not facts.

   Poor: Science involves laboratory work.

   Strongly Agree   Agree   Undecided   Disagree   Strongly Disagree

   Better: Science should be based on laboratory work.

   Strongly Agree   Agree   Undecided   Disagree   Strongly Disagree

2. Each statement is about only one aspect.

   Poor: Science should be based on laboratory work and field experience.

   Strongly Agree   Agree   Undecided   Disagree   Strongly Disagree

   Better: Science should be based on laboratory work.

   Strongly Agree   Agree   Undecided   Disagree   Strongly Disagree

3. Include a mixed number of positively and negatively intended statements.

   Science should NOT be based on paper-and-pencil practice.

   Strongly Agree   Agree   Undecided   Disagree   Strongly Disagree

4. Try to avoid statements that are difficult to decide.

   Poor: Science is beneficial to humankind.

   Strongly Agree   Agree   Undecided   Disagree   Strongly Disagree

   Better: Science is more beneficial than harmful to the environment.

   Strongly Agree   Agree   Undecided   Disagree   Strongly Disagree

Another very important type of learning variable that needs to be closely monitored during science teaching is the classroom learning environment. The classroom learning environment can be both a means and an outcome in science teaching and learning because significant correlations between a positive learning environment and student achievement have been founded (Fraser, 1996). The learning environment can also be differentiated into various types: student-perceived actual learning environment, student-preferred learning environment, and ideal learning environment (expected based on theory). Finding out the match between the actual learning environment and the student-preferred learning environment, as well as between the actual learning environment and the ideal learning environment, can greatly improve the ongoing instruction. The following questions are from a learning environment inventory called My Class Inventory (MCI; Fraser, 1996).

1. The pupils enjoy their schoolwork in my class.	Yes	No
2. Children are always fighting with each other.	Yes	No
3. Children often race to see who can finish first.	Yes	No
4. In our class, the work is hard to do.	Yes	No
5. In my class, everybody is my friend.	Yes	No
6. Some pupils are not happy in class.	Yes	No
7. Some of the children in our class are mean.	Yes	No
8. Most children want their work to be better than their friend's work.	Yes	No
9. Most children can do their schoolwork without help.	Yes	No
10. Some people in my class are not my friends.	Yes	No
11. Children seem to like the class.	Yes	No
12. Many children in our class like to fight.	Yes	No
13. Some pupils feel bad when they do not do as well as the others.	Yes	No
14. Only the smart pupils can do their work.	Yes	No
15. All pupils in my class are close friends.	Yes	No
16. Some of the pupils do not like the class.	Yes	No
17. Certain pupils always want to have their own way.	Yes	No
18. Some pupils always try to do their work better than the others.	Yes	No
19. Schoolwork is hard to do.	Yes	No
20. All of the pupils in my class like one another.	Yes	No
21. The class is fun.	Yes	No
22. Children in our class fight a lot.	Yes	No
23. A few children in my class want to be first all of the time.	Yes	No
24. Most of the pupils in my class know how to do their work.	Yes	No
25. Children in our class like each other as friends.	Yes	No

The above classroom learning environment questionnaire uses a checklist format. A Likert scale may also be used to assess students' preferred learning environment.

APPLICATION AND SELF-REFLECTION 6.4

Why is it important to monitor students' affects and classroom learning environment? Give a description of one scenario in which an affective variable may greatly affect student learning during a unit of instruction and one description of a scenario in which the classroom learning environment is crucial for meaning making in the classroom to take place. Develop a Likert scale to assess the above affective variable and a checklist or a Likert scale to assess the above learning environment. Critique each other's instruments.

THE CASES OF ERIC AND ELISIA: ASSESSMENT OF ONGOING LEARNING

Eric and Elisia finished this chapter with much excitement. Both never thought that assessment and instruction were so closely intertwined, and in fact, many instructional activities they are familiar with, such as concept mapping, are the assessment methods introduced in this chapter. They are pleasantly surprised to see how those instructional activities can provide important information about students' ongoing learning and thus potentially improve their ongoing instruction. However, they also recognize that instructional activities as assessment need to possess additional characteristics such as scorability of student performances. Furthermore, instructional activities as assessment must have a clear assessment target, such as conceptual change, learning trajectory, or learning environment. Eric particularly likes journaling and portfolios as they are common instructional strategies used in elementary classrooms. For Elisia, she particularly likes concept mapping as she sees how it can help students develop understanding of relationships among various concepts, a common weakness in high school students. Both Eric and Elisia cannot wait to try some of the techniques introduced in this chapter in their own classrooms. At the same time, they remain unclear about how various assessment methods, including formative assessment, may be integrated to make grades for students.

Do the experiences of Eric and Elisia sound familiar to you? What were your initial ideas of assessment of ongoing learning, and how have they changed as the result of this chapter?

Chapter Summary

- Journaling as formative assessment has the potential to assess students' conceptual change in developing understanding of a major science concept. Journaling to monitor students' conceptual change can take place in three general forms: open-ended journaling, responsive journaling, and dialogic journaling. Open-ended journaling is when students can decide on a specific focus, format, and length to write about a given concept; responsive journaling is when students answer questions posed by the teacher; and dialogic journaling is when a student and the teacher are engaged in a written conversation.

- Portfolio assessment is a purposeful, collaborative, and self-reflective collection of student work generated during the process of instruction. Portfolio assessment can potentially assess all domains of science learning outcomes, which makes it authentic. Portfolio assessment has the following characteristics: (a) purposeful, (b) student control of content selection, (c) student self-reflection, (d) documentation of both learning outcomes and processes, and (e) communication. Electronic portfolios can address common determents for teachers to implement portfolio assessment, such as time and storage. Specialized commercial portfolio management systems are also available.

- Concept mapping is a process of creating a graphical representation of the relationship between and among concepts. The graphical representation is called a concept map. A concept map includes the following components: (a) concepts, (b) links, (c) cross-links, and (d) hierarchy. Using concept mapping as a formative assessment to assess students' structural knowledge requires the concept mapping task to include three components: an elicitation task, a response format, and a scoring scheme. Concept maps may be revised continuously during a unit of instruction. Computerized concept mapping facilitates the continuous revisions.

- Effective science teaching requires positive individual student disposition and a conducive leaning environment. Two types of questions, the Likert scale and the checklist, are commonly used to assess the above aspects. A Likert scale is a set of statements followed by different degrees of agreement. A checklist is a set of factual statements asking students to indicate whether certain conditions are present. Standardized instruments for assessing students' attitude toward science and various learning environments are also available.

√ Mastery Checklist

- ☐ Use journaling to assess student conceptual change.
- ☐ Use portfolios to assess student learning progression.
- ☐ Use concept mapping to assess student structural knowledge.
- ☐ Develop and use Likert scale and checklist instruments to assess student affective and classroom learning environment variables.

Web-Based Student Study Site

The Companion Web site for *Essentials of Science Classroom Assessment* can be found at **www.sagepub.com/liustudy**.

The site includes a variety of materials to enhance your understanding of the chapter content. Visit the study site to

- complete an online self-assessment of essential knowledge and skills introduced in this chapter
- find Web addresses containing resources pertinent to formative assessment, as well as in science
- find Web addresses containing descriptions as well as scoring rubrics of portfolio assessments in science
- find Web addresses containing information on free and commercial concept mapping programs

Further Readings

Abel, S., & Volkmann, M. J. (2006). *Seamless assessment in science: A guide for elementary and middle school teachers.* Portsmouth, NH: Heinemann.

> This book promotes integrating assessment into inquiry science teaching following the 5E model. It includes 13 vignettes related to various science topics to demonstrate how assessment is an integral part of an instructional unit.

Atkin, M. (Ed.). (2003). *Everyday assessment in the science classroom.* Arlington, VA: NSTA Press.

> This edited book contains chapters related to issues of science assessment. It is an excellent professional reading for practicing teachers to engage in reflection on their assessment practices.

Black, P., Harrison, C., Lee, C., Marshall, B., & Wiliam, D. (2003). *Assessment for learning: Putting it into practice.* Maidenhead, UK: Open University Press.

> This book presents evidence of a comprehensive literature review and empirical studies in schools on the effect of formative assessment for improving student achievements in core school subjects. It also describes teachers' experiences in implementing formative assessment in their classrooms and conceptualizes why and how formative assessment improves student learning.

Fraser, B. J. (1994). Research on classroom and school climate. In D. L. Gabel (Ed.), *Handbook of research in science teaching* (pp. 493–541). New York: Macmillan.

> This chapter in a popular handbook provides a systematic review of theories and methodology on research on classroom and school environments. It also provides detailed technical background (e.g., validity and reliability) to many practical classroom and laboratory learning environments.

McMahon, M., Simmons, P., & Sommers, R. (Eds.). (2006). *Assessment in science: Practical experiences and education research.* Arlington, VA: NSTA Press.

> This edited volume includes 18 chapters written by teams of researchers and school teachers. Each chapter describes a classroom assessment scenario (e.g., portfolio assessment), presents research findings pertaining to various assessment techniques, and discusses dilemmas related to assessments. This book is particularly appropriate for those science teachers who already have some experiences with various assessment techniques.

Mintzes, J. J., Wandersee, J., & Novak, J. D. (Eds.). (2000). *Assessing science understanding: A human constructivist view.* San Diego, CA: Academic Press.

> This edited book is a collection of research articles by various authors summarizing current research on science assessment. Chapters on concept maps, dialogue, portfolios, and writing are particularly relevant to this chapter and provide excellent theoretical backgrounds for them to be used as formative assessment and assessment of understanding in general.

References

Bransford, J. D., Brown, A. L., & Cocking, R. R. (Eds.). (2000). *How people learn: Brain, mind, experience, and school.* Report of the Committee on Developments in the Science of Learning. Washington, DC: National Academy Press.

Champagne, A. B., & Kouba, V. L. (1999). Writing to inquire: Written products as performance measures. In J. J. Mintzes, J. H. Wandersee, & J. D. Novak (Eds.), *Assessing science understanding: A human constructivist view* (pp. 223–248). San Diego, CA: Academic Press.

Enger, S., & Yager, R. (2001). *Assessing student understanding in science.* Thousand Oaks, CA: Corwin.

English, S. (2005). *Using dialogic electronic journal writing to facilitate students understanding of chemical bonding.* Unpublished doctoral dissertation, University at Buffalo, State University of New York.

Fraser, B. J. (1996). Research on classroom and school climate. In D. L. Gabel (Ed.), *Handbook of research on science teaching and learning* (pp. 493–541). New York: Macmillan.

Gallagher, J. D. (1998). *Classroom assessment for teachers.* Upper Saddle River, NJ: Merrill.

Gallagher, J. J. (2007). *Teaching science for understanding: A practical guide for middle and high school teachers.* Upper Saddle River, NJ: Pearson Education.

Jonassen, D. H. (1996). *Computers in the classroom.* Englewood Cliffs, NJ: Merrill.

Likert, R. (1932). A technique for the measurement of attitudes. *Archives of Psychology, 22,* 5–53.

Liu, X., & Hinchey, M. (1996). The internal consistency of a concept mapping scoring scheme and its effect on prediction validity. *International Journal of Science Education, 18*(8), 921–938.

National Research Council (NRC). (1996). *National science education standards.* Washington, DC: National Academy Press.

Norris, S. P., & Phillips, L. M. (2003). How literacy in its fundamental sense is central to scientific literacy. *Science Education, 87*(2), 224–240.

Novak, J., & Gowin, B. D. (1984). *Learning how to learn.* New York: Cambridge University Press.

Stevens, F. I. (1997). *Opportunity to learn science: Connecting research knowledge to classroom practices.* Philadelphia: Mid-Atlantic Lab for Student Success.

Vitale, M. R., & Romance, N. R. (2000). Portfolios in science assessment: A knowledge-based model for classroom practice. In J. J. Mintzes, J. H. Wandersee, & J. D. Novak (Eds.), *Assessing science understanding: A human constructivist view* (pp. 168–197). San Diego, CA: Academic Press.

Yore, L. D., Hand, B. M., & Florence, M. K. (2004). Scientists' views of science, models of writing, and science writing practices. *Journal of Research in Science Teaching, 41*(4), 338–369.

CHAPTER 7

Grading Science Achievement

Chapter 3 discussed the concept of summative assessment and introduced paper-and-pencil tests using multiple-choice and constructed-response questions. Chapter 4 further introduced various methods for assessing science inquiry; Chapter 5 introduced three types of standardized tests, including the high-stakes state standardized test; and Chapter 6 discussed various methods for assessing student ongoing learning—formative assessment. Given the comprehensiveness of science learning standards, it is often necessary to conduct all the above assessment activities to gather information about student learning. Ultimately, a science teacher has to give a student a final grade based on results of the above assessment activities. How is this possible? This chapter will answer this question; it is called grading.

Grading is a process of deciding and communicating how well students have mastered the learning outcomes. The result of grading is a grade. A **grade** is a judgmental statement about a student's achievement in both quantity and quality. There are two aspects in grading: evaluation and communication. The evaluation aspect refers to interpretations or judgments of scores obtained from various assessments, and the communication aspect refers to meanings of the judgments made on the assessment scores; communication particularly pertains to grade reporting. It is obvious that evaluation and communication are closely related; they need to be considered simultaneously. This chapter will discuss various grading methods and approaches to grade reporting.

A common misconception among science teachers is that grading is the same as summative assessment. Another common misconception is that grades are the same as scores. Summative assessment is only one source on which grading may be based. Grading may also reflect students' learning processes assessed by formative assessment. Both summative and formative assessment may produce accurate scores about students' learning and thus inform grading. There are two important reasons that scores are not grades. First, scores are directly tied to test questions. If test questions are difficult, student scores are low and vice versa. Thus, just knowing scores without knowing test questions is not meaningful. Second, it is common that multiple assessment methods are used in a unit or a course; as a result, there are many scores for a unit or course. It is difficult to compare scores without knowing the assessment methods from which scores are derived. The above two reasons suggest that scores are not appropriate for communicating student achievements. It is necessary to translate scores into more meaningful formats (i.e., grades). This translation process is grading. The relationship between assessments, grades, and scores is represented as follows:

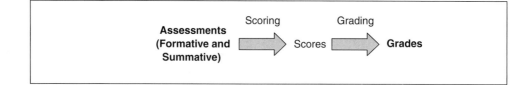

There are three basic types of grading: percentage, criterion referenced, and norm referenced (Gallagher, 1998). **Percentage grading** uses a percentage as the grade to indicate the amount of content (e.g., number of objectives) a student has mastered. Percentage grades are probably the most commonly used grades on middle and high school student report cards because meanings of percentage grades are intuitively self-explanatory. Another type of grading is criterion-referenced grading. **Criterion-referenced grading** uses qualitatively different categories or levels of performances as grades, such as *Pass* and *Fail,* or *Meeting Standard* and *Not Meeting Standard.* Criterion-referenced grading is more commonly used in elementary schools than in secondary schools. **Norm-referenced grading** awards students grades based on their positions on a normal distribution curve among a given group. Norm-referenced grading is a priori grading because for any given group of students, the number of students who fall within different quartiles is predetermined, and students' grades depend on how they are compared with others in the group. Norm-referenced grading is against the basic principle of standards-based science education; it is not recommended for use in K–12 schools. Besides the above three basic types of grading, variations of them are also possible. For example, **rubric grading** is extended criterion-referenced grading. In a rubric, it is possible to incorporate multiple performance levels and percentage grades. This chapter will discuss only percentage grading, criterion-referenced grading, and rubric grading. It will also discuss grade reporting.

PERCENTAGE GRADING

Once you have decided to use percentage grading, or if it is your school or district's policy to use percentage grading, then the first thing you do at the beginning of the school year is

ASSESSMENT STANDARDS ADDRESSED IN CHAPTER 7

NSES Assessment Standard A

Assessment must be consistent with the decisions they are designed to inform. This standard is further elaborated into the following substandards:

- Assessments are deliberately designed.
- Assessments have explicitly stated purposes.
- The relationship between the decisions and the data is clear.
- Assessment procedures are internally consistent. (National Research Council [NRC], 1996, p. 78)

NSES Assessment Standard C

The technical quality of the data collected is well matched to the decisions and actions taken on the basis of their interpretation. This standard is further elaborated into the following substandards:

- The feature that is claimed to be measured is actually measured.
- An individual student's performance is similar on two or more tasks that claim to measure the same aspect of student achievement.
- Students have adequate opportunity to demonstrate their achievements.
- Assessment tasks and methods for presenting them provide data that are sufficiently stable to lead to the same decisions if used at different times. (NRC, 1996, p. 83)

NSES Assessment Standard E

The inferences made from assessments about student achievement and opportunity to learn must be sound. This standard is further elaborated into the following substandard:

- When making inferences from assessment data about student achievement and opportunity to learn science, explicit reference needs to be made to the assumptions on which the inferences are based. (NRC, 1996, p. 86)

to develop a percentage grading system. A percentage grading system is a plan to combine individual assessment scores into a final course or marking period percentage grade. The first step is to quantify learning outcomes for each unit. Depending on what curriculum guideline you follow, you may count the learning outcomes for each unit based on a number of understandings and process skills or a number of concepts and skills to be learned. The number of learning outcomes for the units will become the basis for calculating the weights for grading. A sample weighting system is in Table 7.1.

Assuming that student scores on individual units are based on the same numerical scale, such as in percentages, then a weighted percentage over all earned unit percentage scores will become the final percentage grade for the course or marking period. A sample percentage grading system is in Table 7.2.

TABLE 7.1   A Sample Weighting System

Unit	Number of Learning Outcomes	Weight
1	30	30/195 = 0.154
2	40	40/195 = 0.205
3	25	25/195 = 0.128
4	30	30/195 = 0.154
5	25	25/195 = 0.128
6	45	45/195 = 0.231
Total	195	1

TABLE 7.2   A Sample Percentage Grading System Based on Different Unit Assessment Scores

Unit	Number of Learning Outcomes	Weight	Score (%)	Weighted Scores (%)
1	30	0.154	85	13.1
2	40	0.205	86	17.6
3	25	0.128	95	12.2
4	30	0.154	80	12.3
5	25	0.128	90	11.5
6	45	0.231	88	20.3
Percentage grade				**87**

It is important that a student's earned unit scores are in the same measurement scale, such as percentage. The key to obtaining a percentage grade is to decide weights of individual units.

Another way to obtain a percentage grade is to combine scores from different assessment methods. For example, if a unit or course involves multiple assessment methods such as an end-of-unit test, labs, and quizzes, then appropriate weights for each of the above assessment methods must be decided before a final weighted percentage grade is obtained. The criterion for deciding weights should not be arbitrary. Factors to consider may include the number and importance of learning outcomes assessed, the quality of assessment methods (e.g., how objective is the scoring, how good are the questions), and time spent. Table 7.3 shows a sample grading system based on different assessment methods.

TABLE 7.3   A Sample Percentage Grading Based on Different Assessment Scores

Assessment	Weight (%)	Score (%)	Weighted Scores (%)
Quizzes (5)	25	92	23.0
Projects (2)	30	85	25.5
Homework (20)	20	100	20.0
Classroom participation	5	95	4.8
State test	20	90	18.0
Percentage grade			**91.3**

In the above grading system, the teacher used various assessment methods during the course that included 5 quizzes, 2 projects, and 20 homework assignments, plus classroom participation and the state standardized test. The weights for different assessments were based on cognitive levels involved and how many learning standards they addressed. The inclusion of the state test score in the grading, which counts for 20% of a student's course grade, could be a district policy. The teacher converted students' scores on different assessments (e.g., quizzes) into a percentage score before she calculated the weighted final percentage as the students' course grade.

One important principle in percentage grading is to have one grade for one attribute, such as achievement. If more than one attribute, such as achievement and attitude, is involved, then scores for each attribute should be combined separately to derive separate percentage grades. If you reflect students' attitude into their achievement grades, the grades will become ambiguous and uninterpretable.

A variation of percentage grading is letter grading. Commonly used letter grades are A, B, C, D, and F. More fine-grained letter grading may include such grades as A, A–, B +, B–, and so on. To use letters as grades, you must develop a conversion system to translate percentage grades into letter grades. A sample conversion system is as follows:

Letter Grade	Percentage Grade
A	95.1–100
A–	90.1–95.0
B+	85.1–90.0
B	80.1–85.0
B–	75.1–80.0
C+	70.1–75.0
C	65.1–70.0
D	60.1–65.0
F	0–60.0

It has to be pointed out that there is no universally accepted percentage grade to letter grade conversion system; different teachers may use slightly different conversion systems. It is desirable for a school or a science department in the school to adopt a common conversion system to increase consistency in grading among teachers in the school.

APPLICATION AND SELF-REFLECTION 7.1

A fifth-grade science teacher used the following assessments as a basis for grading: homework, group projects, and end-of-unit tests. However, she is not sure how to decide on weights for different assessment methods. Please provide some suggestions to her and explain the rationale of your suggestions. Create a sample percentage grading system in a table format to illustrate your suggestions.

CRITERION-REFERENCED GRADING

Although percentage grading is intuitively understandable, how high a percentage grade is acceptable is not apparent. Some may think that a 65% grade is acceptable, but others may think that an 80% grade is acceptable. Criterion-referenced grading addresses this issue. It uses explicit criteria for making judgment to answer a question such as how good is good enough. In today's context of standards-based science education, criteria used are naturally the state or district content standards. Content standards specify what students should know and do when completing a course or unit. Criterion-referenced grading decides if students have met these expectations. To make such as decision, you must have evidence about students' mastery of the learning outcomes. Recall the backward design approach based on Understanding by Design (UbD) discussed in Chapter 1, evidence indicating that student mastery should be decided before planning for various teaching and learning activities, which may come from both summative and formative assessments. By the time of criterion-referenced grading, you already should have implemented various assessment plans and, as the result, have scores of student performances on various assessment methods. The task for criterion-referenced grading is to interpret these scores according to the learning standards.

The first step in criterion-referenced grading is to make a list of essential learning outcomes necessary for students to master in order to meet the learning standards. For example, during the course, you have taught 6 units, but each unit contains some essential learning outcomes and some additional learning outcomes beyond the state learning standards. When grading students using a criterion-referenced grading approach, you will list only those essential learning outcomes for meeting the state learning standards and leave out those learning outcomes beyond the state learning standards.

The second step is to match the assessment methods with the essential learning outcomes. Once again, you may have used various assessment methods (e.g., quizzes, projects, end-of-unit tests, homework, progressive concept mapping scores) and obtained various student scores on them. During this step of criterion-referenced grading, you will decide which assessments measure students' mastery of which learning outcomes. For example, you may decide that quizzes, homework, and end-of-unit test scores reflect students' mastery of the essential learning outcomes, while the project scores reflect students' mastery of learning outcomes beyond the state learning standards.

The third step is to calculate the total possible points students may earn, which is the total points from all the assessments. It is possible that you give different weights to different assessment methods based on the nature of the questions. If this is the case, you will need to decide a distribution of points among different assessments and the total points for all assessments for grading. For example, you may decide that total quiz points are 30, end-of-unit test points are 50, and homework points are 20; thus, the total points will be 100. For each assessment such as quizzes, you will need to convert students' scores into a point out of the allotted points for the assessment. For example, if there are five quizzes with each quiz worth 15 points, and the total quiz point total for grading is 30, then the total possible points on quizzes that students can make are 75 points. If a student earned 50 out of 75 on all quizzes, then the student's final quiz point for grading will be $(50/75) \times 30 = 20$.

The last step in criterion-referenced grading is to compare a student's earned weighted point with a cutoff value to decide if a student has met the criterion (i.e., meeting the standard). There is no universally accepted cutoff value. Some teachers may want to use 85%, while others may want to use 65%. The determination of the cutoff value should reflect the rigor of the course; expectations of students by your school, yourself, and parents; students' academic backgrounds; and previous years' student achievement. Although determining a cutoff value is subjective, it should not be arbitrary (i.e., should be based on sound rationales).

The above four-step criterion-referenced grading can be represented in a table format, as in Table 7.4.

TABLE 7.4   Criterion-Referenced Grading for Deciding to Meet Learning Standards

Step 1	Learning outcomes	1.1, 1.2, 2.2, 2.3, 3.2, 3.3, . . .	
Step 2	Assessments	Quizzes, homework, end-of-unit tests	
Step 3	Total points	80	
Step 4	**Student**	**Earned Points (%)**	**Grade (85% as Cutoff)**
	1	70 (87.5%)	Meeting standards ☺
	2	65 (81.3%)	Not meeting standards ☹
	3	. . .	. . .

In the above example, Student 1 earned 87.5% of total points for the learning standards, thus meeting the standards. On the other hand, Student 2 only earned 81.3% of total points, thus not meeting the learning standards.

If separate grades for different learning standards are necessary, the above same four-step grading process can be applied, one for each standard. As we can see, criterion-referenced grading involves subjective judgment. It is possible that a grading system may not be entirely appropriate the first time; it is necessary to monitor the grading system and make adjustments when necessary. There is no single correct grading system; a sound grading system is one that is internally consistent and externally relevant. The internal consistency of a grading system refers to the ability of a grade to accurately indicate the quality and quantity of students' learning as well as your instruction (i.e., a better grade should indicate a higher learning achievement and better instruction). The external relevance of a grading system refers to the agreement of grades with relevant external measures of students' performances, such as students' state test scores, grades on other subjects, grades in subsequent grade levels, and so on. The internal consistency and external relevance together define the validity of grades, an issue that will be further discussed in Chapter 8.

APPLICATION AND SELF-REFLECTION 7.2

Which grading system, percentage or criterion referenced, do you prefer? Describe your teaching philosophy to justify your preference. Create a hypothetical grading system for a seventh-grade science class and explain to the class how it works.

RUBRIC GRADING

Rubric grading is an extended criterion-referenced grading; it specifies more than two levels of student competence, such as beyond standard, meeting standard, and below standard. That is, for each competence level, a cutoff value is used to decide whether the competence level has been reached. One sample rubric grading is the National Assessment of Educational Progress (NAEP) competence-level specification. The competence levels are based on NAEP achievement scores from 0 to 300. The grading system for the fourth-grade science achievement is as follows (National Assessment Governing Board, 2000):

- *Basic (138–170):* Students performing at the basic level demonstrate some of the knowledge and reasoning required for understanding earth, physical, and life sciences at a level appropriate for Grade 4. For example, they can carry out simple investigations and read uncomplicated graphs and diagrams. Students at this level also show a beginning understanding of classification, simple relationships, and energy.

- *Proficient (170–205):* Students performing at the proficient level demonstrate the knowledge and reasoning required for understanding earth, physical, and life sciences at level appropriate for Grade 4. For example, they understand concepts relating to the earth's features, physical properties, structure, and function. In addition, students can formulate solutions to familiar problems as well as show a beginning awareness of issues associated with technology.

- *Advanced (205–300):* Students performing at the advanced level demonstrate a solid understanding of earth, physical, and life sciences as well as the ability to apply their understanding to practical situations at a level appropriate for Grade 4. For example, they can perform and critique simple investigations, make connections from one or more of the sciences to predict or conclude, and apply fundamental concepts to practical applications.

In previous chapters, we have introduced holistic and analytic rubrics for scoring constructed-response questions and performance assessment responses. The difference between a scoring rubric and a grading rubric is that a scoring rubric is for a specific task, such as an essay question or a performance assessment task, while a grading rubric is for a course based on scores from multiple assessments. A scoring rubric produces a score, while a grading rubric produces a grade.

The first step in developing a rubric grading system is to decide on the number of achievement levels. Fewer achievement levels, such as *Meeting Standards* and *Not Meeting Standards,* as in the case of criterion-referenced grading discussed above, may not differentiate students adequately. As a result, advanced students may not feel motivated to do better and may do only minimal efforts to pass. Too many levels, such as *Expert, Advanced, Above Average, Average,* and *Basic,* although desirable, are difficult to define. Three or four levels are more feasible. For example, the New York state regents exams adopt three performance levels: *Meeting Standards With Distinction, Meeting Standards,* and *Below Standard.*

Once performance levels are decided, the next step is to identify essential learning outcomes and order them from easiest to most advanced. The learning outcomes can be general learning standards or more specific substandards within standards. There is no need to include every learning outcome for a grading purpose. The units of learning outcomes should be smaller than unit topics because for any unit topic, there are always learning outcomes related to both basic knowledge and more advanced understandings. Once learning outcomes are arranged in a hierarchical order, a decision is made on what you would expect students at each performance level to be able to achieve. For example, you may want your students at the meeting standards with distinction level to be able to master 85% of the learning outcomes, while students at the meeting standards level to be able to master 75% of learning outcomes. These decisions result in cutoff points within the learning outcomes. The above process can be represented in Figure 7.1.

In Figure 7.1, students are the target of grading. Basically, grading is to divide students into three categories: not meeting standard, meeting standard, and meeting standard with distinction. The ruler in the middle represents test scores from various assessments; it is the basis for grouping students. Learning outcomes are from learning standards; they are arranged from more basic (bottom) to more advanced (top).

One issue remains outstanding—how to decide if students have mastered the learning outcomes deemed necessary for a given performance level (e.g., meeting standard). Obviously, learning outcomes for each performance level may be distributed in various curriculum units and assessed by various assessment methods, and thus we need to desegregate unit test scores into smaller components (i.e., by assessment tasks or questions). The

FIGURE 7.1   Rubric Grading

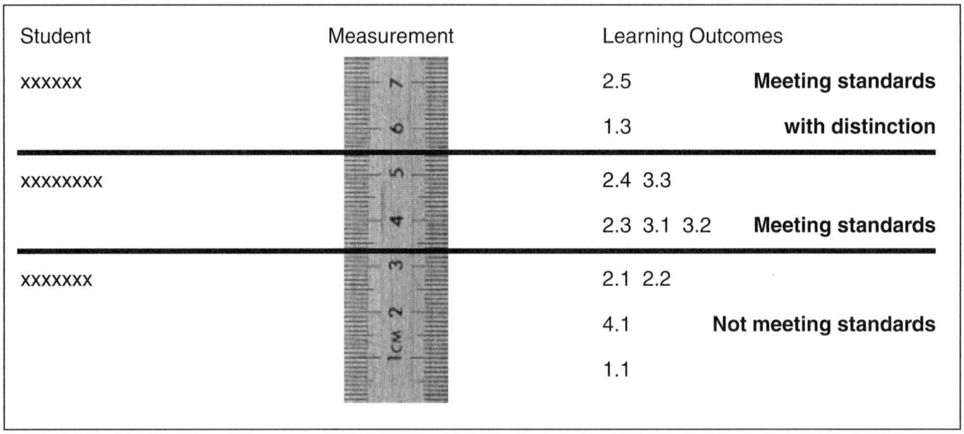

Note: X represents students.

TABLE 7.5   A Sample Rubric Grading

Student Name:					
Performance Level	Learning Outcomes	Total Points	Earned Points	% Points	Grade (80% as Cutoff)
Meeting standards with distinction	1.3, 2.4, 3.3, . . .	50	25	50	
Meeting standards	1.2, 2.2, 3.2, . . .	80	65	81.3	☺
Below standards	1.1, 2.1, 3.1, . . .	140	130	92.9	

strategy is to group all assessment tasks related to learning outcomes for a given performance level and obtain one score from them. Once a score is obtained for each performance level, a cutoff score (e.g., 80%) is then applied to decide if a student has reached the performance level. This process can be represented in Table 7.5.

The student in Table 7.5 achieved 81% of learning outcomes required for meeting standards but only 50% of outcomes required for meeting standards with distinction, and thus the student's highest competence level or final grade is meeting standards.

The above rubric grading assumes that learning outcomes can be arranged from more basic to more advanced, and students are not expected to learn all of them. This assumption is reasonable when teachers adopt differentiated instruction and thus differentiated assessment. Under differentiated instruction, more advanced students learn additional materials beyond common curriculum expectations; they also take part in more advanced assessment tasks such as bonus questions, projects, and so on. That is, rubric grading requires students to learn different learning outcomes that are assessed by different assessment methods.

When differentiated instruction is not conducted, and all students learn the same set of learning outcomes, the above rubric grading may not be applicable. However, if you conceptualize meeting standards to be a learning progression, then rubric grading is still applicable. A learning progression is a pathway along which students' competence of meeting the learning standards is developed continuously. That is, students need to take multiple interim steps to meet the expected learning standards. This idea is best demonstrated by Jim Minstrell's (2001) facet learning. Facet learning describes a possible learning continuum from most naive conceptions to scientific conceptions (i.e., the learning standards). The following facet cluster is for developing understanding by students on forces:

FACET CLUSTER ON FORCES

00 Students can identify forces on an object and compare their relative sizes.

01 Students can identify the sources of forces on an object.

02 Students can correctly identify the direction a force is acting.

03 Students can compare the relative sizes of forces on static objects.

40 The student reports that objects cannot exert forces along or parallel to its surface.

50 For an object at rest or moving horizontally, the student believes the downward force is greater than the upward force.

60 The student believes that force is a property of an object and its size is indicated by the magnitude of other properties of the object.

61 If an object has more mass than another object, it also has more force.

62 If an object is more active (moves faster) than another object, it also has more force.

70 The student reports an energy source as a force.

71 The engine or battery exerts a force on the object.

80 The student believes that passive objects cannot exert a force even though they touch another object.

81 For an object at rest on a surface (e.g., a book on a table), the surface (e.g., table) does not exert an upward force.

82 Passive objects (e.g., ropes) connecting two other objects do not exert forces, but instead transmit the active force. (For example, in the situation of a person pulling on a rope connected to a cart, the student identifies the person as exerting the force on the cart, not the rope.)

90 The student believes that motion determines the existence of a force or forces.

91 If an object is moving there is a "force of motion."

92 When the "force of motion" runs out, the object will stop.

93 If an object is not moving, no forces are involved in the situation.

Source: http://www.diagnoser.com/diagnoser/index.jsp. Reproduced by permission.

In the above facet cluster on force, explicit learning goals and various intermediate understandings (i.e., different sorts of reasoning, conceptual and procedural difficulties) form a learning progression. Each cluster contains the intuitive ideas students have as they move toward scientifically accurate learning targets. Each facet has a two-digit number. The 0X and 1X facets are the learning targets. The facets that begin with the numbers 2X through 9X indicate ideas that have more problematic aspects. In general, higher facet numbers (e.g., 9X, 8X, 7X) are the more problematic facets. The X0s indicate more general statements of student ideas. Often these are followed by more specific examples, which are coded X1 through X9. Therefore, nine categories of student performances are differentiated in this example. The nine categories may form the basis for a rubric grading. Although nine performance levels may be too many to define, the idea of learning progression for grading remains applicable.

Applying the idea of learning progression to rubric grading follows a similar process as described above for rubric grading within the context of differentiated instruction and assessment.

The first step is still to decide the number of student competence levels. Again, this number should not be too few or too many; three to four levels are more appropriate. The next step is to make a list of student performances necessary for meeting the learning standards. Student performances should relate to assessment tasks, such as being able to answer 80% of the questions on the end-of-unit test related to plant parts, score 4 out of 5 on the performance assessment on animal functions, and complete 90% of homework. Once student performances deemed necessary for meeting the standards are decided, the third step is to sort students based on their performances on various assessments into two groups: meeting the standards and not meeting the standards. Depending on the number of competence levels you have decided, the next step, the fourth step, is to further sort students in the above resulted groups into subgroups by following the same Steps 2 to 3 described above. For example, if you have decided three competence levels for grading, and the three levels are meeting standards with distinction, meeting standards, and below standards, then your Step 4 is to decide student performances necessary to qualify for meeting standards with distinction. Using those performances as criteria, you will then sort those students who have been classified as meeting standards into two subgroups: meeting standards with distinction and meeting standards. Table 7.6 presents a sample grading system for an eighth-grade science course:

Like developing a scoring rubric, developing a good grading rubric is not a simple task; you need to consider many factors when developing a grading rubric. First, you need to have a clear understanding of the expected standards. This typically requires review and analysis of the state and/or school district content and performance standards. Because most state content standards are general and are without accompanying performance standards, translating content standards into competence levels is not simple. Second, you need to have your assessments aligned with the standards. Then you need to develop your descriptions of student competence levels using specific performances demonstrated by students in various assessments. Descriptions should be directly based on students' actual performances on various assessments. After you have graded students, you still make adjustment to the grading rubric if necessary so that the grades students receive are fully justified.

APPLICATION AND SELF-REFLECTION 7.3

Now that you are familiar with two types of rubric grading, develop a rubric grading system for a fourth-grade class with differentiated instruction and a rubric grading system for the same fourth-grade class based on learning progression by using the relevant learning standards below. Your grading systems can be assumed for a marking period. Present your grading systems to the class. Compare the two rubric grading systems and discuss the pros and cons of each grading system.

The relevant learning standards for the fourth-grade classes are as follows:

Standard 1: Students are expected to ask questions about objects, organisms, and events and conduct appropriate measurements.

Standard 2: Students are expected to identify salient properties of objects and be able to describe changes of objects.

Standard 3: Students are expected to describe salient characteristics of living organisms and their life cycles.

TABLE 7.6   A Sample Grading Rubric for an Eighth-Grade Science Course

---

Meeting standards with distinction (scored 85% on tests and 85% on projects):

Students at this level have demonstrated an advanced understanding of fundamental concepts related to natural phenomena and living things. They have also demonstrated an advanced level of inquiry skills. More specifically, students at this level are able to identify forms of energy and explain how energy is conserved during its transfer from one form to another in both living and nonliving systems. Students are also able to use theories about the structure of matter to explain the state of matter and the physical and chemical changes of matter. Students can also describe the diversity and variation of various living things. Students at this level can pose a meaningful question, design sophisticated procedures to answer the question, and communicate the findings effectively.

Meeting standards (scored 65% on tests and 65% on projects):

Students at this level have demonstrated an adequate understanding of fundamental concepts related to natural phenomena and living things. They have also demonstrated an adequate level of inquiry skills. More specifically, students at this level are able to identify forms of energy and analyze how energy is transferred from one form to another during various changes in the natural environment and living systems. Students are able to identify different types of matter based on their physical and chemical properties, as well as differentiate between two basic forms of changes (i.e., physical and chemical changes). Students can also identify different characteristics of plants and animals. Furthermore, students at this level can pose a meaningful question, design appropriate procedures to answer the question, and communicate the findings effectively.

Below standards (scored < 65% on test or < 65% on projects):

Students at this level have demonstrated a preliminary understanding of fundamental concepts related to natural phenomena and living things. They have also demonstrated a preliminary level of inquiry skills. More specifically, students at this level are able to identify sources of energy and understand in general that energy can be transferred. Students are able to identify different states of matter and know that there are two types of change in matter (i.e., physical and chemical changes). Students are also familiar with some characteristics of plants and animals. Students at this level can also follow instructions to collect and analyze data in order to make conclusions.

GRADE REPORTING

One important purpose of making grades is to communicate with stakeholders (e.g., students and parents) and other interested parties (e.g., other teachers, college admissions officers). Theses stakeholders and interested parties are audiences of grades. **Grade reporting** refers to ways in which student grades are communicated to various audiences. Although every grade a teacher makes may be based on a sound rationale, the meanings of grades may still not be immediately apparent to audiences. Grade reporting is to convey not only what student grades are but also what grades mean, how they are made, and why they are made. Behind every grade are stories about a student's learning, such as how well the student has learned, what are the strengths and weaknesses in the student's learning, what are the implications of the grade, and so on. Different audiences are interested in different stories of grades; methods of grade reporting need to vary according to types of audiences. In general, there are three important types of audiences: (a) the parents/students, (b) other teachers in the school system, and (c) university admissions officers.

Grade Reporting to Parents/Students

Parents and students are key stakeholders in student learning. Reporting grades to parents and students needs to take into consideration the potential uses or expected uses of student grades. If we consider that parents are partners in student learning, then reporting grades to parents should be more than just informing them how their children are doing in science. Empowering parents to play an active role in student learning requires teachers to provide more information about their children's grades. Such information may pertain to the following questions: (a) What does the grade mean (e.g., percentage grading, criterion-referenced grading, rubric grading)? (b) How is the grade made (e.g., assessments the grade is based on, weights given to different assessments)? (c) Why is this the grade (e.g., attendance record, class participation, course expectation and rigor)? (d) In what ways can parents help improve the student's grade (e.g., homework monitoring, purchasing learning resources)? Report cards sent to homes typically include the student's grades in all subjects plus some information on the student's attendance record. Because of limited space and the need for consistency across all subjects, report cards do not convey all information pertaining to the above questions. This leaves only one option for science teachers: supplementing the school report card with a narrative report. A **narrative report** explains meanings of grades and suggests how to improve them. A narrative report attempts to answer the questions listed above. In elementary grades, a parent-teacher conference typically fulfills the function of a narrative report. During a parent-teacher conference, the teacher explains to the parents the above questions; the teacher may also show samples of student course work to illustrate the above information. When the student progresses to middle and high schools, parent-teacher conferences become less common, and a narrative report becomes imperative. Although individualized narrative reports are ideal, they may not be practical due to time constraint of teachers. If an individualized narrative report is not feasible, a generic or standard narrative report in the form of an information sheet is possible. A sample generic narrative report for a seventh-grade science class is as follows:

Dear Parents/Guardians,

In a few days, you will receive your child's report card for this marking period. In this letter, I would like to explain how grades are made, what they mean, and how you may help improve them. During this marking period, we focused on the state learning Standard 1—Science Inquiry and learning Standard 4—Physical Science. The science inquiry standard expects students to be able to independently pose meaningful questions, design appropriate procedures to collect and analyze data, and make conclusions. The physical science standard expects students to identify various forms of energy and their transfer from one form to another. The assessment methods include an end-of-unit test, an open-ended inquiry project throughout the marking period, and homework. Your child's grade is in a percentage. You may interpret the percentage as the amount of expected learning outcomes based on the learning standards your child has mastered. The percentage grade is calculated based on the following weights:

End-of-unit tests	50%
Project	30%
Homework	20%

A percentage of 85% is considered to be acceptable, or meeting the learning standards. At this level, students can identify forms of energy and analyze how energy is transferred from one form to another during various changes in the natural environment. Students are also able to pose a meaningful question, design appropriate procedures to answer the question, and communicate the findings effectively.

In addition to your child's grade, you will also see your child's attendance record. In general, the more days missing, the more likely your child's grade will be low. Also, active participation in class by raising and asking questions is a positive factor affecting grades. This topic of energy is conceptually challenging; hands-on experiences are essential to develop good understanding. Although I have provided many such experiences in class, more hands-on experiences at home are also helpful. Given the emphasis of assessment on the long-term project and homework, constantly monitoring and supporting your child in completing the project and homework should be very helpful.

During the next marking period, we will use a similar grading system as the one for this marking period. Although the topic will be on a different one—the human body—your help in monitoring your child's homework completion and independent research project will be beneficial for your child to achieve a high grade.

If you have any questions about your child's grade, please do not hesitate to contact me at xxx xxxx. Thanks for your cooperation. Together, we can make a difference in your child's learning.

Seventh-Grade Science Teacher
xxx

From the above narrative report, we see that the teacher explains the meaning of a percentage grade, how the grade is calculated, and what factors may have contributed to the grade. The teacher also suggests ways to improve student grades. The specificity of the narrative reports should be appropriate at the level of most parents. Too technical in educational terms or too in-depth in science content may throw most parents off and achieve no pur-pose of communication. Also, narrative reports should be direct and concise; no parents would like to read pages of explanations.

Grade Reporting to Other Teachers

Teachers of other subjects, particularly at higher grade levels, often need to know students' grades in a particular course or at previous grade levels to better plan for individualized instruction. Typically, the school or district maintains student academic records electroni-cally. Although teachers may access students' electronic records for grades and other demo-graphical data, additional information on what students have learned during a previous course or marking periods and how the grades are made is more informative but usually not available in the electronic database. Besides electronic student records, schools typically also maintain physical records or student files containing additional academic matters such as student awards, individualized education plans (IEPs), disciplinary actions, important corre-spondence between the school and the parents, and so on. Although it is not mandatory for teachers to provide any written explanation of student grades to be inserted into students' files, doing so can be beneficial for other teachers to plan better student future learning. This type of grade reporting is not a direct and official communication like that to parents; it is mainly for record keeping. When a teacher finds a student struggling in class or doing extra-ordinary work in class, information about students' previous academic grades and learning could help the teacher to decide if special attention is needed for the student. Even a gen-eral knowledge of what students have learned in previous years and how students have been graded can inform the teacher in making important instructional decisions. Too often, teach-ers do not talk to each other, even though they are in the same building; as a result, curric-ula from grade to grade are not coherent (e.g., overlapping in content and emphasis, gaps or blanks in topics taught, too high or too low expectations). Most effective and efficient learn-ing takes place when curricula over the years are progressive and coherent.

A narrative report accompanying a student's report card, which will become part of the student's record, can be considered. Important information to be included in such a nar-rative report are (a) topics learned during the course or marking period, (b) the assessment methods and grading system used, and (c) individualized comments. Parts a and b are generic; they are common to all students. Individual comments are specific to the student, providing such background information as in-class participation, group work, attitude and interest, parent cooperation, and so forth. Individualized comments do not have to be long; they should focus on important factors that may help explain the student's grade—high, low, or average.

Grade Reporting to University Admissions Officers

Communicating student grades to university admissions officers is an important and seri-ous purpose of a high school student's transcript. Although the student's transcript is not the only piece of information universities make admission decisions on, the student's tran-script provides very important information about the courses the student has taken and how well the student has done in them.

Grades recorded on a high school transcript should convey at least three pieces of information: (a) courses taken and the nature of the courses, (b) student achievement on the courses, and (c) student ranking in the class. Many high schools offer science courses in tracks, with some courses being more advanced than others (e.g., honors, Advanced Placement, remedial). If this is the case, it is important to indicate on the transcript what types of courses the student has taken. It should also be helpful for the university admissions officers to know what courses are required for high school graduation and which courses are electives. In terms of the student's actual grades, it should be apparent to the admissions officers whether a grade is a percentage grade, a criterion-referenced grade, or a rubric grade. If you report letter grades, you should provide a note on how the letter grades correspond to percentage grades. Criterion-referenced grades and rubric grades are not common on high school transcripts; if they are used, explanatory notes should be provided to explain what the grades mean. The last piece of information, student ranking in the class, is not commonly seen on high school transcripts. This may be due to the belief that comparing students against each other is unethical or unfair. On the other hand, no information on relative rankings in class may unintentionally underrepresent those more advanced students because a same percentage grade (e.g., 90%) from different schools can mean quite different things in terms of what students have learned and what the student's potential is. Variation in expectations of a same course, assessment methods, and grading can be great from teacher to teacher and from school to school; a same grade from different teachers and schools does not mean a same achievement level. The relative student ranking in class provides supplementary information about a student's actual learning achievement and potential. Given that teacher-made assessment and grading may not be technically high in quality (to be discussed in Chapter 8), exact ranking of students may not be creditable. Reporting student relative ranking in terms of quartile rank (i.e., lower 25%, 25%–50%, 50%–75%, and 75%–100%) can be an option.

THE CASES OF ERIC AND ELISIA: GRADING

At the beginning of this chapter, Eric and Elisia were unsure about what new knowledge and skills they would develop in this chapter. They have seen grades from elementary school to university that are all in numbers. They know that grades appear on report cards and transcripts. The first thing they learned in this chapter is the difference between a score and a grade. They can see how making such a differentiation can improve the accuracy and relevance of grades. This differentiation also helps them understand the relationship between assessment and uses of assessment results. The percentage grading system is most familiar to them, but the idea of different grades for different attributes is new to them. During student teaching in a third-grade class, Eric has seen criterion-referenced grading used by his cooperation teacher. He can see how rubric grading is a natural extension of criterion-referenced grading. Elisia, being a high school preservice teacher, does not see how criterion-referenced grading and rubric grading are applicable. Transcripts are used universally, and overall averages or GPA are computed for each student. However, she can see how criterion-referenced grading and rubric grading may be useful as interim grading during a science course. Eric and Elisia both understand the value of grade reporting. One concern for both of them about the suggested grade reporting approach (i.e., narrative reports) is time. They wish that some assistance, such as software, would be available in schools for them to write narrative reports for students. One additional insight they have developed from this chapter is how various assessment methods may be integrated during the grading process. Never before have they seen how assessment and grading are so complex, but overall they seem to feel more prepared than before.

Do the experiences of Eric and Elisia sound familiar to you? What were your initial ideas of grading, and how have they changed as the result of this chapter?

Chapter Summary

- Scoring and grading are two different processes. Grading is a process of deciding and communicating how well students have mastered the learning objectives; the result of grading is a grade. Scoring is a process of quantifying a student's performance on an assessment task; the result of scoring is a score.

- Percentage grading uses a percentage as the grade to indicate the amount of content or number of objectives mastered. A percentage grading system is a plan to combine individual assessment scores into a final percentage. Percentage grading involves calculating a weighted total score as the grade from scores students have earned on individual units or different assessments. The commonly used letter grading is a variation of percentage grading.

- Criterion-referenced grading uses qualitatively different categories or levels of performances as grades, such as *Pass* and *Fail* or *Meeting Standard* and *Not Meeting Standard*. Criterion-referenced grading involves identifying learning outcomes essential for students to master, calculating the total student-earned scores on the learning outcomes, and comparing the weighted total earned score with a criterion cutoff score to decide if students have mastered the learning standard.

- Rubric grading is an extension of criterion-referenced grading; it specifies more than two levels of student competence, such as beyond standard, meeting standard, and below standard. Rubric grading involves deciding levels of student competence, ordering learning outcomes from easiest to most advanced, dividing the learning outcomes by levels of competence, comparing student performances on learning outcomes at each competence level with a criterion cutoff score, and deciding the student's highest competence level. Rubric grading may also be based on a learning progression from novice competence to expert competence.

- Grade reporting refers to ways in which student grades are communicated to various audiences. Grade reporting conveys information on not only what student grades are but also what grades mean, how they are made, and why they are achieved. Report cards and transcripts are common ways of reporting grades. Depending on types of audiences, narrative reports or explanatory notes to report cards and transcripts can provide additional information about students' learning.

√ Mastery Checklist

- ☐ Develop a sound percentage grading system.
- ☐ Develop a sound criterion-referenced grading system.
- ☐ Develop a sound rubric grading system.
- ☐ Be able to report grades effectively.

Web-Based Student Study Site

The Companion Web site for *Essentials of Science Classroom Assessment* can be found at **www.sagepub.com/liustudy.**

The site includes a variety of materials to enhance your understanding of the chapter content. Visit the study site to complete an online self-assessment of essential knowledge and skills introduced in this chapter. The study materials also include flash cards, Web resources, and more.

Further Reading

Cizek, G. J., & Bunch, M. B. (2007). *Standard setting.* Thousand Oaks, CA: Sage.

This book should be of interest to those who are interested in psychometric theories and their applications to criterion-referenced grading (i.e., standard setting). It introduces commonly used methods to set performance standards in standardized testing situations.

References

Gallagher, J. D. (1998). *Classroom assessment for teachers.* Upper Saddle River, NJ: Merrill.

Minstrell, J. (2001). Facets of students' thinking: Designing to cross the gap from research to standard-based practice. In K. Crowley, C. D. Schunn, & T. Okada (Eds.), *Designing for science: Implications from everyday, classroom, and professional settings* (pp. 415–443). Mahwah, NJ: Lawrence Erlbaum.

National Assessment Governing Board. (2000). *Science framework for the 1996 and 2000 National Assessment of Educational Progress.* Washington, DC: Author.

National Research Council (NRC). (1996). *National science education standards.* Washington, DC: National Academy Press.

CHAPTER 8

Using Data to Improve Assessment and Instruction

One important result of assessment is data. In previous chapters, we have introduced various types of assessment; all of them produce data. Assessment data can help answer many important questions such as the following: How good are the test questions? Has the test achieved what it is intended to assess? What are the strengths and weaknesses of student learning? To answer questions above, you need to analyze statistically students' responses to the test questions. For teacher-prepared tests, statistical analysis can help identify strengths and weaknesses of individual test questions and the whole test. If flaws in test questions (e.g., confusing or too difficult) or in a test (e.g., scores are internally inconsistent) are identified, revisions may be made before the test is used again. Test development and improvement should take place in cycles to ensure a continuous increase in quality of tests.

When conducting data analysis, you assume the role of a data user. Being a "data user" allows you to conduct an inquiry using your own students' data to improve instruction. You can potentially become a leader by identifying specific areas for immediate instructional improvement rather than having an instructional improvement plan imposed on you by the district or state that might not be directly relevant to your students. Assessment of students and improvement of instruction are interconnected. You need to monitor student learning on an ongoing basis to evaluate and adjust your teaching for improved student learning.

Teacher inquiry is a way of knowing—a process of gaining new knowledge and insights about teaching and student learning. It is also called *action research*. You often have specific concerns about student learning. For example, in which areas are my students weak or strong? Which learning standards have my students mastered? Answering these questions requires you to go through an inquiry process. Similarly, in terms of instruction, you may have hunches about what works. Will spending more time on computers improve student learning? Have I given students sufficient opportunities to learn what they are tested on? Obtaining clear answers to those questions requires you to gather and analyze data as part of inquiry. Data-driven instructional improvement approaches every change in instruction as a testable hypothesis that can be supported (or refuted) by student assessment data.

This chapter introduces techniques for conducting basic item and test analysis. These techniques enable you to become a reflective practitioner in order to constantly improve the quality of your assessment and instruction.

BASIC STATISTICS FOR ITEM AND TEST ANALYSIS

In a test, each student receives a score for each question or item, as well as a score for the entire test. Statistical analysis is based on such scores for all students. The **mean** is the arithmetic average of a set of scores over all students. It represents the central tendency of individual scores among the students. A mean represents the scores well if there are no outliers (i.e., unusually large or small) within the scores. Otherwise, the mean will be distorted by those outliers. When outliers exist, two other statistics may be more appropriate (i.e., less sensitive to outliers). One is median, and another is mode. **Median** is the score that is located at the middle when all scores are rank-ordered from highest to lowest. To find the median, you need to order scores from lowest to highest or from highest to lowest and then count which score is in the middle, which is the median. If two scores are in the middle, the median is the average of the two scores in the middle. **Mode** is the score that has the most occurrences. To find the mode for a set of scores, you need to count the frequencies of all scores, and the score with the highest frequency is the mode. Mode is more accurate when there are a large number of scores.

Another set of statistics describes the variation among a set of scores. **Standard deviation** is the averaged difference between individual scores and the mean of the scores. A **range** is the difference between the maximum score and minimum score.

Table 8.1 is a hypothetical set of scores from a class. At the bottom are descriptive statistics about the three sets of test scores.

Another commonly used statistic for item and test analysis is Pearson's product-moment correlation coefficient. This correlation coefficient represents the overall linear relationship between two sets of scores. The two sets of scores are also called incidences of variables. Correlation coefficient ranges from -1 to $+1$, with negative values indicating an inverse (i.e., downward) linear relationship and a positive value indicating an upward linear relationship. The absolute value indicates the degree of the linear relationship, with 1 being perfectly linear and 0 being no relationship at all. A visual display on the relationship between two sets of scores can show both the direction and magnitude of the relationship. Figure 8.1 shows the relationship between Test 2 scores and state test scores in Table 8.1.

ASSESSMENT STANDARDS ADDRESSED IN CHAPTER 8

NSES Assessment Standard C
   The technical quality of the data collected is well matched to the decisions and actions taken on the basis of their interpretation. This standard is further elaborated into the following substandards:

- The feature that is claimed to be measured is actually measured.
- An individual student's performance is similar on two or more tasks that claim to measure the same aspect of student achievement.
- Assessment tasks and methods for presenting them provide data that are sufficiently stable to lead to the same decisions if used at different times. (National Research Council [NRC], 1996, p. 83)

NSES Assessment Standard D
   Assessment practices must be fair. This standard is further elaborated into the following substandards:

- Assessment tasks must be reviewed for the use of stereotypes, for assumptions that reflect the perspectives or experiences of a particular group, for language that might be offensive to a particular group, and for other features that might distract students from the intended tasks.
- Large-scale assessments must use statistical techniques to identify potential bias among subgroups.
- Assessment tasks must be appropriately modified to accommodate the needs of students with physical disabilities, learning disabilities, or limited English proficiency.
- Assessment tasks must be set in a variety of contexts, be engaging to students with different interests and experiences, and must not assume the perspective or experience of a particular gender, racial, or ethnic group. (NRC, 1996, p. 85)

Figure 8.1 shows that overall, there appears to be a positive linear relationship between the two variables (i.e., Test 2 scores and state test scores). The trend line is upward, indicating a positive relationship. Also, the plots gather around the trend line and only deviate from the trend line slightly, indicating a strong linear relationship. The Pearson correlation coefficient is 0.96, suggesting a very strong positive linear relationship.

   In addition to studying relationships between variables, another important question that can be answered by statistics is the difference between two sets of scores. Are the two sets of scores significantly different? Statistically, a significant difference means that the difference is unlikely the result of a random effect or by chance. One statistical procedure, called a t test, calculates the probability of two means of two sets of scores completely by chance. The probability ranges from 0 to 1, with 0 meaning no chance at all to result in the difference by chance and 1 meaning a certainty to result in the difference by chance. Most times, the calculated probability is between 0 and 1. A cutoff value of 0.05 is commonly used to make a conclusion about whether there is a significant difference. If the calculated probability

TABLE 8.1   Hypothetical Test Scores for a Class of 18 Students

Student	Test 1 (%)	Test 2 (%)	State Test (%)
1	67	68	70
2	56	65	67
3	88	85	80
4	92	90	89
5	93	95	94
6	78	77	80
7	88	84	88
8	66	68	68
9	89	83	80
10	88	84	83
11	95	96	94
12	68	69	65
13	85	86	87
14	79	77	70
15	84	81	82
16	56	57	56
17	91	90	94
18	67	68	70
Mean	80.2	79.7	79.2
Median	85.0	83.0	80.0
Mode	88.0	68.0	80.0
Standard deviation	11.3	10.6	11.4
Maximum	95.0	96.0	94.0
Minimum	56.0	57.0	56.0
Range	39.0	39.0	38.0

FIGURE 8.1   Relationship Between Two Sets of Scores

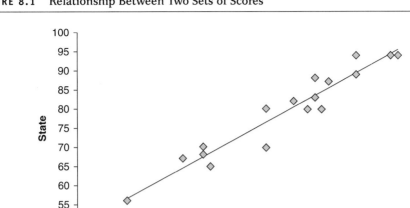

is smaller than 0.05, then we can conclude that the difference is unlikely due to chance, meaning that there is a statistically significant difference between the two means. If the calculated probability is equal to or greater than 0.05, then we can conclude that the difference is likely due to chance (i.e., there is no statistically significantly difference between the two means). In the hypothetical test results in Table 8.1, the means for Test 1 and Test 2 are different (80.2 and 79.7). The probability calculated by the *t* test to result in the difference between 80.2 and 79.7 by chance is 0.58, which is > 0.05, and thus the difference between 80.2 and 79.7 is not statistically significant—the difference is likely due to chance.

Many statistical programs are available for data analysis, from generic to specialized. There is no need to purchase specialized software such as SPSS for conducting classroom assessment data analysis; a generic program such as MS Excel is more than sufficient. The text Web site provides a step-by-step tutorial on how to use MS Excel to conduct item and test analysis.

CONDUCTING DATA ANALYSIS

Data analysis typically involves the following steps: entering student responses, scoring student responses, conducting item analysis, conducting test analysis, interpreting data analysis results, and planning for assessment and instruction improvement.

Entering Student Responses

Whatever computer program you choose to use, the first step in data analysis is always entering student responses to test questions into a data table. Designating rows/columns to be students or test questions is arbitrary. Additional information, such as scoring keys to multiple-choice questions and points to constructed-response questions, also needs to be entered in a row or column. For multiple-choice questions, letters (e.g., A, B, C, and D) or numbers (i.e., 1, 2, 3, and 4) indicating students' choices should be entered. For constructed-response questions, points students have actually earned (e.g., 0, 1, 2, 3) should be entered.

Scoring Student Responses

The next step is to score students' responses to multiple-choice questions by comparing students' responses with the answer keys by assigning credits (usually 1 point) for a correct response and 0 credits for an incorrect response. Because the credits that the students earned on the constructed-response questions have been entered directly in the data table, no scoring for the constructed-response questions is necessary. A student's total score is the sum of credits earned on both the multiple-choice and constructed-response questions. A student's percentage score is the total score divided by the total number of points available.

Once students' responses are scored, statistical analyses can be performed on individual items (item analysis), groups of items, or the entire test (test analysis).

Conducting Item Analysis

Now that you have inputted and scored student responses, you are ready to analyze student performances by items.

Analyzing Item Difficulty

Item difficulty refers to the percentage or proportion of students who have answered a question correctly. If 100 students answer a test question, but only 80 students answer the item correctly, then the item difficulty is 80% or 0.80. In this example, the percentage of students responding incorrectly would be 20% or 0.20. For constructed-response questions, if the maximum point for a question is more than 1, the difficulty can still be expressed as a percentage of the average points earned by students over the maximum points and be interpreted in the same way as that for multiple-choice questions. Although items are not particularly useful for instructional improvement when all or almost all of your students answer the item correctly, those questions are targets of assessment improvement. The most intriguing (and useful) items for instructional improvement are often those with difficulties between 0.30 and 0.70 because they tend to differentiate students by ability.

Analyzing Item Discrimination

Item discrimination refers to how the item can differentiate between students whose overall abilities are high and those whose overall abilities are low. There are many indices for measuring item discrimination. One is to use the correlation between students' performance on an item with their overall performance on the test. That is, for each item, there is a set of students' scores (e.g., 1s or 0s if the item is a multiple-choice question). Also, for any test, there is a set of students' test scores. A correlation between these two sets of scores can be used as an index of item discrimination. Assuming a class size of 25 or more, correlations of negative values or positive values less than 0.40 may suggest that the test question is flawed—confusing, too difficult or too easy, or the concept may not have been taught correctly. If class size is smaller than 25, the expected correlation coefficient should be even higher. Three sample questions (Q1, Q2, and Q3) and their item statistics are list in Table 8.2.

The discrimination coefficient in correlation for Item Q1 is 0.60, a modestly high correlation, suggesting that the stronger students answered the question correctly more often than the weaker students. Approximately half of the students answered the question correctly, and about an equal number of students selected each of the incorrect choices. These data suggest that the question is "working well."

The discrimination coefficient for Item Q2, on the other hand, is only 0.18. This low discrimination is attributable to the fact that 97% (154 out of 159) of the students answered the item correctly. The high success rate of the students suggests that the question is easy and that it does not differentiate students who have a good understanding from those who do not; the question is not particularly useful in guiding instructional improvement. Item Q3 demonstrates a low to moderate discrimination value, meaning that a large number of stronger students missed the question. Closer examination of this question is likely to yield insights for how to improve your instruction. Both Q2 and Q3 may need improvement for future use.

Analyzing Response Pattern

The response pattern for an item indicates the number of students selecting each of the alternative responses for multiple-choice items or the number of students receiving no, partial, or full credit for constructed-response items. Response patterns can indicate to what degree students have a good understanding of a concept or the number of students with common misconceptions. In the example in Table 8.2, the response patterns may indicate that students had a good understanding on the concept related to Q2, but choices B, C, and D for Q1 and choice B for Q3 could be a common misconception among students. Questions with choices by no students or constructed-response questions with scoring categories earned by no students need to be revised for future use.

Conducting Test Analysis

In addition to examining student performance on individual test items, you can also examine student performance on groups of questions related to various learning standards or

TABLE 8.2   Sample Item Statistics

Item	Key	Difficulty	Discrimination	A	B	C	D
Q1	A	0.50	0.60	79 (49.6%)	26 (16.4%)	27 (17.0%)	27 (17.0%)
Q2	A	0.97	0.18	154 (96.9%)	3 (1.9%)	1 (0.6%)	1 (0.6%)
Q3	A	0.52	0.35	82 (51.6%)	44 (27.6%)	19 (12.0%)	14 (8.8%)
. . .							

review the achievement of different groups of students (Class 1 vs. Class 2, boys vs. girls, etc.). Test analysis also involves analyzing the validity and reliability of the test.

Analyzing Mastery of Standards

Items on a test can be grouped based on curriculum standards, and the average of difficulties of the items can be calculated. This average difficulty can be interpreted as the percentage of students who have answered the questions related to the standard correctly; the higher the percentage, the better mastery level students have achieved.

A similar analysis may also be conducted by different cognitive levels such as Bloom's taxonomy. Questions at a particular cognitive level are grouped together, and the average of the difficulties of those questions is calculated as a measure of students' performance on the cognitive level. For example, it may be useful to find out if students have done well on items that require application and analysis.

Analyzing Student Group Performances

Often, it is interesting to find how students of different groups (e.g., male and female; Session 1 and Session 2 of a same course) have performed on a test. Statistics for describing group performances are mean, standard deviation, and range (the difference between the maximum and the minimum). A *t* test produces a probability for which the difference between two means is due to chance. If the calculated probability is smaller than 0.05, you can conclude that the difference is statistically significant; otherwise, the difference is not statistically significant (i.e., caused by chance).

Analyzing Test Validity

Test validity is a measure of how the test scores are useful for making meaningful inferences. Validity is a unitary construct, which means that it is a holistic measure of scores of the entire test. Evidence must be established to claim validity of a test. This process is called validation. Validation may be conducted through analyzing test content, response processes, internal structures of items, relations to other tests, and consequences of test result use.

Content validation of a test involves examining the test grid to see if the coverage (i.e., content and cognitive skills) of the test is appropriate and if the test items follow the test grid. A valid test must have a justified test grid and a good match between the test grid and test items in the test. In Chapter 5, we introduced a method to analyze the alignment between instruction and the content standard. Content validity may also be demonstrated by the alignment between assessment and the content standard. This is because the test grid is supposed to follow the content standard. A direct analysis of the alignment between a test and the content standard is an appropriate way of assessing content validity.

Validation of the student response process and internal structure of test items involves examination of students' reasoning processes and response patterns to individual items. The science assessment targets are usually invisible and assumed to exist based on theories. Because of this, the target of assessment is also called the construct. For example, when you assess students' problem solving, we assume that a problem-solving ability exists based on our science education theories, and since it is invisible, we have to develop indicators to assess it. Validation based on students' response processes and response patterns to individual test items means establishing the evidence that the test items and the whole test assess the target construct. Advanced statistics are usually needed for this type of validation, which is beyond the scope of this introductory book.

Validation based on relations to other test results involves comparing student test performances on the test with students' performances on other tests or benchmarks. The key to this type of validation is identifying a reasonable criterion as the benchmark that is related to the intended use of the test. The statistical analysis involved is usually a calculation of correlation coefficients. For example, if the purpose of a test is to award students grades that may be used for placement of students into different levels of courses, then a reasonable criterion or benchmark can be students' grades on the different levels of courses, and if the correlation between the two sets of grades is high, then we can claim that the original test used for student placement is valid.

Finally, validation based on consequences means examining if the use of test scores has resulted in negative consequences, such as certain groups that have been systematically denied access into some programs. A hypothetical example related to this type of validation is that female students' scores on the state test have been consistently lower than male students' scores. The consequence of this result could be that female students have been systematically penalized in university admissions because state test scores may be used in university admission decisions. In this case, the state test would be claimed to be consequentially invalid. The statistical analysis involved for consequence validation is to compare the performances on the test between individual groups to see if the difference is statistically significant. Statistical significance means that the difference is not likely to happen by chance. A *t* test usually is used to test the difference between the means of two groups. If a *t* test shows the difference to be statistically significant, then the test could result in negative consequences and thus lack consequential validity.

Analyzing Test Reliability

Reliability is concerned with consistency of test scores. Various factors cause inconsistency in student test scores. First of all, inconsistency in scoring may be due to different scores given by different raters, which is called *interrater reliability.* Another important type of reliability that science teachers need to be concerned with is called *internal consistency of items.* A reliable test requires that all items in a test assess related attributes. If so, students' responses to different items should be consistent with each other, and the test items collectively measure students' ability on one construct. The statistical measure for internal consistency is commonly Cronbach's alpha. Cronbach's alpha is defined as

$$\alpha = \frac{k}{k-1}\left(\frac{1 - \sum_{1}^{k} \sigma_i^2}{\sigma_x^2}\right),$$

where *k* is the total number of questions on the test, σ_i^2 is the squared standard deviation (also called variance) of students' scores on item *i,* and σ_x^2 is the squared standard deviation of students' scores on the entire test. Cronbach's alpha can be interpreted as the variation of students' scores on individual items in relation to the variation of students' scores on the entire test. Student scores on the test indicate students' abilities. The smaller the variation on individual items in relation to the variation in students' abilities, the higher the internal consistency. Cronbach's alpha ranges from 0 to 1, with 0 indicating no internal consistency among items and 1 indicating complete internal consistency among items. State standardized tests typically have an alpha above .8.

INTERPRETING DATA ANALYSIS RESULTS AND PLANNING FOR ASSESSMENT AND INSTRUCTIONAL IMPROVEMENT

Data analysis is only the beginning of the data-driven assessment and instructional improvement process. Once data analysis results are available, it is necessary for you to "make sense" of them. In general, students' performances on items and tests are due to a variety of factors, such as the quality of test items, teacher instruction, and student learning. A Data Analysis Results Interpretation Sheet, such as the one shown in Table 8.3, can be used as a guide for interpreting data analysis results.

In the table, the first column is the category of analysis, which can be individual test questions, standards, cognitive levels, student subgroups, and so on. The second column is the data analysis results indicating students' performances such as percentage correct. The other three columns are possible reasons contributing to the performance levels in column 2. Student factors include considerations such as students' content knowledge, the reading level or readability of a particular question, misconceptions, the amount of effort students bring to the assessment, student reasoning pattern, and so on. Testing factors may include item-specific issues such as item difficulty, discrimination, and the placement of an

TABLE 8.3 Data Analysis Results Interpretation Sheet

Category	Student Performance	Student Factors	Test Factors	Instructional Factors	Assessment or Instructional Improvement Plan
Item 1	97% correct	None	Item flaw	None	Revise the item
Item 2	50% correct	Misconception Unable to differentiate concepts	Diagram difficult to read	Not enough time spent differentiating concepts	Use computer simulation
. . .					

item on the test (is a difficult item placed too close to the beginning of a test?) and test-specific issues such as validity and reliability. In addition, teachers may have not taught the concept, may have covered the topic too briefly, or may have taught the idea incorrectly. A sincere self-reflection is needed. A frank discussion of these issues with colleagues may also be beneficial. Once causes for students' poor performances have been identified through this type of root cause analysis, teachers need to decide what to do next (the last column in the table), which leads to assessment and/or instructional improvement plans.

Interpreting data analysis results of individual items usually starts with items at both ends of the difficulty spectrum—those questions on which students performed extremely well and those items that students found to be the most challenging. A sample easy item is as follows:

Which of the following is not an animal?
   a. Boy
   b. Flower
   c. Snake
   d. Tiger

This question was on a third-grade science test. The difficulty from a teacher's data for this item was 0.88; the discrimination calculated from the sample was 0.11. Among 24 students in class, 21 selected the correct answer *b*, 1 student chose *c*, 2 students chose *d*, and no student chose *a*. This was a very easy question, because the vast majority of students were able to answer this question correctly. However, this may not necessarily indicate that the students have a good understanding of animals because the discrimination index was so low (0.11), indicating that this question might not differentiate students in terms of their various levels of understanding. For example, a student may not think a boy is an animal, but since flower is a plant, she would still choose *b*. The two students who chose *d* might have missed the key word *not* in the item stem and only thought a tiger was an animal. The student who chose *c* could be simply due to recoding error or randomly guessing. Thus, this question is clearly flawed.

If analysis indicates that students' poor or good performance is due to flaws in test questions, further evidence may be needed before teachers disregard the poor or good performance of students. In the above example, a better question format, such as a matching question or an improved multiple-choice question, is in order. Similarly, if a teacher believes that the grammar, the diagram, the size of the text, or any other factor is the primary reason that students may have missed an item, the teacher may alter the item accordingly and "retest" the item.

Here is another example paraphrased from the New York state eighth-grade science test:

Which factor has the greatest influence on the direction of the air-mass track in the gulf coast?
   a. Upper air current
   b. Ocean currents
   c. Sea breezes
   d. Mountain barriers

The data from a school sample indicate an item difficulty of 0.50 and a discrimination of 0.34. Seventy-nine students selected the correct answer *a,* 40 selected response *b,* 34 selected response *c,* and 6 selected choice *d.* Only half of the students in this sample recognized the role of upper air currents in moving the tropical air mass from the gulf inland. The discrimination value for this item was a bit lower (0.34), indicating that some stronger students might have *answered* the question incorrectly. The majority of the students answering this question incorrectly indicated the role of either ocean currents or sea breezes. Less than 5% of the students suggested that mountain barriers played a role in this process. The response pattern is clearly not random—students selected choices *a, b,* and *c* much more frequently. In this case, the teacher did explain the three concepts but did not expect students to differentiate these ideas on their own. The data support the conclusion that most students recognized that the air mass did not cross mountain barriers. It is also apparent that students are not differentiating between upper air currents, ocean currents, and sea breezes. A misconception may exist among students for treating air currents, ocean currents, and sea breezes the same. Accordingly, one instructional improvement plan may involve computer simulations showing students the differences of the three concepts.

The same process as above can be used to interpret statistical analysis results on student mastery of standards, test validity, test reliability, test bias, and so on. Using assessment data to improve your assessment and modify instruction reflects a role change from teacher as "data giver" to a "data user." Typically, you act as a data giver when you report students' assessment results to the district, state, students, or parents. You act as a data user when you test hypotheses and conduct investigations using your own students' data to improve instruction. Assessment of students and effective instruction are fundamentally interconnected. By monitoring student learning on an ongoing basis, you can evaluate and adjust your teaching.

As stated in the National Science Education Standards, "Far too often, more educational data are collected than analyzed or used to make decisions or take action" (NRC, 1996, p. 90). Figure 8.2 presents four scenarios for testing and analysis. Increased standardized testing has moved all teachers toward more testing and data generation. As a teacher, you can choose between doing less analysis (Quadrant IV) or more analysis (Quadrant I). In choosing Quadrant I, you move from data giver to data user, allowing you to identify areas for immediate instructional improvement rather than having an instructional improvement plan imposed on you. In the process, you are exerting professional leadership and contributing to the cause of science education reform.

Research has shown that inquiry into practice can be an effective tool to improve instruction, and assessment data can be a powerful source to gain knowledge and insights about teaching and student learning. As teachers, we often have specific student learning concerns. For example, in which areas are my students weak or strong? Which learning standards have my students mastered? Answering these questions requires you to go through an inquiry process. Similarly, in terms of instruction, you may have hunches about what works. Will spending more time on computers improve student learning? How is my teaching aligned with the state standards? Have I provided students sufficient opportunities to learn what they will be tested on? Designing and conduct appropriate assessment and analyzing results can help answer the above questions.

FIGURE 8.2   Four Scenarios Involving Testing and Analysis

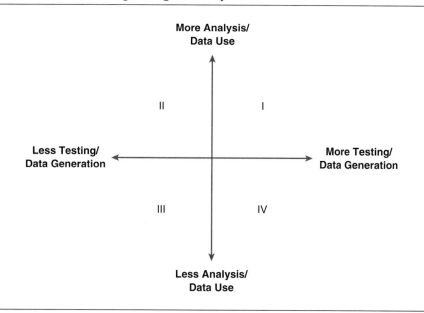

ASSESSMENT AS A PART OF SCIENCE TEACHER COMPETENCE

From the above discussion, once again we see a close relationship between assessment and instruction. Science assessment competence is an important part of science teacher teaching competence. In Chapter 1, we had an overview of the assessment standards expected in the National Science Education Standards (NRC, 1996). Chapters 2 to 8 intend to help you develop knowledge and skills to meet those standards. You have come a long way to this point of the book. Let's take a moment to think about those assessment standards again to see if we can relate the various assessment concepts and skills we have discussed in Chapters 1 to 8 to them.

Assessment Standard A: Assessment must be consistent with the decisions they are designed to inform. This standard is further elaborated into the following substandards:
   a. Assessments are deliberately designed.
   b. Assessments have explicitly stated purposes.

    c. The relationship between the decisions and the data is clear.

    d. Assessment procedures are internally consistent.

What would a science teacher do if the teacher has met this standard? First of all, the teacher should be aware of various decisions that are made based on test data. Improving student learning is one of most important decisions a science teacher routinely makes. This decision may take place at the beginning of teaching a unit, during a unit, and at the end of a unit. Accordingly, the science teacher needs to deliberately design an appropriate assessment to collect data to help plan science teaching (assessment of preconceptions), implement science teaching (assessment of ongoing learning), and evaluate the outcome of science teaching (summative assessment). For each assessment, the science teacher needs to follow appropriate procedures (e.g., developing a test grid for a summative assessment) to ensure that the data to be collected are relevant and will inform the intended decision making. In addition, assessment data also inform making other important decisions, such as state accountability, program evaluation, and international comparison. Furthermore, science teachers also participate in standardized testing at the state, national, and international levels. The science teacher needs to be clear on how different assessments are related to each other as different assessments inform different decisions.

> Assessment Standard B: Achievement and opportunity to learn science must be assessed. This standard is further elaborated into the following substandards:
>   a. Achievement data collected focus on the science content that is most important for students to learn.
>   b. Opportunity-to-learn data collected focus on the most powerful indicators of learning.
>   c. Equal attention must be given to the assessment of opportunity to learn and to the assessment of student achievement.

A science teacher who has met this standard should be able to conduct an assessment of student achievement in a variety of domains as defined in the national, state, and/or district science content standards. For example, science inquiry is an important ability students should develop, in addition to adequate understanding of fundamental science concepts and theories. Thus, the science teacher should be able to design effective assessments to measure various aspects of science inquiry, such as laboratory skills, inquiry performances, and reasoning about science inquiry. Furthermore, a science teacher who has met this standard should be able to collect relevant data pertaining to important student opportunity-to-learn variables. Examples of these variables are students' preconceptions, attitude toward science, classroom learning environment, and the alignment between science instruction and content standards. When reporting student grades, the science teacher should also be able to explain what a student's grade means and how the student has achieved the grade.

> Assessment Standard C: The technical quality of the data collected is well matched to the decisions and actions taken on the basis of their interpretation. This standard is further elaborated into the following substandards:
>   a. The feature that is claimed to be measured is actually measured.
>   b. An individual student's performance is similar on two or more tasks that claim to measure the same aspect of student achievement.

   c. Students have adequate opportunity to demonstrate their achievements.

   d. Assessment tasks and methods for presenting them provide data that are sufficiently stable to lead to the same decisions if used at different times.

This standard is essentially about the technical quality of science assessment. A science teacher who has met this standard should understand what defines technical quality of science assessment, such as validity, reliability, and absence of bias. For example, the science teacher should be able to design a test grid and create a summative test that aligns with the test grid to ensure the content validity. The science teacher should also be able to design a good scoring rubric for performance assessment so that scores given by different raters do not vary considerably. The science teacher should also be able to design a test that is internally coherent so that students' performances on various test questions are consistent (i.e., internally consistency reliability). Given that so many different assessment methods are available, the science teacher who has met this standard should be able to choose the most appropriate assessment formats for the assessment targets for specific students' learning conditions.

Assessment Standard D: Assessment practices must be fair. This standard is further elaborated into the following substandards:

   a. Assessment tasks must be reviewed for the use of stereotypes, for assumptions that reflect the perspectives or experiences of a particular group, for language that might be offensive to a particular group, and for other features that might distract students from the intended tasks.

   b. Large-scale assessments must use statistical techniques to identify potential bias among subgroups.

   c. Assessment tasks must be appropriately modified to accommodate the needs of students with physical disabilities, learning disabilities, or limited English proficiency.

   d. Assessment tasks must be set in a variety of contexts, be engaging to students with different interests and experiences, and must not assume the perspective or experience of a particular gender, racial, or ethnic group.

A science teacher who has met this assessment standard should be able to conduct science assessment appropriate for the characteristics of students. The science teacher should be knowledgeable about various types of individual differences such as physical, racial, and cognitive differences. For example, the science teacher should be able to conduct differentiated science assessment for students who are talented and gifted or for students who are less able. The science teacher should also be familiar with various assessment accommodations and adaptations for both classroom and standardized tests. The science teacher should also be able to conduct data analysis to test if test bias exists.

Assessment Standard E: The inferences made from assessments about student achievement and opportunity to learn must be sound. This standard is further elaborated in the following substandards:

   a. When making inferences from assessment data about student achievement and opportunity to learn science, explicit reference needs to be made to the assumptions on which the inferences are based.

The science teacher who has met this standard should be able to create a grading system appropriate for the science teaching and learning that has taken place. The science teacher should understand the difference between scores and grades and is able to effectively communicate grades to different audiences in order for them to make the most appropriate use of the grades.

As can be seen from the above, this book has attempted to address all the assessment standards by introducing fundamental concepts and essential skills. It is hoped that by now you feel adequately prepared and equipped to conduct science assessment. Your competence in conducting science assessment consistent with the above assessment standards is the ultimate goal of this book.

APPLICATION AND SELF-REFLECTION 8.2

At the beginning of this book, you did a self-evaluation on how you had met the assessment standards. Now, at the end of this book, let's do another self-evaluation to see if you have made progress in meeting the assessment standards. Which standards do you think you have met? Which standards do you think you are not sure if you have met? Which standards do you think you have not met? Place a √ to indicate Met, ? Maybe, and – Not Met.

Standard	Status
Aa. Deliberately design assessment.	
Ab. Use assessments for explicit purposes.	
Ac. Relate clearly decisions to data.	
Ad. Follow internally consistent assessment procedures.	
Ba. Collect achievement data on the science content that is most important for students to learn.	
Bb. Collect opportunity-to-learn data as the most powerful indicators of learning.	
Bc. Assess both opportunity-to-learn and student achievement.	
Ca. Ensure that the feature claimed to be measured is actually measured.	
Cb. Ensure that individual student's performance is similar on two or more tasks that claim to measure the same aspect of student achievement.	
Cc. Ensure that students have adequate opportunity to demonstrate their achievements.	
Cd. Ensure that assessment tasks and methods for presenting them provide data that are sufficiently stable to lead to the same decisions if used at different times.	

Standard	Status
Da. Review assessment tasks for the use of stereotypes, for assumptions that reflect the perspectives or experiences of a particular group, for language that might be offensive to a particular group, and for other features that might distract students from the intended tasks.	
Db. Use statistical techniques in large-scale assessments to identify potential bias among various subgroups.	
Dc. Appropriately modify assessment tasks to accommodate needs of students with physical disabilities, learning disabilities, or limited English proficiency.	
Dd. Set assessment tasks in a variety of contexts, to engage students with different interests and experiences and not to assume the perspective or experience of a particular gender or racial or ethnic group.	
Ea. Make sound inferences based on assessment data about student achievement and opportunity to learn science.	

THE CASES OF ERIC AND ELISIA: USING ASSESSMENT DATA TO IMPROVE INSTRUCTION

Like many other preservice teachers, Eric and Elisia do not have a positive attitude toward statistics. They remember those dreadful experiences associated with statistical formulae. Apparently, they were not sure how statistics might help them in terms of assessment and instruction. However, the statistics reviewed at the beginning of this chapter seem to be very basic; if analyzing assessment data involves only those statistics, they think they can handle that. They were pleased to know that MS Excel is all they need to conduct basic statistical analysis because they have used MS Excel extensively, although they have not specifically used statistical functions. They are anxious to try the MS Excel data analysis template made available on the Web. The item and test analysis techniques introduced in this chapter have helped them see values of the data analysis because those analyses would provide relevant evidence about various claims teachers commonly make about tests and instruction. Because evidence-based practices for assessment and instruction are consistent with the basic scientific principle, they cannot argue against such use. Also, this chapter has helped them to see how various assessment concepts and techniques introduced in previous chapters share a commonality in terms of data and how they are related to assessment standards. This chapter has taken them back to Chapter 1, in which assessment and instruction are claimed to be interrelated. Overall, the journey through this book on developing science assessment competence has been a beneficial one, as they have seen clear improvement on meeting the assessment standards based on their self-evaluation. A few substandards remain unclear to them; they look forward to continue professional development in further developing their knowledge and skills on them.

Do the experiences of Eric and Elisia sound familiar to you? What were your initial ideas of data analysis, and how have they changed as the result of this chapter?

Chapter Summary

- Analyzing assessment data is important for planning effective assessment and instructional improvement. Quality assessment does not occur at once; it requires following a systematic process by identifying the strengths and weaknesses of test items and the test as a whole and revising them accordingly. Similarly, effective instruction does not happen by intuition; it requires systematic inquiry into teacher teaching and student learning, and analyzing student assessment data is a critical component of the inquiry process.

- Statistics involved in conducting data analysis of assessment data are in four categories: statistics for describing central tendency, statistics for describing variation, statistics for describing relationships, and statistics for testing the significance of differences. Mean, median, and mode describe the central tendency of a set of test scores; standard deviation, range, maximum, and minimum describe variation of a set of test scores. Pearson product-moment correlation coefficient describes the linear relationship between two variables, and the t test produces the probability for the difference between two means to occur by chance.

- Assessment data analysis typically follows the following procedures: (a) entering student responses to individual items of a test, (b) scoring student responses, (c) analyzing student performances by items (item analysis), (d) analyzing student performances by groups of items or the entire test (test analysis), and (e) interpreting data analysis results for planning assessment and instruction improvement.

- Item analysis usually involves calculating item difficulty, item discrimination, and item response patterns. Item difficulty is measured by the percentage of students answering an item correctly, item discrimination is measured by a correlation between students' scores on the item and their total test scores, and the item response pattern is the distribution of students choosing different choices of a multiple-choice question or earning different points on a constructed-response question.

- Test analysis typically involves analyzing students' mastery of groups of items, test validity, test reliability, and student group performances. Grouping of items for analyzing mastery may be based on curriculum standards, cognitive levels, question types, and so on. Test validity is a property of test scores collectively; it can be established by examining the test content coverage, student response processes, relationship with other tests, and consequences. Test reliability is concerned with student score consistency. The internal consistency reliability can be calculated using Cronbach's alpha, which is a measure for interitem variation in relation to the possible variation among students.

- Interpreting data analysis results involves examining student performances by item and by test, identifying factors contributing to the performances, and deciding appropriate actions to follow. Factors affecting students' performances on items and the test may be related to item and test quality (e.g., discrimination, reliability, and response pattern), student misconceptions or other learning difficulties, or teacher factors such as insufficient instructional coverage. If an item or test is found to be flawed, assessment improvement is in order; if students or instructions are found responsible for the poor performance, instructional improvement is in order.

√ Mastery Checklist

☐ Conduct basic item analysis to answer questions about item difficulty, item discrimination, and item response pattern.

☐ Conduct basic test analysis to answer questions about mastery of learning standards, test validity, reliability, and absence of bias.

☐ Use data analysis results to improve assessment and instruction.

Web-Based Student Study Site

The Companion Web site for *Essentials of Science Classroom Assessment* can be found at **www.sagepub.com/liustudy**.

The site includes a variety of materials to enhance your understanding of the chapter content. Visit the study site to

- complete an online self-assessment of essential knowledge and skills introduced in this chapter
- find a step-by-step tutorial on using MS Excel to conduct item and test analysis
- find an MS Excel data analysis template to automate common item and test analysis: short version for classroom assessment data analysis and long version for state assessment data analysis, plus a sample completed data analysis using the template
- find Web addresses for resources related to teacher action research in their classrooms and schools

Further Readings

Love, N. (2002). *Using data/getting results: A practical guide for school improvement in mathematics and science.* Norwood, MA: Christopher-Gordon.

> This book provides useful conceptual frameworks and practical techniques on how data may be used to improve teaching and learning at the school level.

Stringer, E. (2008). *Action research in education.* Upper Saddle River, NJ: Prentice Hall.

> This is an easy-to-read book for those teachers who are interested in conducting action research in their classrooms and schools. It first introduces a conceptual framework for action research and then provides detailed elaboration on various stages of a typical action research process. The book also contains real examples of teacher action research as case studies.

Reference

National Research Council (NRC). (1996). *National science education standards.* Washington, DC: National Academy Press.

Glossary

Analytic scoring rubric: an elaborated scoring scheme that contains two dimensions: construct and proficiency.

Application: the ability to use knowledge effectively in a new situation to solve a problem.

Assessment: a systematic, multistep, and multifaceted process involving the collection and interpretation of data.

Benchmarking: comparing one group of students' performance with the state, national, or international average.

Cognition: theories on how students learn.

Cognitive style: the organization and control of cognitive processes pertaining to information receiving, contexts, and information processing.

Concept mapping: a process of creating a graphical representation of the relationship between and among concepts.

Criterion-referenced grading: uses qualitatively different categories or levels of performances as grades.

Diagnostic assessment: conducted specifically to identify students' strengths and weaknesses on the intended learning objectives so that effective planning for instruction may take place.

Dialogic journaling: involves two persons (i.e., a student and the teacher) who ask questions to each other and discuss ideas.

Differentiated assessment: an approach to conducting assessment according to student individual differences.

Discrepant event: a surprising, counterintuitive, unexpected, and paradoxical phenomenon.

Empathy: the ability to get inside another person's feelings and worldviews.

Episodes: memories of events experienced directly or vicariously.

Evaluation: the process of interpreting measurement data based on a set of criteria to make certain judgments.

Explanation: a person's ability to provide knowledgeable and justifiable accounts of events, actions, and ideas.

Formative assessment: takes place as part of ongoing instruction in order to monitor and make adjustments to the ongoing instruction.

Grade: a judgmental statement about a student's achievement in both quantity and quality.

Grade reporting: the ways in which student grades are communicated to various audiences.

Grading: a process of deciding and communicating how well students have mastered the learning outcomes.

Holistic scoring rubric: a one-dimensional hierarchical differentiation that defines qualitatively different degrees of performances in terms of global characteristics.

Images: mental representations of sensory perceptions.

Intellectual skills: mental processes performed to solve a problem or conduct a task.

Interpretation: the narratives or translations that provide meaning to events or objects.

Interviews: conversations on a specific topic between the science teacher and a student (i.e., individual interview) or between the science teacher and a whole class (i.e., group interview).

Item difficulty: the percentage or proportion of students who have answered a question correctly.

Item discrimination: the way in which an item can differentiate between students whose overall abilities are high and those whose overall abilities are low.

Laboratory skills: both the manipulative and thinking skills involved in laboratory activities; they are also called *process skills.*

Lake Wobegon effect: people's tendency to overestimate themselves in relation to others.

Learning style: the preferred approaches to the acquisition and organization of knowledge. Simply put, learning style is about how students learn best.

Likert scale: a set of statements followed by different degrees of agreement.

Mean: the arithmetic average of a set of scores over all students. It represents the central tendency of individual scores among the students.

Measurement: a process of quantifying the degree to which a student possesses a given characteristic, quality, or feature.

Median: a score that is located at the middle when all scores are rank-ordered from highest to lowest.

Mode: the score that has the most occurrences.

Motor skills: procedures followed to conduct a physical task.

Narrative report: explains meanings of grades and suggests how to improve them.

Norm-referenced grading: awards students grades based on their positions on a normal distribution curve among a given group.

Observation: assessment tasks through which students' attainment of learning outcomes is elicited.

Open-ended journaling: process in which students can decide on a specific focus, format, and length to write about a given concept.

Opportunity to learn: the provision of conditions, resources, and practices that maximizes students' likelihood to achieve the expected learning competence.

Percentage grading: uses a percentage as the grade to indicate the amount of content (e.g., number of objectives) a student has mastered.

Perspectives: the ability to appreciate different points of view.

Prediction-observation-explanation: a specialized group interview aimed at probing students' understanding of a natural phenomenon.

Propositions: facts, opinions, and beliefs.

Range: the difference between the maximum and minimum score.

Responsive journaling: process in which students answer questions posed by the teacher, while both open-ended journaling and responsive journaling take place individually.

Rubric: a continuum along which different levels of competence in performing a task are differentiated.

Rubric grading: extended criterion-referenced grading that incorporates multiple performance levels and percentage grades.

Self-knowledge: a person's ability to identify his or her own weaknesses and to actively seek improvement.

Standard deviation: the averaged difference between individual scores and the mean of the scores.

Standardized test: a measurement tool that requires uniform administration, scoring, and interpretation.

Strings: fundamental statements or generalizations that do not vary from situation to situation. Strings are usually in the form of proverbs, laws, and rules.

Structure knowledge: the knowledge of how concepts within a domain are interrelated.

Student preconceptions: the different ideas students that bring with them before they learn the new concept or content.

Summative assessment: takes place at the conclusion of instruction in order to grade students for mastering instructional objectives and make decisions for student future learning.

Test: a set of questions or tasks that elicits student responses plus a set of scoring keys or schemes to score them.

Test grid: consists of a topic dimension and a cognitive reasoning dimension.

Two-tiered MC question: a combination of two conventional multiple-choice questions, with the first one asking students to answer a question by selecting the best answer and the second one asking students to justify the given answer by selecting all applicable reasons.

Index

About the Author

Xiufeng Liu is associate professor of science education at the State University of New York at Buffalo. He received his doctorate in science education from the University of British Columbia in 1993. He was a high school chemistry teacher in China, a research associate at the China National Institute for Educational Research (CNIER), and a science teacher educator in Canada before his current position. He conducts research in the closely related areas of technology-enhanced science assessment, applications of measurement models in science education, conceptual change in science, and science curriculum policies. He has published more than 30 refereed articles in key science education journals, 5 books, and 15 book chapters, and he has presented numerous papers at national and international conferences. Dr. Liu teaches courses entitled Measurement and Evaluation of Science Teaching, Seminar on Science Teaching, Seminar on Science Curricula, and Technology for Science Teaching. In addition, he conducts an annual summer science assessment workshop for teachers and is frequently invited to give talks and workshops on science assessment, including Rasch measurement, in the United States and abroad.